BRING ON
UNITED

BRING ON
UNITED

Ferguson's Golden Generation in Their Own Words

ANDY MITTEN

Harper
North

HarperNorth
Windmill Green
24 Mount Street
Manchester M2 3NX

A division of
HarperCollins*Publishers*
1 London Bridge Street
London SE1 9GF

www.harpercollins.co.uk

HarperCollinsPublishers
Macken House, 39/40 Mayor Street Upper
Dublin 1, D01 C9W8, Ireland

First published by HarperNorth in 2024

1 3 5 7 9 10 8 6 4 2

A catalogue record for this book is
available from the British Library

HB ISBN: 978-0-00-872607-2
TPB ISBN: 978-0-00-872608-9

Printed and bound in the UK using 100%
renewable electricity at CPI Group (UK) Ltd

For Ba, Olivia, Clara and Annie

And for Reds everywhere, who lived through this

CONTENTS

FOREWORD

by Ruud van Nistelrooy

My time at Manchester United as a player was so special, so happy. It didn't start that way, though: I failed my medical in 2000 and then, the next day, tore my cruciate ligament playing for PSV. After that, I doubted I'd ever get the opportunity to join United, and I wondered whether I could even get back to the same level at all. United were a top European team so it seemed natural to me that they wouldn't wait for any one player. But they did wait for me and I appreciated the support, especially from Sir Alex Ferguson and David Gill. They kept in touch, but even then I was thinking 'They're just trying to be nice,' and, while I appreciated their kindness, I didn't believe that things would work out as they did.

In the end I signed for a British record fee. I was relatively unknown because I was coming from the Dutch league, but it was a big transfer with big expectations. People wanted to see what I was about and it was important for me to show what I could do as quickly as possible. I was ambitious and confident that I could contribute to the team and willing to do everything I could to achieve that. From the start, I felt sharp and ready, scoring in the

1

friendlies and the first games. That gave a signal to my teammates, the fans and media that I could succeed in the team. It all helped me get off to a flying start.

I moved with my girlfriend, now wife, and we lived in an apartment building where we met people we're still friends with now. Because you're away so much as a footballer, it was important that my partner was happy and she was. We both were. We liked living in Manchester, which was a very different city then. It has changed a lot with all the new buildings, but it was always a football city.

We'd invite friends from Holland to experience the Old Trafford atmosphere; the noise, the roar when we scored, the banter and the songs. They travelled over often, they loved it. As a player, you felt pushed forward by the fans. It's hard to explain, but that's how I felt.

We didn't win the league in my first year and when we reached the Champions League semi-final we went out to Leverkusen. That – and not reaching a Champions League final while I was at United – was my biggest disappointment. I had a poor game in Leverkusen and it all hurt because we were so close.

But there were plenty of highs. I was at United from the age of 25 to 30; my peak years at the highest level. It helped that I was surrounded by quality players, a quality manager and staff. Our mentality was that if we were knocked back then we'd come back stronger.

And the culture came from Sir Alex. He was the club and embodied everything about it. He demanded everything of you every day because he knew what was needed to be successful. He would inspire, motivate. He'd give me freedom to play – which is really what you want as a forward. He wouldn't stuff you with too much information. He wanted you to work hard, be a good teammate and be the best you could be. He'd compliment you, and he'd correct you where needed. It could be brutal as you had to reach the highest standards every day.

FOREWORD

And there were strong characters in the dressing room too. The core was all United, with the Class of '92, Roy Keane, Dennis Irwin and Wes Brown coming through. These United boys set the tone for the new boys like me. We had good fun on the road and spent a lot of time together. Then I was up front with Cole, Yorke and Solskjaer. It was amazing, they were so easy to play with. I felt a connection with them in training, without even looking.

As a team we won the league in 2003 and I won the golden boot too, scoring 44 goals in what was the best season of my career. I won the PFA and Player of the Season awards too, which felt wonderful of course, but the most important thing was that we were a team who played, won and celebrated together. We had some fun nights out, I'm sure you'll read about them in this book. Then we had the youngest players coming through, Cristiano Ronaldo and Wayne Rooney. They needed time to reach the level to win things, but they learned so quickly.

It was difficult for me at the end, but that's part of professional life. I held no grudges and everyone moved on. United had an excellent season and won the league, while I had a top season at Real Madrid and won La Liga.

My United memories are happy ones. My favourite moments were towards the end of games we were about to win with the MUFC fans in full voice and the rest of the stadium empty. Happy, happy times.

I spent much of my time at United being set up by others. Now it's my turn to make an assist, to set up the stories of the other lads, most of whom I played with. Great times, great memories. I hope you enjoy reading about them.

Ruud Van Nistelrooy
Manchester, 2024

PREFACE

Champions of Planet Earth

At the start of this century, Manchester United were English Premier League and European champions. After winning the treble in Barcelona, Sir Alex Ferguson's team went to Tokyo and defeated Brazilian side Palmeiras on 30 November 1999, in the very last Intercontinental Cup, to add the title of world champions to the list. That honour was to be short-lived; within weeks it would be passed on to another Brazilian team, Corinthians, as they triumphed in the inaugural FIFA Club World Championship, in which United also competed. Yet in December 2008, on the eve of the final year of the noughties, United became world champions again in Yokohama, Japan; the high-water mark of a decade bookended by brilliance.

In January 2000, I headed to Rio de Janeiro for 17 days with a few hundred other United fans. The Club World Championship was controversial, United cast as villains for turning their backs on the FA Cup. But the truth was more prosaic: the English authorities, including the government, had pushed United into it.

What had been happening to the club – and their fans – was scarcely believable. Exactly ten years earlier in 1990, Mark Robins had kept United in the FA Cup as Sir Alex Ferguson and his side struggled to finish thirteenth in the league. In 1988 one of football's biggest clubs had been obliged to pay European giants AC Milan to play a friendly at Old Trafford, and that wasn't the only example of the club's diminished status.

But by the time I asked Peter Kenyon, the club's leading executive, on the eve of United's second of four pre-season games in 2000, 'Who are the biggest clubs in the world?', he answered confidently: 'Us and Real Madrid.' And, as the 400,000 who watched that tour in Australia and China would testify, the stats bear his assertion out, judged by revenue or by trophies. United and Real Madrid would go on to become champions of England and Spain respectively in 2001, 2003, 2007 and 2008. And United won the league twice more, in 2000 and 2009.

United were so successful potential buyers began to circle. Old Trafford was expanded in 1995, 2000 and 2005, rising from 44,000 seats in 1993 to c. 76,000 a dozen years later. The modest club shop, now a Megastore, was expanded and moved four times.

This was a club on the march. At the end of the 1999–2000 season, Vodafone was announced as shirt sponsor, replacing 18-year partner Sharp. Then, in summer 2002, as longtime chairman Martin Edwards stood down, a new kit deal with Nike was agreed, amounting to a record-breaking £303 million, 13-year partnership that dwarfed any previously agreed by the sports brand. It was described as a 'strategic alliance between two global brands.'

While the finances exploded, uncertainty prevailed as Ferguson surprised everyone, not least his stunned bosses, by saying he wanted to leave at the end of the 2001–02 season. Arsène Wenger was the club's first choice to replace him, Sven-Göran Eriksson the second, but Ferguson changed his mind after a chat with his wife, Cathy. At the next game in February 2002 the travelling United fans at Charlton's Valley stadium began to sing 'Every single one of us, loves Cathy Ferguson'.

While there was consistency on the pitch, as the team never finished below third place in the noughties (with a stellar record which reads: 1st, 1st, 3rd, 1st, 3rd, 3rd, 2nd, 1st, 1st and 1st), there were monumental shifts. Imports from well beyond the United Kingdom and Republic of Ireland were transforming the national makeup and the habits and attitudes of the squad.

'The foreign lads at this club have helped tremendously in terms of diets,' Roy Keane told me in 2004. 'I know people harp on about it but they are so far ahead of us, especially the French lads like Mikaël [Silvestre]. Laurent Blanc was, too.'

As fans, we rode the wave and travelled wherever the team played – which was all over the world. In Rio, at the turn of the millennium, we had the time of our lives. Not for we fans the actual worry of having to play football in the high Brazilian summer. It felt like a holiday, a reward to older fans who'd gone 26 years without seeing United win the league before 1993. We walked into a hotel where South Melbourne FC were staying and spotted their young manager, a certain Ange Postecoglou. We went into a huge nightclub called Help, on Copacabana beach just next to our hotel. It took us a while to realise that there were few other men in there and that the girls were working. We visited the house of the Great Train Robber Ronnie Biggs, a pitiable sight surviving off the proceeds of t-shirt sales to the few Brits attracted by the novelty of his notoriety. We woke up in apartments on Leblon beach, where pasty-skinned Mancunians stood out a mile. We went to samba schools in favelas, met the main ultras from Flamengo and, when it came to going home, a delay of 24 hours to the flight saw us put up in a cool hotel along with the air stewardesses. They settled around the swimming pool; we didn't speak to a single one of them.

We'd bumped into Reds around Rio, smiles as wide as Christ the Redeemer's outstretched arms. Inside the Maracaná, we did our best to get the atmosphere going, but it was a hopeless task against tens of thousands of Vasco da Gama fans singing the most beautiful, soulful songs I've ever heard inside a football stadium. Everyone was relaxed. Everyone except Sir Alex Ferguson who, rightly, never dropped his guard as far as United were concerned. Without him, none of us would have tasted these sweets. We lived a life of reflected glory but, there in Rio at least, we created our own culture; the permanent thread, through thick and thin. Players came and went, we were permanent. And it seemed like the Manchester United juggernaut would roll on and on.

It was a more innocent time. Still looking like scrawny teenagers, we went to the FIFA hotel and asked its head, Michel Platini, for an interview for the *United We Stand* fanzine. He agreed, just like that, and we did an hour-long interview. By contrast, at the 2024 FIFA three-day conference, tight-lipped incumbent Gianni Infantino refused to speak to any global media.

I went to Rio with John Paul O'Neill who'd edit the *Red Issue* fanzine. By 2005, he'd have the idea to form a breakaway club, FC United of Manchester, amid protests over a mooted takeover by the American billionaire Malcolm Glazer. My brother Joz was one of their first ever signings, dropping down five leagues to play for a start-up paid for mostly by working-class Mancunians and discussed over rounds of beer rather than rounds of investor funding. The split in United's fanbase was acute and it lasted years. I've watched non-league football since I first went with my dad aged three, but I continued to go to Old Trafford.

In the middle of the noughties, I wrote a book about United in the 1980s. The interviews staggered me as I spoke to players for up to four hours at a time, among them Bryan Robson, John Gidman, Arnold Muhren, Billy Garton and Frank Stapleton. They were funny, fascinating and sometimes tinged with sadness. Gordon McQueen, who died in 2023, insisted on having four pints before we started, then more during the course of the interview. When his wife Yvonne picked us up, she noted that he'd been drinking.

'It's close season,' he explained.

PREFACE

'You retired 18 years ago.'

She dropped me back to Yarm station herself. There were no agents involved, no public relations advisors. There was no social media to steal and twist the quotes. I could have twisted their truth myself, but I didn't misplace the trust of any of those boys. And I made sure I always kept an eye out for them, since several had lost all contact with the club they once played for. They weren't forgotten heroes to me, just heroes. When McQueen passed away, his family asked me to speak on television as soon as the news broke. I received a message from one of his daughters to say that they were sitting watching, crying and smiling. In a modern football news cycle in which fans obsess about transfers, there should be space to remember those men who paid a heavy mental, financial and physical price for the entertainment they brought to millions.

A book on the 1990s followed in 2009. I had little time for Andy Cole ... until I met him and spoke with him for hours. Now, I consider him one of the most impressive people I know. Then, in 2011, I wrote a book on United in the 1970s to complete the trilogy, before raising a family took priority.

It was a joy meeting the lads of the noughties who rose to the top of their trade, talking to them about the amazing moments they experienced and looking back at what I and others had written about them at the time. In Moscow, I'd seen United become champions of Europe and yet, as everyone celebrated, I couldn't get back to my hotel because, at 3 a.m., a feral dog blocked my path. Moscow's authorities estimate that 30,000 strays populate the city and that many of them congregate around Metro stations – some of them even go up and down the escalators. This mutt was snarling at me. Maybe it was a Scouse dog and the 'Scouse Free Zone' flag in the Chelsea end of the Luzhniki Stadium had been wrong. The beast resembled a cross between a wolf and hyena. If I moved, it growled. I tried to edge away, but the hound had none of it and barked so loud that workmen 100 metres away looked over. I couldn't speak

Russian, so I could hardly shout for help. You'll get a players' perspective on Moscow in this book, which doesn't involve dogs.

We put the triumphant players on the cover of the following *United We Stand* with 'The Pride of Europe' above the three stars for United's three European Cup wins. A decade later, I saw that cover framed in a bar in Cork, Ireland, and recalled vividly the times we'd had.

Dressing room behaviour was and continues to be moderated. I found no outrageous stories of the kind that belonged to earlier decades, like Russell Beardsmore being put in a washing machine by his teammates or players hitting Ferguson in the face with snowballs. But, as you'll read, the jokes and pranks continued and they were integral to the indomitable team spirit which took United to the very top.

For me, the top was in Japan. I remember walking around Yokohama at 6 a.m. after Manchester United had just become world champions. The fisherman were out by the quayside and 'Weird Fishes' by Radiohead came on my headphones. Forget the jetlag, life felt fantastic.

I roomed with Stuart Mathieson from the *Manchester Evening News*, a decent man trusted by the players. He told me it was like sharing a house with a teenager since I was coming in at all hours. And why not? It was my birthday in Japan and I looked around a bar in Shibuya to see friends I'd known forever on the cusp of watching their team become world champions. It was a long way from Halifax in the League Cup in front of under 7,000 in 1990. I'm talking about terrace legends no longer with us like Mick Burgess from Blackpool, an unlikely start for Bill Buford's book about football hooliganism, *Among the Thugs*. Former hooligans and current hooligans: John Taylor, a famous Cockney Red who'd been so good to me during the treble year; Beanhead, Messer, Clive, Kiddo, Romford, Chad, Phil and Barmy Kev were all there. The O'Neills were singing. Rob Brundish, who loved Japan so much he'd move there, talked with Nige about old times. Mike Dobbin, probably United's greatest fan in terms of games attended, on his final trip. He'd pass within a month, his team world champions. And there were so many more. As the Reds sang, 'It's a long way to Yokohama, it's a long way to go, It's a long way to Yokohama, where all the best teams go. Goodbye Man City, farewell Liverpool too' and 'Ob-la-di, Ob-la-da Man United, Champions of Planet Earth'.

Some 800 fans had found £2,000 each to make the trip. One mate, Steve Armstrong, flew to Tokyo, watched the match and flew home again in the space of a few hours because, for once, his wife thought it unreasonable to travel when it was her brother's wedding. He reckoned his body clock was still messed up months later. I know one lad who had to declare himself insolvent after watching United around the world. There were just so many games and trips and when he said he'd watch United from the banks of the River Irwell to the shores of Sicily, he really meant it. He was one of the lucky ones. Most United fans couldn't stretch themselves like this, not get to all these games.

But I was also a journalist, regularly on the road with other work, trying to get Lionel Messi, David Villa, Ronaldinho, Xavi, Daniele De Rossi and just about anyone who was decent to join United when the interviews ended and the tapes went off – and only half in jest. I'd go and interview Brazilians in Spain who had no idea who I supported and they'd tell me that Rio Ferdinand from 'Manchester' was the best defender they'd come up against. And it seemed totally normal to see United's players held in such high esteem.

Some mates would turn right before a game to drink and scrap – but I'd turn left. There was still some major disorder in the noughties as United lads attacked hooligans from Leeds in Leeds and from Roma in Rome.

I was working and I had to keep a straight compass far from home, this time in Japan. Even when Paddy Crerand told me that Sir Alex Ferguson was speaking Spanish in a press conference.

'No, Paddy, that's the translator's voice,' I replied, adjusting his settings so he could hear his fellow Glaswegian not just his interpreter. Crerand, a United legend, was priceless on that trip.

'Cristiano!' he shouted at Ronaldo, who everyone knew was going to Madrid. 'I'm Paddy from Real Madrid TV.' The Portuguese loved that one.

I was working with Nina Warhurst, a Manchester girl and Red with enough personality to charm the world's biggest city, who now presents the Breakfast Show on BBC1. Andy Dickman was there too, a lifelong Liverpool and football anorak who prides himself on his programme collection. What must it have been like for him watching United win and win and win? Dicko was always magnanimous and professional. We met the fans of the Mexican side Pachuca, who turned out to also be the club's directors. We found that out at 4 a.m. when Dicko and Nina got them singing 'La Bamba'. What did Mexicans make of Gareth from Levenshulme singing 'Yo no soy Marinero, soy capitan' over tequila shots?

And was I seeing things when I walked back past the United team hotel, where Dimitar Berbatov was confined to his bed with a virus for the entire trip, and the immaculate concierge in a top hat proudly wore a Manchester United scarf?

No. And people really weren't seeing things when they looked into the hotel to see jetlagged Paul Scholes and Ryan Giggs passing the time by painting at 2 a.m. This is the sort of stuff that would quickly go viral now. Then, people thought I was odd if I got my camera out at a game.

'We're the best team in the world,' said man of the match Wayne Rooney, pronounced as 'Threwny' on the stadium PA. And we were.

United were brilliant and we couldn't wait to see more. As Reds sang all over the world: Bring On United.

Andy Mitten
Manchester, September 2024

1

YOU ARE MY SOLSKJAER

Ole Gunnar Solskjaer

'The best moment in my football career was in 2007.' Ole Gunnar Solskjaer is unwavering. 'I know what you're thinking, surely it has to be the Champions League final [in 1999] and I understand why you think that but let me explain.

'My dad used to be a wrestler and I saw all his cuttings from newspapers about his career, but I never actually saw him wrestle. That was deep inside of me that I never saw him and I didn't want my oldest son Noah to remember his dad just from videos or paper clippings. I wanted him to remember me playing at Old Trafford. But he couldn't because I was injured for so long. But when we beat Newcastle at home 2–0 – and I got credited both goals – that changed. The first one came from a Ronaldo shot that came back off the post, the second from Nemanja Vidić, whose shot hit my shin pad and changed direction. Noah was in the family stand, aged six. As I walked off, I saw his hands in the air, celebrating his dad scoring two. That was the moment where I thought that three years of rehab had been worth it. That's the best moment I had. And he can remember it clearly. He was my main motivation to get back to play for the first team at Old Trafford and play in a game in front of him. I did it. That moment epitomised me and what motivates me more than anything.'

Ole Gunnar's father influenced him in other ways. 'I wrestled with him and he'd easily beat me because he was strong. I felt he was big once but when I stand up now my dad is much smaller than me. He was a good influence on me. Only once did he need to have a word and that was when I came home late from a party. My friends were going out a lot. He saw me in the morning and asked: "Do you think this is the way to make a success of your life?" I never forgot that.'

It was six months after Ole Gunnar Solskjaer had won the treble for Manchester United and he was in Rio de Janeiro for the Club World Championship when the team received a visit from Martin Edwards. The United chairman had been splashed all over the news back home, having been spotted in the company of working girls by the Copacabana. He hardly kept it a secret. When United fans, myself included, walked into a giant club called Help! next door to our hotel thinking it was a normal nightclub, we couldn't believe that the ratio of girls to men was maybe eight-to-one. One of the men was Edwards, who waved and asked us fans if we were having a good time in Rio. Edwards' street cred went up with plenty of supporters that night, with him out on the town and the players in bed.

'Martin came to all us players and said, "Well, at least I've kept you out of the headlines, boys!"' Solskjaer says, laughing out loud. 'My memories of that trip are Jaap [Stam] and I stupidly thinking about the actual games in detail and how we'd do instead of visiting the Sugarloaf Mountain or Christ the Redeemer statue. Or paragliding off the top of a mountain near our hotel. In fact, as the gaffer was telling us to behave in Brazil, Nicky Butt came flying overhead on a paraglider.

'I took it seriously because I was still fighting for my place in the team. There was no room for me to relax. Every training session and game was an opportunity to prove to the gaffer that I should play more. I was playing well and scoring when I was picked – I even got four against Everton – but I also knew that when the biggest games came I would be left out.

'Maybe the gaffer looked at Brazil as a break in the season and a chance to recharge because the league and retaining the Champions League were the priorities. The club got battered for not playing in the FA Cup. Missing the FA Cup was sad and I know some of the lads felt we should have put young players in the early rounds, but what if we'd drawn Liverpool?'

Brazil wasn't United's finest hour, but there was plenty of sun.

'We returned to Manchester and Carrington, the start of a new training ground and a new era. For the first time, fans couldn't come and watch us train. That was sad but also probably necessary because times were changing. At The Cliff, we were never worried about people watching training. We tried to sign all the autographs too and we lost that at Carrington with all the security, but I also remember helicopters flying above us a couple of times, trying to find out our tactics and who was going to start. Carrington was a step up in professionalism and for 2000 it was good. For 2024 it was probably not good enough.'

Solskjaer played 46 United games in 1999–2000, scoring 15.

'I kept a diary which I've still got and I've got a page here from March 2000 where it says, "I've had enough now of low confidence and bad performances. Now I'm going to really work on my mentality". I was talking to the psychologist, Bill Beswick, and Steve McClaren, and it was Bill who encouraged me to write down how I felt. Before that, I used to keep training diaries where I wrote down what we did rather than just think about things. This was my feelings, written on the day. I wasn't only thinking something, but writing it down so that I thought about it two or three times more. It really helped me to get down on paper what I was thinking. I found it a useful mental coaching tool.

'I was number 12, 13 or 14 in the squad. The danger was that if you miss a couple of chances then you hide because you don't want to make more mistakes. You know you'd have Roy Keane battering you because he wanted the best for the team. But if I wrote all that down I'd read it back and think, "I'm not going to improve if I'm going to hide when I lose the ball." I started to force myself to push through that, getting the ball again, never hiding. Prove to the gaffer and to Roy, the captain, that I always wanted to get on the ball. It helped me a lot and my relationship with Roy has turned out well and we're in regular contact. When we played we used to have a few fights. He demanded 100 per cent every single day. He pushed the players and wanted to count on his teammates all the time. And the day Roy stopped moaning at you – you knew you were in trouble. That meant he'd given up on you. He never gave up on me, never stopped shouting at me. So he saw something in me. When I saw him stop shouting at certain individuals, I thought, "You're finished, you're done." And they usually were.'

In April 2000, Real Madrid knocked holders United out of the Champions League, winning at Old Trafford in the quarter-final second leg after a 0–0 draw in the Bernabéu.

'The home game was where Redondo did the backheel past Henning. Henning wasn't a right-back but he was in the right-back position when that happened and this was his last full season at United. He had a tough time at that moment. Henning was a very good player and a good guy. He was 100 per cent, he didn't want headlines, but you could trust him, on and off the pitch. But the next season he came on at half-time at West Ham away when we were winning 2–0 but we drew 2–2 and got battered by the gaffer after that game. He said, "Don't even bother turning up again, find yourself a new club when you are away with your national team." I was watching that thinking, "He doesn't really mean that, he's saying it in the heat of the moment," which I think it was. The next day, Steve McClaren rang our home phone at my mum and dad's in Norway. I didn't have a mobile phone, I wasn't too bothered about people being able to get hold of me. Steve asked me to speak to Henning and say that the gaffer didn't mean it and to calm the situation, which I did. But Henning never played another game for United.'

Three days after that Real Madrid defeat in April 2000, United won the league at Southampton.

'I scored on the Saturday and we played Chelsea on the Monday. This was the first time that I went against the gaffer. I knew that Ruud van Nistelrooy was going to be signed because the gaffer told me. When he did, he said that he needed to challenge me to prove that I was a Man United player. He also said that I wasn't aggressive enough and traced that back to a friendly game against Inter Milan in 1997 when I got an ankle injury. He said I'd lost a little aggression after that injury and that he wanted to see more from me, that he'd play me more and test me until Ruud arrived. I had no problem with Ruud signing. I'd seen strikers come and go and I was going to take up the challenge. Of course, Ruud was going to be a starter, but I was playing lots of games, I'd signed a long-term deal and it was up to me. I was professional enough to always give my best in training or in games. I would never let myself or the gaffer down by sulking.'

Ferguson gathered his strikers before the Chelsea game.

'He said that we've done well and that we have four great strikers. Then he said: "Coley and Ole, you started against Southampton, so against Chelsea I'll go with Yorkey and Teddy. Everyone OK with that?" The others nodded. I waited for them to walk out of the room and said: "No, I'm not happy with this. You've just told me that you're going to sign Ruud, said that I'll play more games and you challenged me to be more aggressive. I played Saturday and I want to play again. You've just challenged me to do that."'

'You're right, son,' said Sir Alex, 'Go and get Teddy for me.'

'I went into the dressing room and said, "Teddy, the gaffer wants to see you." Me? I played, I scored. And that was the meeting where

I proved that I had the mentality to be a Man United player, on and off the pitch. That was the only time I went against the gaffer until the Roy Keane meetings in 2005.

'In December 2000, I was in form and scored in four different league games. Then we played Newcastle away in the final game of the year. It was one I didn't score in. We got a penalty and I should have taken it. Becks took it and put it in the top right corner.

'I was thinking that I might be player of the month. I did an interview with the Norwegian press that was translated into some of the British newspapers and spun into headlines that were way worse than what I'd said. The question to me was: "Now that you are a regular …" and I answered, "No, not really, I'll probably be on the bench soon and I don't look at myself as a regular." The gaffer came to see me and he snapped big time because it was on the back of all the newspapers that I'd said he'd probably leave me out soon. I think he only read the headlines. He then looked at me as a defeatist who accepted being a sub instead of pushing on and saying that I should play every game but for me it was a way of saying that I'm loyal to whatever the gaffer does and doing whatever I'm asked to. One of the beauties of the manager was that you could never read him.'

Van Nistelrooy's arrival was delayed a year and Solskjaer played 47 times in 2000–01, the same again the following season when he scored 25 goals. And he played a career high of 57 United games in a season during 2002–03. And all this at a time when competition for a place in United's front line was acute and big-name strikers were leaving and arriving at the club.

'Life was very good. I was becoming more mature, more regular in the team. Teddy Sheringham had a great season in 2000–01, then he left. We were a winning team; we just didn't win the second Champions League and that was the main aim. After '99, we knew we'd be winning the league again. No doubts. We didn't talk of that being a target, we talked about winning it better. We won the league in '99, 2000 and 2001.'

Then van Nistelrooy arrived.

'The partnership between Ruud and I is underrated. We were good friends, on and off the pitch. Our girlfriends, too. We all spent a lot of time together. I clicked with all the Dutch lads – Jaap, Jordi, Ruud. There was something about their personality which fitted me. They were probably doing all the talking and I was doing all the listening. Most of us lived in Bramhall. We didn't go out drinking like some of the English lads, more in local restaurants in Bramhall or Hale with our now wives. I'd see fans and that was fine. I was never a big superstar and didn't behave like one. People would put their thumbs up to me and ask for a photograph. Ruud and I scored 60-odd goals together. Ruud got 30-odd, I got 26.'

Twenty-five, according to the books.

'Well, that's a mistake because I got 26. They must have nicked one off me or put it as an own goal when it's mine!'

But United didn't win the league, nor the Champions League.

'We should have won the Champions League in 2002. Juan Sebastián Verón hit the inside of the post and the ball bounced to the inside of the other post. Leverkusen counter-attacked and scored: 2–2. They're the fine margins in football. One centimetre the other way and Juan would have put us 3–1 up. In the away game, I missed a chance. Roy Keane still bothers me about it. I shot and missed the target. It was a good chance near the end of the game, better than I thought on the night so Roy has a point, though if he'd had the chance he wouldn't have scored it. I should have done it. Diego Forlán had a chance which rebounded and went wide. The cross came in and I chested it and shot a half volley with my left, which went half a yard over. I should have forced it down.'

It's painful hearing this.

'Very painful, but these are the moments I remember. I don't remember all the times winning the league as much as the missed chances. I felt we improved by not winning because we were used to winning. When we won, we got on with it. When we lost, it brought us together.'

Teddy Sheringham and Andy Cole left the club in 2001, and Dwight Yorke departed in July 2002, leaving Solskjaer as the only one of the treble-winning forwards left.

'Good teammates, good players, good friends, memories and good times, but when they go, they go. That's football. The four of us all had different personalities, but I always respected them and always spoke to them. I hope that all my teammates that I've ever had would say that I behaved respectfully to all of them. Teddy and I leaned into each other more because we'd play the not so important games and Coley and Yorkey would play the biggest games. And it meant more opportunities for me because I was still at the club and never wanted to leave. I'd turned Spurs down [in December '98] and that helped my relationship with the gaffer. He brought me into his office and said, "Tottenham and Alan Sugar have put a bid in for £5.5 million. Martin Edwards has said yes and the club want the money, but I don't want you to go. If you stay here then you will play and be an important part of the squad." So we agreed for me to stay. Then he said, "Please don't tell anyone" as he'd just lost the club all that money. I finished that season scoring the last goal of it in Barcelona. You must look after number one in football but I knew that all I could do was do my best.'

Diego Forlán joined the club in January 2002.

'He was a very nice guy and when the lads came in from abroad, we'd try to talk to them because I knew what it was like to come in as an outsider. He could shoot with both feet, but unfortunately it didn't work out for him at United. We knew what a good player he was and he'd go on to be the best player in the 20120 World Cup to prove that. I remember the chat I had with the gaffer about play-ers after they'd left and he said: "Diego Forlán was a great player. It was my mistake that I never managed to get the best out of him." I felt something in common with Diego. He was a team player who did his extras after training. The British and Irish lads left everything on the pitch in training and then went back to the dressing room. Diego was more like me. If he was unhappy with a session or wanted to practise something specific, he'd do extra shootings. Players might shout "why doesn't he shoot in training?" in a light-hearted, but with an element of truth, kind of way because they felt he didn't get the best out of himself when it mattered. Maybe he lacked the confidence with us and that confidence came later. It was too bad, but that's football. Alan Smith was another striker at United. He was like me in mentality. Different player, but always ready to give our best. I could have left at several points, but decided to stay, no matter what the changes were around me. Until I got my injury.'

United played Deportivo La Coruña six times in an 18-month period at the start of the noughties. The sides had never met before, nor since.

'We had some lovely trips there and Deportivo had some fantastic players. I swapped shirts with Djalminha. They had Fran, Tristan, Mackay and Valerón. Nice games, good attacking teams. We only looked at winning the Champions League as being good enough.'

In the summer of 2002 another Norwegian, Ronny Johnsen, left the club.

'A brick wall as a player, a man mountain. Quick, strong, everything you want in a defender. He was a quiet guy, someone who you wanted in your team. His partnership with Jaap at the back was superb. What a pair of centre-backs. You could play them two v two and nobody would beat them. I'd play for the national team with Ronny and Henning so we'd see a lot of each other and were friends, though not socially, because they were three or four years older than me, I was more with the Dutch players at United.'

Humour was a key part of the dressing room.

'It was brilliant at United. Cristiano came in. Young, Portuguese and wanting to look good. Big "A" for Armani brands and bright colours to stand out. But that was a chance for us to test their mentality. We did it with all new players. Rio joined for a record fee. Someone blasted a ball into him which he obviously couldn't control. I shouted, "How much?" We were testing people, our way of knowing whether we could trust you when the going got tough.'

And he got some stick himself.

'When I first arrived at the club I was young and naïve. I would wear my knitted Christmas jumpers from back home. I wore whatever I felt comfortable with. Well, whatever my wife bought for me. The more Norwegian my clothes, the more I got hammered. If you wore something which you got hammered for, but didn't wear it again, you'd lose their respect. Coming back in with a jumper on showed that you could handle it. I never gave them the satisfaction and I think – well, I know – that they expected me to come in one day like Michael Douglas in *The Game* and snap on everyone. But I loved that dressing room mood. Everyone would get battered and ripped to pieces. Giggs, Butty and Maysie were the culprits. Brutal, but brilliant. Roy was dry, witty and cutting. If I could choose one teammate from everyone who I played with to be the first name on the team sheet, it would be Roy every time. He was so influential and respected. If you missed a penalty in a game you'd be hammered for it the next day. The idea was that you took the next one and were strong enough mentally to take it. I don't think the gaffer knew that any of this was going on because the dressing room was our place.'

There were changes among coaches.

'Steve McClaren moved to Middlesbrough but with his replacement Carlos Queiroz, I also felt that I was moving more towards a starting player in the team, becoming more and more of a Man United player. Carlos was very professional, thorough and methodical. It was the first time we'd had real structure and periodising of the training. Before it was more about gut feeling, a kind of "the lads need a round robin now". Carlos had none of that. We'd never had specific tactical sessions before Carlos. He was all about "This is a process; I'm telling you exactly what you need". Sir Alex once told me that Carlos had stayed so late after a game that he didn't go home because he was so worried about getting the tactics right. The gaffer taught Carlos to relax a little and trust the players a little more, but he was a football addict.'

The wife of one of the older staff close to Ferguson said that Carlos had lots of female admirers, but that he was only interested in his football.

'The training session Carlos gave the team before Barcelona away in 2008 is legendary. He convinced the team by saying: "If we follow this, then we'll get a result." We did and beat them 1–0. Iniesta, Xavi and all those players didn't get any joy in those pockets in behind.

'Some of the English lads didn't like his style, but I did and he liked me as a person. He also called me by my first name, which he didn't with some of the lads as they found it disrespectful. It was probably easier for him to say Ole than Gunnar Solskjaer.

'And there were other good coaches. René Meulensteen could sell sand in the Sahara, but he'd convince you with his methods, which is important for a coach to do. Later, René influenced me a lot in my coaching.'

Manchester United v Real Madrid in 2003 was a turning point for two players.

'I started, Becks didn't. That was the beginning of the end for him at United. It was the first time that I started a big, big game – apart from when others had been injured. We had head tennis in the morning and I was in Becks' team when the gaffer called him over to say that he wasn't going to start against Real Madrid and that I was starting. The shit hit the fan, but it wasn't something I could have done anything about and needed to think of my own game. Which was one of the best games that I ever played, but I should have scored two or three because I had some decent chances.'

Solskjaer, playing on the right wing in place of Beckham, needed to score after a 3–1 defeat away in the first leg.

'I was up against Roberto Carlos at left-back and Zinedine Zidane as the left midfielder. We had me and Wes [Brown] on the right. We weren't really regulars and we needed to win by two and I gave Ruud an assist so it was 1–1 at half-time. We still believed, but Ronaldo scored some screamers and United fans had the class to applaud him. Man United class, the way you do things and conduct yourself. It's not just about winning 1–0. It sounds idealistic, but Man United should do things differently and with class. We turned the game to win 4–3 and I believed that we could get five and six. We never ever stopped believing. It was one of the most memorable games that I'd played in and had I scored just one of those chances, I think I'd remember it as the most memorable from my performance point of view.'

With Beckham Madrid-bound, Solskjaer became the first-choice right winger.

'And then we signed Cristiano,' he says, laughing. 'We could see that he was a massive talent and would become a superstar, but I was not going to step aside. I was stubborn and my stubbornness killed me in one game against Wolves [August 2003, Old Trafford]. Cristiano was on the left. He played against Denis Irwin, then at Wolves. Cristiano didn't get any change out of Denis, so he kept changing position to try and get away from him. Cristiano wasn't tracking back as he should, so I ended up tracking his position and running more than I had done in any other game. I felt a sense of loyalty to the team. Towards the end, I was fucked. I should have asked to be subbed, but I thought, "This young cocky player is not going to be the reason that I ask to be subbed." Scholesy played a ball in behind for me to run onto. I cut inside and stretched but felt my thighs and legs give in. I could feel my thigh bone and my knee. But I cut inside and shot with my left, missed the target and then jogged off to get changed. That was the moment when I first fucked my knee up. That was the start of three years of injury hell. All because I wasn't prepared for Man United to lose a game because a young player was not tracking back, which meant I did his job.'

Solskjaer went on an international break soon after.

'My knee had gone – cartilage. I didn't want to miss games for Norway so I tried to play. I came back, played for United against Panathinaikos and it was in that match, just before half-time, that the pain was unbearable. I had to come off.'

Solskjaer went into hospital and wasn't sure what was going to happen.

'I woke up after the anaesthetic and knew that I'd not just been out for 45 minutes, but for hours. I felt my knees and knew they'd operated on it. I carried on and recuperated for four months, then played again in the FA Cup semi-final against Arsenal at Villa Park [in 2004]. I played up front on my own and did well.'

Underdogs United won 1–0.

'The gaffer praised me at half-time. He said that I'd shown a masterclass of how you lead the line on your own. That gave me a feeling that I was important for the team. The fans were brilliant that day, too.'

The atmosphere was so loud that the *Guardian*'s Richard Williams chose it as the focus of his match report. 'The fervour that fuelled United's effort, reinforced by the incessant ardour of their fans, made this one of the season's great occasions,' he wrote. United, out-of-form, were playing an Arsenal team who would win the league by 11 points and finish 15 points ahead of Ferguson's third-placed side. The indifferent form brought out strength in adversity from 17,000 travelling fans.

Solskjaer had previous at Villa Park. In January 2002, he started the comeback from 2–0 down in an FA Cup third-round tie with a goal in the 77th minute. Van Nistelrooy added two after 80 and 82. Travelling Reds ran onto the pitch, mobbing the players as millions watched on TV, puritans squealing in disgust.

'My first experience of the FA Cup has been beautiful,' said Ruud, without a trace of hype.

'What was it about pitch invasions and Villa Park?' laughs Solskjaer. 'With fans, I felt that United supporters could see in me someone who gave 100 per cent and put the team first – maybe since that sending off against Newcastle after I'd stopped Robert Lee running on goal. That was in 1998.

'It had to be done. There were a couple of games left in the league. We were two points behind Arsenal and had to catch up on them. And I had to catch Rob Lee before he got to the box. Becks came up to me as I was sent off and I told him: "I had to."

'Yet I paid for it after. The gaffer hammered me in the dressing room and I was fined two weeks' wages the next day. Then he said: "Raimond van der Gouw was in a good position, son. And Robert Lee has a bad goalscoring record." How could I think about Robert Lee's goalscoring record when I saw him running towards goal? I wasn't going to let him try. I think deep down, Sir Alex knew I did that for the team.'

Millwall were the opponents in the 2004 FA Cup final at Cardiff. Solskjaer had been joined by another striker, Louis Saha.

'Good lad. Very talented player. We once blitzed Reading away in an FA Cup game and were 3–0 up inside six minutes. We played up front and both scored. He was perfect for me because he was strong, quick. I could assist for him. I enjoyed playing with Louis a lot more than I enjoyed driving with Louis. He lived around the corner from me. He had this rapid Mercedes car with a big engine. He arranged to pick me up one day for an away game. I was reliable and on time. No fuss. He had to collect me at 3 p.m., but he was late. I told him that we'd never make the meet on time and that they might leave without us. He was laughing and said: "Don't worry, we'll make it." I've never been so afraid and scared in my whole life. The way he drove down the A34 was like a Formula One driver. He could see I was worried but he just laughed. We made it.

'I didn't really like playing at Cardiff in those finals. It was a dry, slow pitch. I came on in the final for Ronaldo and, as we celebrated, I thought, "This might be the last game that I ever play for Man United" because I knew, given the pain still in my knee, that I needed a massive operation and there was a likelihood of never playing again because my knee was not going to be 100 per cent and you need to be 100 per cent to play for United.'

He went to Sweden for the second procedure.

'A transplant. Then it was another 18 months of not playing properly before I had four months, on and off, playing as a sub or for the reserves, at the end of the 2005–06 season. But I was never the same again.'

A banner appeared on the Stretford End with the words: 'OLEGEND'. He was a patron of the United Supporters Trust (MUST) too. Was that awkward when the takeover, which the fans had fought, went through in 2005?

'The players didn't speak about it a lot. They just wanted to stay focused on winning. And if the gaffer was happy with the takeover then we were.'

A few months after the May 2005 takeover, Solskjaer returned to action for a reserve game against Liverpool. A larger than usual crowd of 3,000 showed up to see him. He won his place back in the first team. He came back as a substitute against Birmingham City in December 2005 and made a start in a cup game against Burton Albion the following month. In March 2006 his cheekbone was broken accidentally by Ugo Ehiogu of Middlesbrough in a reserve game.

'Mike Phelan drove up to watch me and he did see me for two minutes until the accident. He then had to drive me to hospital in my full kit. Not a good day for Mick – that's why I had to bring him back as assistant manager years later.'

Solskjaer did get back into the first team for 2006–07.

'I was captain on occasion. I took that as a compliment from the gaffer. I remember one friendly where I was only going to play 45 minutes and Giuseppe Rossi played. The gaffer asked me to play a full game and he slaughtered Rossi for five minutes at half-time because he was fannying and flicking and trying daft things. Giuseppe was crying. So, I stayed on and then the manager said to me in private after: "Ole, you explain to Giuseppe why I said those things." I told him that the manager did believe in him but he wanted him to learn the United game and stop with the flicks and tricks. He would learn and he had a very good career, but I don't think he'll ever forget that talk from the manager. I believe that the manager had, on occasion, to be cruel to be kind because some players responded to that.'

When the Norwegian scored against Charlton Athletic in August 2006 it was his first Premier League goal since 2003.

'Ole has been through a torrid time with injuries for the last two years,' said Ferguson. 'But he's persevered, never lost faith and got his repayment tonight. Everyone is over the moon for him.'

'I was playing well and back into scoring double figures,' Solskjaer explains. 'People were surprised. We played Orlando Pirates during the 2006 pre-season tour of South Africa and I wanted to make a good impression. I was fitter than ever and scored twice. That performance put something in the gaffer's mind where he thought – and he said it publicly – that he would reconsider his plans because he could now count on me again. That season went well until I did my hamstring again against Copenhagen.'

Fellow Scandinavian Henrik Larsson arrived on loan, in part because Solskjaer was struggling with injury, in 2007.

'When Henrik left, the coaches had a far higher opinion of him than when he arrived,' says Solskjaer. 'Before, there were people saying: "He's only done it at Celtic, it's only the Scottish league" – even though he'd done well at Barcelona. The key to Henrik was his movement and the simplicity of his play. Paul McGuinness [reserve team manager] made a video of his play and every time he touched the ball, he only touched it once. He never had two touches. It was all about layoffs, link-up play and he could score. He was quiet, shy even. But he made a difference, just as Cantona had done. And he was a fantastic teammate.

'I mentioned Paul McGuinness because he played a key role in the development of so many young United players. I think they'd all say that they have more respect for Paul now than when they had him as a manager because he was never about being liked. He was about knowing what they needed and when you're 16, 17 or 18, you'd hate Paul's strictness and discipline. But Paul knew that you had to go through a process to be a Man United player and that once you made it, the players understood.'

Solskjaer's last United appearance came in the 2007 FA Cup final.

'I came on for the last five minutes of extra-time to take a penalty. The gaffer told me to make sure I took one. Then [Didier] Drogba scored after 116 minutes and penalties weren't needed. That could have been a great send-off but it wasn't to be. I didn't know that was going to be my last game since I still had a contract for the following season. I felt that I could be a good sub for a year.'

Another injury, this time in training, changed all that.

'I heard a crack in a four v four game and went to get a scan at a clinic in Whalley Range the next day. I got the results and drove back to Carrington, thinking: "How am I going to tell the gaffer that I'm finished?" I was so not looking forward to it and wasn't sure how to phrase it. As I drove in, the gaffer was walking out to the car park and he waited for me.'

'How are you, son?' asked Ferguson.

'Not good, boss, I need another operation and I'm not going to do it,' replied Solskjaer. 'I'm going to finish.'

'Don't worry, son,' replied Ferguson. 'You've had a fantastic career. You've made your family proud. You had a great season last year with 11 goals. Why don't you coach my forwards?'

'I'd been out of work for about five seconds,' laughs Solskjaer, 'and I was back in a new job at United, coaching the forwards, which I did for a year. I loved helping players who wanted to be helped. Not all players do. After a year I was offered the job of reserve team manager. If you'd asked my teammates I'm certain that not one of them would have said that I'd be a manager, especially the lads I played with in the 90s. I was quiet, I listened and did my job. But towards the end of my career more of my football personality came out and I started helping younger players. I'd always been football mad, a coach before I was a player. I played *Football Manager* and wrote my own team sheets out from the age of eight, always been a *Football Manager* guy, not a *FIFA* guy.'

Aged 13, he formed a Kristiansund street team he called 'Maranico' – an abbreviation of Maradona, Platini and Zico. He'd cycle around the town, getting the best players to play for it.

'Management was more my dream,' he says. 'I've always been fascinated by picking teams, buying players, selling players and my dream was to be the Man United manager. Of course, you prefer to be a player because you're young and fit and can run around, plus you only must concentrate on looking after yourself and being a good teammate, but being a coach is what I was meant to do.

'There are others like me and if I'm honest, I would not have seen Phil Neville becoming a coach like he has. He was a quiet one, Gary the noisy one. Phil had similar personality to me, quietly confident. He just wanted to get on with things, he didn't want headlines. We were number 12, 13, 14 players, the loyal players who the gaffer needed for 20–30 starts per year. Nicky

Butt was another, though Nicky was also a big entertainer in the dressing room.'

Solskjaer received a testimonial against Espanyol at Old Trafford in 2008.

'I spoke to Barcelona and other clubs but they didn't want to commit. Espanyol, with Iván de la Peña, did, and I appreciated that. My friend is a doctor and he gave me a cortisone injection before the game so that I had no pain in my knee in almost five years. Those 20 minutes I played were a joy. I loved it, apart from the goalkeeper not reading the script because I turned, swivelled and shot on goal. It should have been the winning goal, in my testimonial. But he made a great save! Fraizer Campbell scored the winner and when I took him to Cardiff City years later, I told him that I should have never played him because he didn't pass to me. But a good memory.'

Solskjaer was known as a super sub, but in 2002 coach Queiroz came to him and said: 'We're going to get rid of this super sub tag. You're more than a sub.' Solskjaer says: 'He believed in me.'

Had Solskjaer been offended by this term?

'No, I liked it. I'd rather be a super sub than an average Joe because I knew that I affected games and I knew how to influence the gaffer. If we weren't winning, then I'd start jogging down the line and the fans would start singing for me. He would take notice of that, so would my teammates and so would the opponents when I came on for the last 20 minutes. My reputation helped us more than if there was no such thing as me coming off the bench. It was all part of the mental side of football. When Erling Haaland was taken off for Norway against Scotland in an important game, with Norway leading 1–0, it wasn't just a football decision. Scotland knew that Norway's biggest threat was off the pitch and that they would have a chance. And they did.'

Solskjaer was coach of United's reserves from 2008–11 with Warren Joyce.

'Carlos convinced the manager that I would be a coach,' he explains. 'That caused a little bit of conflict behind the scenes. Danny Simpson was one of my players and he was brought down to play with the reserves in a tournament in Holland. I asked him if it was the lowest point of his career, playing with lads four to five years younger. It wasn't ideal for him but I wanted him to be humble and have good habits. He listened to me and would ultimately have a good career, but on that trip Warren and I saw a big taxi pull up outside a restaurant we were in. Danny, with his bigger wages, was treating the players to a night out in Amsterdam. We hammered him for this and had all the lads running hard the next morning. Danny's career had found another low that morning, but I think experience helped Danny. I was proud when he became a Premier League winner, same with other players I coached: Danny Drinkwater, Matty James and Ritchie De Laet. They had other coaches, but some of what Warren and I did made a difference to their game. I felt the same when I saw Paul Pogba become a World Cup winner or Danny Welbeck being an established Premier League player. Sam Johnstone had a good career, Ron-Robert Zieler won a World Cup with Germany, Josh King had a good career, Rafael and Fabio too.'

Other reserve players chose to leave professional football, including Oliver Gill, son of the club's CEO, David.

'Oliver could play and was on the bench for the first team. He was quick with a good left foot but he was too clever to be a centre-back and probably not tough enough with his mentality to be a top footballer. Oliver was a coach's dream because if you told him something he'd take it all in and try to do it to the best of his ability.'

Federico Macheda was one of his players. He'd later follow him to Cardiff, testing his manager's patience, but knowing that Solskjaer rated him as a finisher.

'Ole was in charge of United's reserves and helped me a lot,' explains Macheda. 'He also took me to Cardiff City. He paid attention to strikers because he'd been a great one himself. He told me the secrets of striking, he coached us after training, getting us to do extra finishing and encouraged us to score the scruffy goals too. I knew how to finish but he made me better. I wish every young striker would have someone like Ole working with them.'

Macheda was responsible for one of the great moments of United's noughties.

'People still ask me about it all the time,' he says. 'I understand why people see me as a guy who scored one important goal but I don't see me like that,' he says. 'It was a great moment and my friends in Rome were calling me, crying. My life completely changed. Even now I remember details that I've not told anyone. Like me crying in the dressing room showers as all the emotion came out from what had just happened.'

Let us remind you what did happen.

It's 5 April 2009 and Manchester United are playing Aston Villa at Old Trafford. After an hour, Villa have come from behind and lead 2–1 when Macheda, 17, is brought on for his United debut. He'll play up front with Ronaldo and Tevez. United had lost their two previous matches and slipped to second behind a Liverpool team who'd won 4–1 at Old Trafford weeks earlier. It was squeaky bum time, alright: Alex Ferguson's side had to win.

Macheda was on the bench because he'd been doing well in the reserves under Ole Gunnar Solskjaer, having moved from Rome with his family aged 15. He was learning English and things were going so well that Sir Alex Ferguson had said to him: 'If you do well tonight then there's a big chance that you're going to be on the bench on Sunday against Villa.' Macheda scored three goals that night against Newcastle United's reserves.

That's why, combined with Wayne Rooney being suspended and Dimitar Berbatov injured, he was on the bench.

'I was actually supporting Aston Villa because I wanted to get on the pitch,' he explains. 'If Villa were winning – and they were – then I'd have a better chance. I just wanted to play one game for United. I wanted that so much that I'd left Lazio, the team I've supported all my life and still support. I was just happy to be there. Even at half-time I stayed on the pitch kicking the ball around.'

Ferguson shouted to him after Villa had scored their second.

'"Kiko! Kiko!" he said. I looked around; I thought he was shouting to someone else, but there was only one Kiko, me! And he shouted again, more angrily, "Kiko! Kiko! Get changed. You're going on."'

United's number 41 whipped his tracksuit off and crossed himself. He'd only told his parents, who were only 34 themselves, five years younger than United's goalkeeper Edwin van der Sar, the night before that he was on the bench. They'd been working as a security guard and hotel maid in the tough Roman district of Ponte di Nona before their move to Manchester. Money was tight, there were no family holidays. The move had been a huge change for them, too, as they watched from the stand as their son replaced Nani.

Macheda told himself, 'Get on the ball as soon as you can' and went to the halfway line, shouting to Patrice Evra for the ball.

'I needed a first touch, then I knew that I could play.' He appealed unsuccessfully for a penalty after a challenge from Curtis Davies.

'My touches were good, I was pressing, defending and confident. Ronaldo scored and it was 2–2.' That was after 80 minutes; United needed a win, not a draw.

'I went to celebrate with Ronaldo and wanted to hug him but didn't have the confidence to smash into his chest as I didn't know him that well. I honestly thought: "If my career ends now then my friends will see me on the pitch next to Ronaldo."'

'Let's go!' screamed Ronaldo. But Macheda couldn't.

'I was fucked!' he says. 'I'd run like a happy dog for 20 minutes. They wanted more from me. But they weren't my usual teammates. They were the first team. I didn't really know them; I'd only trained with them for two days.'

Roared on by the crowd, United attacked and attacked. In the 90th minute Patrice Evra passed forward to Michael Carrick, who switched the ball to Gary Neville.

'I thought I was fit but I was running forward and I couldn't breathe,' explains Macheda. 'I was so tired. Neville passed to me and I tried to turn but lost the ball. It went to Giggsy. My back was against the goal, I couldn't really do anything.'

Giggs returned the ball to the Italian.

'I tried a crazy back heel but then I turned and shot,' he says. 'It was instinct, I wasn't even looking at the goal, but I knew I'd hit it well. I knew that as soon as I raised my head and saw the ball going towards goal.' The back heel had helped him turn behind a defender before he curled a shot like Kobbie Mainoo, from the same spot, in front of the Stretford End, Macheda's flying past Brad Friedel. And like Mainoo, he was already turning away to celebrate.

'I began to run towards my family but everyone grabbed me. Darren Fletcher pulled me to the floor. I was struggling to breathe. His arm was around my neck. I said to Danny Welbeck, who was hugging me, "I can't breathe, man, tell him to move." Finally, they let go and I ran to my father, who jumped over the fence and hugged me. The noise was crazy.'

That was his United high point. At least he had it. Another of Solskjaer's reserve team players was Rodrigo Possebon. I've met the Brazilian several times in his own country, where he's doing well as a sports director in the top division. He's from Porto Alegre, like Anderson.

'My career started there at Internacional, the world champions, when I was in their youth ranks,' he said. 'Many players went from

Inter's youth system to Europe: Pato, Oscar, Nilmar, Fred, Sandro and Lucio. At 15, I heard that a scout from United was following my steps in youth tournaments around Brazil. Since being young, my biggest aim was to play for a big club in Europe, but I never expected it could happen so fast.

'The scout, John Calvert Toulmin, tried to make contact with Internacional, but the club didn't want to talk. They said I was young and they didn't want to negotiate. After a year of negotiations, they saw that I really wanted to go to United and there was nothing that they could do. I travelled twice to Manchester before signing, to meet the club and see everything.

'I was 17 and I lived things at United that money could not buy. It was the greatest experience of my life in terms of football, to live together with such great players and a legend as a manager.

'The Manchester weather took some getting used to but I lived well in England. I always had in mind that when you go out to another country you should absorb the new culture and deal with it as quickly as possible, that attitude accelerates your adaptation. I liked fish and chips, but not with any sauce.

'My two compatriots Rafael and Fabio were at the club, as were their family, which helped me a lot. I was always at their house; we were close, the same with Anderson. Cristiano Ronaldo was a very good guy, always helping, chatting, advising and being close to us.

'I tried to settle in fast and put my mind into the football part. United gave me everything I needed to just focus on my job. I did my best in training and games, learned day-by-day surrounded by great players who helped me improve and grow.

'English football was completely different to Brazilian. The tactics, type of players, a different type of grass. The game was quicker in terms of movement, passing and style of play. In Brazil you have more time on the ball, it's warmer and the pitches are heavier than England. That makes it a bit slower, but not easier, just different. Moving young to Manchester helped me to understand those things. As you are young you still have time to adjust your style. You will not change as a player and you don't want to because United signed you because of your style, but you need to adapt and adjust.

'After six months I started to train with the first team, the best level you can get with some of the best players in the world: Cristiano, Scholes, Ferdinand, Rooney, Anderson, the twins [Fabio and Rafael], van der Sar, Vidić, Giggs, Tevez and a lot more. Fletcher, O'Shea and Wes Brown were funny and very nice with me.

'Ferguson was receptive with all the young players, always talking and asking how everything was, or if I needed something. In 2008, just after United became European champions, someone told me that I was travelling the next day to Johannesburg to join the first team squad on the pre-season. I just packed things, took the yellow fever injection and went to Africa, where I played two friendly matches. It was my first experience with the squad and was great. I was in Africa for the first time and with the first team squad for the first time.

'The games went well and I was a substitute in the opening Premier League game. Giggs had to come off. I looked around and there was only me as a midfielder. The manager called me. There were 75,000 supporters and not much time to think. I was on. When you play with such good players alongside you things get easy, you are almost every time comfortable on the ball, and you need to make the right decisions. Rio spoke to me a lot when I was on the pitch. That impressed me, how he could play at such a high level and concentration and still give me advice as he did.

'I broke into the first team and was in good shape. Unfortunately, in football you are never fully protected against injuries and I suffered a bad tackle against Middlesbrough. But it could be much worse, that tackle could have broken my leg as people thought at the time. That didn't happen, thank God. I was left with a deep cut in my leg and it was a month before I came back. And one month is a long time in football, especially for me at that time as I was doing well.

'Ferguson was furious with the tackle and the Middlesbrough manager Gareth Southgate apologised. My United career never really got going after that.'

Such was Possebon's opinion of Solskjaer, he called me in 2014 to ask if I'd put a word in for him at Cardiff. It wasn't really my place and I'd not got Solskjaer's latest phone number. Possebon persisted and I called Cardiff, who put me straight through to the manager.

'Andy,' he said, 'I'm still following you. If I need to fall asleep then I just read one of your articles.'

Relationships formed at United would stay with the Norwegian as he moved through various clubs in management.

'I took Quinton Fortune to Cardiff as a coach,' he says. 'And that was after I brought him as a coach at United when I was with the reserves. I respect Quinton a lot, if that's not obvious. As a player, he could play almost everywhere. He was strong as an ox, a beast who could irritate the fuck out of you because you couldn't take the ball off him. I once hurt myself as I tried to kick him. He stood strong and I twisted a ligament. Quinton felt nothing.'

We're coming to the end of the chat. I've kept in touch with Ole Gunnar since he left United as manager, but I also knew him when he played. We were delighted to hear that he'd been in the old Sportspages bookshop in Manchester to buy one of our fanzine t-shirts from Camp Nou in '99. We printed a simple message in black print on a grey t-shirt which read 'This Is The One' (a title of a Stone Roses song) 'Solskjaer and Sheringham. Camp Nou 26/5/99'. No fuss, he went in as a customer of a shop which sold fanzines, but the shop assistants obviously recognised him. Most footballers don't understand fan culture. They talk in clichés about the fans being wonderful and how they appreciate their support. In reality, they have misgivings because their only interaction with fans is limited to persistent requests for selfies or autographs. And the type of people who spend an hour waiting to have an autograph signed are not the type of people with whom a young, rich footballer necessarily wants to identify. But Solskjaer was different. He knew what a fanzine was, what MUST did and remained close to the fans at United's huge Scandinavian supporters club. His reputation remained sound on the Manchester grapevine as a decent family man.

In 2000, I wrote his personal website with him, when players had such things. That was a day at Carrington going through his career and winding him up about the difference between Kristiansand and Kristiansund.

John Taylor is one of the main Cockney Reds who long went to every single United game home and away including friendlies. He wasn't one for wearing colours or autographs, but when he found out I was spending a day with Solskjaer, he asked if I could get him a picture of his goal in Barcelona signed together with the message 'Who put the ball in the Germans' net?'

Ole Gunnar smiled at the request, but said it was disrespectful. Instead, he wrote, 'To John, I hope you enjoyed this moment as much as me.' He did. We all did. And how could we not?

He'll never not be asked about that moment and in 2024 I travelled to India with him to see the adulation he received. And, in quieter moments, hear more of his cultural hinterland.

'Do you know Tom Waits?' he asks on a flight between Mumbai and Delhi. 'It's 50 years since the debut album. I like him a lot.' In nearly 30 years of knowing Solskjaer, it's the first time that the talk has not been about football, the subject which consumes his life, and about listening to gravelly-voiced Californian singers.

But even that India trip was rare for him since he's perfectly happy being at home on Norway's Atlantic Coast.

'Nobody stops me for photos in Kristiansund,' he says. That's not the case away from the town, where people either a) ask him for photos or b) tell him that he looks like Ole Gunnar Solskjaer.

'My kids love that,' he says as we conclude. 'I'm not one for looking back, but I enjoyed reminiscing. And I should say that I would never have been able to have my career without my wife's support as a player and a coach. She always stood by me. It's why I could turn down offers after I left United as a manager. I didn't need to take them for the sake of working. I wasn't about money, we – not I – wanted an adventure. We certainly had that at United.'

2

YIP JAAP

Jaap Stam

Jaap Stam's mum was on the phone.

'I'm worried about you,' she said, calling from the Stam family home in the small Dutch town of Kampen. 'What are you eating in England? Do they have meat over there? Chicken? Beef?'

'No, they don't sell either,' replied the world's most expensive defender, who had transferred to United a couple of weeks before. 'If I want meat in England then I have to go out and find a cow and cook it.'

Mrs Stam saw through that one. Proud parents of four children, Jaap's mum and dad had never been abroad, didn't speak English and had never been on a plane until they went to see their youngest son in Manchester in 1998.

'They got lost at both airports,' laughs Stam. We're sitting on a terrace in Zwolle, the city where he now lives, close to where he grew up. It's an important rail hub in Holland, an hour from Amsterdam by train next to the IJssel, a major tributary of the Rhine.

'I once went to pick them up at Manchester Airport and they weren't there. I could see their bag moving around the carousel when the doors opened, but no parents. This was for half an hour. They had decided to take a walk to the other side of the airport. My dad just wanted a cigarette. He was a heavy smoker and struggled not smoking for the 45-minute flight from Amsterdam. He wasn't allowed to smoke in Manchester Airport but he thought nobody could see him.'

There was unease among some of Stam's siblings about how their parents would survive on their expedition to Manchester, with one of them asking her father what they'd do if something went wrong.

'I'll just drive home,' said Stam Senior.

'But you don't have a car and they drive on the opposite side of the road,' said his daughter.

'I'll rent a car and if we have a problem, I'll just call the guys.'

'But the guys are your friends in Kampen. They fix the streetlights and they're not in Manchester. It's a different country.'

Nevertheless, Stam's parents soon found their feet on their visit to Northern England.

'Dad drank a strong Dutch liquor called Jenever,' explains Jaap. 'He signalled for a small one, which is a known signal for a Jenever in Holland. In Kampen, the bartenders understood this since they also knew that my father drank it as he was a regular. But in the Mottram Hall hotel where I stayed when I first moved to England, the waiters couldn't understand his signal. And why would they?'

Stam's father took control of the situation.

'Son, he understands that I want a Jenever.'

'No, Dad, they don't have it over here.'

'OK, I'll have a whisky then.'

The Stams must have been impressed with England since they returned a few months later at Christmas. That was after Jaap had been back to Holland, where his father had a surprise for him.

'My parents invited me to re-watch my United games with them,' he says. 'I never re-watched games. I had played in them and remembered them. They meant well and they were proud, but I didn't want to spend my precious time back in Holland watching myself play football on TV.'

For his first Christmas in England, United gave each player an ample-sized turkey.

'I took it home and put it in the fridge. My dad saw it and his eyes lit up. I said he could take it back to Holland as I wasn't going to prepare it and cook it.'

Stam's father had no qualms about carrying a large dead bird.

'He placed the turkey on the conveyor belt along with the suit-cases. The check-in girl asked him what it was and he replied, "Kalkoen." Which is turkey in Dutch, but we were not in Holland. I said that it was a turkey and she said that you can't check a turkey in like a suitcase. My father picked it up, carried it through security and took it on the plane as hand luggage. Once home, he prepared it for all the family, this special English turkey from Manchester United. And then the whole family had the shits in the days after.'

Stam talks with affection about his parents, who have passed away.

'They were from a different world to the one I ended up living in. They had little, so saved everything and left nothing to waste. I'm so glad that they got to see some of the world and visit the places where I played in England and Italy. They were really enjoy-ing life by that stage after many tough times.'

Stam describes his background.

'I was born in Kampen, a small place of 40,000 close to Zwolle. I still have friends there and see them. My family was working-class: Dad a carpenter, Mum a house mum. We didn't have money; you'll hear that from many footballers. Dad worked every day, including weekends. I have three older sisters and childhood was enjoyable. Now, my boys want good football boots, which are expensive. My boots cost 15 Guilders, around €7. My jeans were handed down to me from my sisters, my sweaters too. Except for a special one which was bought for me, which I was allowed to wear on Sundays to visit family. I was always out, playing football with friends.

'There were no steaks to eat, just potatoes. No eating out, no trips abroad. I met my now wife Ellis at 16 and my first trip abroad was at 18 when I travelled to England for a trial at Sheffield Wednesday. The manager, Trevor Francis, invited me because Jimmy Calderwood was assistant manager at Zwolle, my first professional team. The plane had a propeller and I was frightened.'

Stam was progressing quickly.

'When I was 12, I was the smallest in my team but I started growing at 16 and quickly moved up to play for Dos Kampen, before joining Zwolle.'

Sheffield Wednesday asked Stam to come back but he wanted to stay at Zwolle in the Dutch second division.

'I had a positive impression of Wednesday: Trevor Francis, training, the quality of the first team who had finished third in England and the people at the club, but it was my first season in professional football. I was at home and felt I was in the right place. I was only earning €750 per month before tax, but I still felt rich because I was still at school – an OK student, but someone better with his hands like my dad. I was always trying to fix things or speed things up like motorbikes. But when I started getting money for football, I could go out and eat food if I wanted or buy a shirt for the first time ever. Life was good.'

Stam was a childhood Ajax fan but attending matches was out of his reach: 'a different world to the one I was in. None of my friends went to Ajax.

'The manager, Theo de Jong, took me to Zwolle and I signed a contract, but then he left to join Cambuur, so I had a new manager. He said: "I don't know what I should do with him because he's coming from the amateurs", so I had to prove myself again. I was 20 but I proved that I was capable of handling that level. After one season, Cambuur's manager de Jong came back in for me and took me to the Eredivisie. Zwolle sold me for £100,000, so they made a big profit.

'I was now in the top division but I struggled at the start. I had an ankle injury which didn't help, but jumping from the amateur league to the Eredivisie in two seasons was a huge leap. I had to adapt to the more intense and physical football and I had to be fitter and that took a couple of months. I played as a right-back but a managerial change meant I was put at centre-back and stayed there.'

Stam's stock continued to rise and he was sold after two seasons for £400,000 to Willem II in Tilburg.

'I was there for just six months and continued to do well. We even beat Louis van Gaal's Ajax team, who were European champions. There was a lot of interest in me during the winter break. Celtic were interested. I was sold to PSV for the equivalent of £1 million. They had injuries and needed a new centre-back. There was a release clause and PSV knew that. I was happy to move because I always wanted to make steps and if things didn't work out then I could always go back.'

At PSV, Stam again started out as a right-back.

'A couple of games before a centre-back got injured, I moved to centre-back and left the full-back position. PSV had a very good team: Phillip Cocu, Wim Jonk, Jan Wouters, Luc Nilis and Ronaldo. He was a kid, a great player who replaced another Brazilian forward, Romário. Ronaldo was always complaining about how cold Eindhoven was compared to Brazil, but he was so talented. He was telling people that he'd score 35 goals and we were laughing at him, but he was right and he did. Ronaldo was so fast, even with the ball at his feet, and so unpredictable that it was perfect for me to play against him in training. Against Ronaldo, I learned when to go tight, how to mark spaces and to be better positioned. We had real battles in training sessions which we both enjoyed, two young players.'

PSV won the cup in Stam's first season, the league in his second, when he was given the Dutch Footballer of the Year award. In the third they didn't win anything but reached the Champions League and played Newcastle United.

'PSV was a top club with great people and players. I was paid €150,000 per year, then deducted almost 50 per cent tax. It was good money but not crazy at all because you also had to pay 50 per cent of your wages into a pension, which is normal in Dutch professional football to prevent players spending or losing all their money.'

Stam's agent, Tom van Dalen, called him and said that there was a team interested in him. Stam told him that he was happy at PSV. The agent insisted that this team was worth thinking about: Manchester United. Stam agreed that United were indeed worth thinking about.

'I watched English football on TV and United were the biggest club, popular in Holland. But I said no to Sir Alex – via my agent – because I didn't feel ready. I was 23 and I made decisions with my heart. PSV was a wonderful club; [Ellis and I] got married and bought our first house together too. I had no urge to go abroad and wanted to establish myself in the national team first. I was aware that was a risk, that there might not be another chance and I was comfortable with that.'

United didn't give up. Ferguson had plans to replace Gary Pallister and sent his brother Martin to watch Stam in person several times in the following season. The player knew this was happening but never spoke to him.

'Eventually, Sir Alex called me a couple of times during the season. I was told that he was going to call and was more nervous about that conversation than I was about playing games. He called me and I couldn't really understand him. I would pick up certain words like "game" and "play" and I answered what I thought was the answer to his question. The calls continued after matches and I was so nervous that I was dripping in sweat. My wife couldn't understand why I was nervous when I was used to playing in front of huge crowds, but I was. I can laugh about it now, but my career was a big deal. PSV knew of United's interest and at the start said that they were not going to let me go as they'd renewed my contract. That came because they'd said I would get a bigger contract if I did well and got into the national team. And feelings in football can change quickly, the way you feel about situations and people. I went from being completely happy at PSV to wanting to join Manchester United within six months because I felt I was ready to play in England. Eventually, I told PSV that I wanted to leave. They were angry, which was understandable. They said they didn't want me to go and that whoever bought me would have to pay a lot of money – €15 million – record transfer fees. And because of the money, I didn't think I'd move. I knew that talks were going on because my agent was telling me.'

United kept in touch.

'Sir Alex flew to Amsterdam and we met in an apartment of one of my friends. We could look each other in the eye and he said that he wanted to sign me because he wanted the team to play at a higher level and he thought I could help him out.'

There were other suitors.

'Liverpool. Italian and Spanish clubs. It felt good to be wanted and life felt good. My relationship with my wife was excellent. And talks made progress with United before I was told: "They want to have your fee as well". In my contract I was entitled to 10 per cent of any transfer fee paid. Over a million pounds, more or less. More money than I'd ever received in my life. And I had to let it go if I was to move to United and get nothing. PSV told me that I wasn't allowed to talk about confidential details in my contract, but then one of the PSV directors did just that.'

Stam joined United for £11 million, a world record fee for a defender.

'The most important thing for me wasn't the money, but to join United, one of the biggest clubs in the world. I wanted to win the biggest trophies. That's why I'd got into professional football. But I got a wage increase when I joined United anyway.'

Stam played in the 1998 World Cup finals, had ten days off and then met up with his new United teammates in Bergen on a pre-season. After that he went back home for two days at the suggestion of Ferguson, then moved to England to live in the Mottram Hall hotel located on a golf course where a lot of the new players were placed by United. Stam went alone, his wife stayed at home with their newly born first child, Lisa.

'I didn't play golf and I didn't drive, so Jordi Cruyff or Nicky Butt, who lived nearby, would give me a lift to training. Jordi was proud that while his car didn't look as flash as some of the other players, it was at least as fast. I learned Mancunian from Nicky, but living in a hotel quickly irritated. I knew the menu back to front and ordered everything off it. I tried every pie going and I felt a bit miserable. Different language, country, club, culture, players and I was away from the baby. Training was OK, pre-season too, but we lost 3–0 to Arsenal in the Charity Shield and I didn't have my best game. I needed to get used to the intensity of English football and the quality of the opposition. I went from feeling like I could beat any team in Holland to playing against Dennis Bergkamp and Thierry Henry. It was an eye-opener and I needed to step up. Criticism started immediately in the newspapers given my big fee and I felt pretty miserable. I'd read the newspapers alone in a hotel because I wanted to read about football, but my name was in the headlines and they were talking shit about me. More than once I wondered if I'd made the right decision moving away from a good life in Eindhoven. I also spoke to the manager and he said: "Jaap, don't read the papers. We know what you can bring, we trust you, we've watched you for a long time. Just focus on yourself."'

After a few months, things picked up.

'Lisa was old enough to fly over with my wife and we found a nice house in Bramhall. We liked it. It was an ordinary house with no big gates or anything. We wanted to live normally, but at times strangers would turn up. Later on, one man came to give me advice on how to get over an injury – as if United didn't have doctors.

'I started playing better. I didn't read any newspapers. It's very difficult for young players now to avoid what is said about them on social media because even if they don't see it, the people around them are likely to say something.

'I was in a great team and felt supported by the players and manager. I adapted to the way of playing and fitted into a social circle with Ole, Henning [Berg], Ronny [Johnsen] and Jordi. I was close mates with them and they lived locally. I met Jordi's dad Johan, all his family, and we'd spend Christmas with them. Those Cruyffs can certainly talk.

'And I ignored the media – the manager was right. I found the way the press delved into my private life to be offensive. I went to the cinema and bought two bags of sweets, which I took home and filled bowls around the house and intended to last for weeks. The *Daily Star* made it a front-page story, saying I'd eaten two bags of sweets while watching a film and quoted the price. It was bizarre. I only realised when I went into the dressing room and the lads were asking me about my sweet tooth. When I went home and told Ellis, she said: "I wondered what all this was about" and handed me a bag of sweets which a journalist had just delivered to our front door. There was a photographer hiding behind a bush waiting to take a picture of me receiving the sweets. It was a good job I wasn't at home.'

At work, Stam was impressed by his teammates.

'Henning was perfect to work with. He was reserved as a person off the pitch but never stopped talking on it. He was clever positionally and I learned from him in the early days.'

* * *

Berg felt the same and the pair played in both games against Inter Milan in the 1999 Champions League quarter-finals.

'If there's anything United fans remember me for then it's those two games against Inter,' Berg told me. 'I was involved in both, I was having a good period. My first year at United had not been good because we finished second to Arsenal. Everybody was miserable the way that ended.

'Then we got some new signings. Jaap Stam came in and made a difference. Jaap brought the physical presence that the manager was looking for, he tackled at the right time, he was fast, which Ferguson appreciated as he needed to frequently defend one v one.

'Dwight Yorke arrived too. Dwight changed the atmosphere. He was smiling all the time, even when Ferguson told him off. He'd just smile, which relaxed Ferguson.

'Dwight linked up well with Andy Cole. I did not play much at the start of that season, my best period at United was between January '99 and the end of the season.

'Against Inter I saved a shot on the line. I got injured at home to Juventus in the semi-final so I missed the away leg and the Arsenal semi-final, the Champions League. I would have not played every game but I would have played many of them as I was in the team. I was a central defender playing alongside Jaap.'

Berg, like Stam, had been the most expensive defender in British football history when he signed for United from Blackburn Rovers in 1997. He sums up his time at United thus: 'Very good but also difficult. I was there for three years and played around 100 games but I was not a regular playing all the time. This was the first time in my career that this had happened.

'Every game at United is a big one. The level was higher, the teammates better. And we had to compete in Europe too. For me to succeed at United, I had to be at my very best level. If I dropped a little bit, I was not good enough.

'United were a little more defensive than Blackburn, more solid. A bit like Norway. The central defenders took care of the strikers, yet the team was more open in front.'

And Berg, like Stam, took time to settle.

'I went to see Ferguson after a few months to talk about the style of play because I was used to playing differently. He explained how United play. Steve McClaren came in a few months later and we worked on team shape. That made a big difference for our results in Europe. In England, we were better player for player. In Europe, we'd play teams like Juventus, Barcelona, Inter and Milan. We needed to be better tactically and collectively. When Steve came in, he helped a lot. A lot.'

Berg left United in 2000.

'I didn't play enough,' he explains. 'But I still played in several quarter-finals in the Champions League. Ferguson maybe liked me more in Europe against good technical players where I read the game, whereas physically I was not the strongest or fastest for England.

'But by 2000 I was in and out of the team and I said to the manager: "It's good to be here and I like to play, but I feel I should be playing more regularly and if I can't then it's better to go some-where else." Ferguson agreed with me. Blackburn came back for me. They were in the Championship but I went there again and we got promoted. It was much better for me to be part of the Blackburn team and playing. Andy Cole came to Blackburn, then Dwight Yorke. It wasn't like United, there was no Europe and games against Zidane and Del Piero, but we finished sixth in my last season in the Premier League.'

Berg also speaks warmly about his compatriot, Johnsen.

'Ronny was top. If he hadn't had all those injuries, Ronny would have been regarded as one of the better central defenders in Europe. Playing with Ronny felt natural after a while, we didn't even need to speak. He was underestimated as a player. He was fast, physical and we called him "the Leech" in training because he wouldn't let go of you. The other players would shout "Fucking hell, Ronny, go and mark somebody else, you leech". He was also called the Iceman. People thought it was because he was cool, but it was because he had so many ice packs on his knees and ankles after matches.'

Stam explains how United played.

'We played on the front foot going forward, which meant the full-backs bombed on. Even Roy Keane wanted to move forward and I'd shout at him to sit, to which he responded by saying: "Fucking hell, you should be able to handle that at the back." Opponents would play with two strikers and a ball would be put over the top, so we had to be trusted to defend well and we did. I was from a culture in Holland where people expect the centre-back to do everything – tackle, head well, pass well, dribble and be the extra man in midfield. Yet at United I wasn't allowed to do all of those. I drove into midfield once and carried on moving forward, then I saw Fergie come down from the bench and give me a bollocking from the touchline. "Give the ball to Scholesy!" he shouted, "we've got other players to score, not you." For Sir Alex, a centre-back was there to defend. He wanted me to stick to the task that I did best.'

There were other defenders.

'David May was an important man in the dressing room. He brought light, fun and air. He'd call every player out and try to provoke us all. He'd tell me to stop moaning and accused me of always moaning. Maysie was good on the ball, his passing and timing excellent because he wasn't the tallest centre-back. A good person and he still is.

'Gary Neville, young but confident and talked. Always had an opinion. If I passed the ball he'd shout: "Why did you pass it like that?" And I'd respond and say that it was the right pass. And we'd argue – in a positive way. That's why I said in my book that he was a busy cunt. It wasn't disrespectful like the headlines suggested, he was busy in a positive way. Gary and Phil were nice people who helped me when I arrived. And lads like Gary, Giggsy and Butty calling you out for everything kept you on your toes. If I came in with a new shirt on they'd whistle at me and say, in strong Manchester accents: "Fucking hell, Jaap, new shirt. Going out in town?". The key was not to show a reaction because if you went red, everyone would join in and it'd all go loose. At least I could understand them. When I arrived at United I thought I spoke English decently, but struggled with some of the accents. I was saying "pardon" all the time.

'I'd go home and tell my wife some of the things I'd seen at training and we'd both laugh. Like Nicky Butt being chased by a naked Peter Schmeichel after he burned his backside with a giant metal teapot.'

Stam's first season could not have gone better as the team won the treble. He played 90 minutes of every single game in the Champions League campaign, all 13 of them, as United charged towards Camp Nou.

'I felt I was improving but always that I wanted to prove myself. I was always worried about my performances. I'm a thinker and always thought about different possibilities. I put pressure on myself. I admire the players who don't care, who don't feel pressure. I was not one of them because if I made a mistake in a game, I would think about it until the next game. We had players like Yorkey [Dwight Yorke], who was totally different to me. He was like "OK, I've had a bad game, next game I'll do better but still enjoy the rest of my day". My way was for me and it brought me to the level I reached.'

Stam's captain was Roy Keane.

'A great player and a great person. I got on well with him and still do. I see him now because we both do work for television. He invites me for a coffee at his house, he's very kind. As a teammate, he wasn't always easy for a lot of people. He had his way of thinking about life and football, he's honest and tells you what he thinks. That can be difficult for some. I had arguments with him myself on the pitch if, for instance, I gave someone else the ball and they lost the ball. Like it was my fault! I would argue back and we'd go at each other for minutes. That's fine. He was always testing himself and other players. He had a remarkable attitude and we saw that most in Turin, that semi-final game [in 1999]. Juventus had a team full of world-class players but Roy really stepped up for the team, not for himself, and we needed that. He made sacrifices so that others could win trophies and we had other players like that. One of our strengths was that we had very good players in the squad, but we didn't have one player who thought he was the best in the team. And if someone acted like they were more special, the others would let him know.'

Stam was playing for the best team in the world, coming up against the strongest possible opponents. He picks out the strikers who gave him most problems.

'The Arsenal forwards. I knew Dennis Bergkamp from the national team, so I knew he was world-class. He took positions that were difficult to mark and had effective partnerships within the team.

'Alan Shearer was also difficult to mark. He was not the biggest, but he was very good in the air because he was clever in his timings. He'd run from the sides and was difficult to predict. His centre-backs would play the ball into an area where he could run at it. He'd run at the ball and head it or flick it on towards one of his teammates. Your positioning had to be perfect if you wanted to win the header and you learn things like this by playing against the best in the business.'

And Stam was thriving. Fans sang one of their more inventive songs: 'Yip Jaap Stam is a big Dutchman, Get past him if you fucking can. Try a little trick and he'll make you look a dick. Yip Yap, Jaap Stam.'

There was also a t-shirt on the swag stall of Sir Matt Busby Way featuring a picture of Stam and the suggestion that one needed a map to get around him.

'That's a good one,' says Stam when he's shown a picture of the shirt. 'The fans were really good to me.'

And forever, Stam is a treble winner.

'I never once thought about winning the treble, more about adjusting myself so that I could play for my new club. My priority was winning the league in my first season and we did that. I never once spoke about winning the Champions League to my family, but you could see that things were clicking. The camaraderie among the players, the patterns clicking between players during matches. And because of that, confidence grew. We didn't give many goals away, we could see that opponents looked frightened when they came to Old Trafford. They might give it a go at the start of the game, but then revert to drop deeper. We'd push and push. We didn't create loads of opportunities but we always created enough to win games and we had players up front to finish them. It's surreal that we won it. It was then and it is now. It's a difficult thing to process and because players are always looking forward, trying to win the next games, you don't look back to process it for years, but people remind you of it all the time – and all over the world. They remember details you don't and comment on specifics. Like the time they met you. Someone asked me about the hotel we stayed at in Spain the night before the final. I couldn't tell you the name or where it was, just that you could see the sea, that there were bright colours, that it was high-rise and that we weren't allowed to leave it. There was tension and pressure. That's all I remember. Your brain prioritises what it needs and as a player, you simply don't see the impact of playing for or winning trophies for United.'

United were losing after 90 minutes. Did Stam feel it was lost?

'Yes. I mean no. I had the feeling that we were always creating opportunities because the team did. But there was a reality that the game was almost over and part of me was doubting. Belief and doubt at the same time. We didn't play well, they scored, they hit the post and crossbar too. They deserved their lead. Carsten Jancker was difficult to play against. Big, strong and difficult to get in front of when the ball was played into him. Bayern had top players: Khan in goal, Lothar Matthäus, Sammy Kuffour, Stefan Effenberg, Mario Basler, Mehmet Scholl. They had physical players. We didn't have Roy or Scholes.'

What happened at half-time?

'Everybody has got their own version of the team meeting. My memory is that Fergie said "It's one game. We're not playing our best football, but it's only 1–0 and it might be the only opportunity that you have in your lifetime for you to play in a Champions League final. Don't pass that trophy with any regrets. Make sure that tomorrow, when you look in the mirror, you can say that you gave everything." He could have talked tactics, but that's what he said.

'He was right. I wasn't playing my best football, but finals are rarely top games. That's because of the pressure that comes with them, the quality of the opposition, the importance of the result. Players are more reserved in how they play because they know that if they make a mistake and the other team scores, that's what they'll be remembered for. As a defender, you might be more reserved when you go in on a one v one.'

United got the breakthrough.

'Excellent subs from the manager. He trusted every player. He gave the players who started a chance, but when they couldn't deliver in the game he brought Teddy and Ole on. They made the difference; they were in the right place at the right time.

'It was pure joy when they scored. Normally, I'm not that joyful. I'm quite reserved, even when we scored winning goals. I'd tell everybody to stand up again and do your job. But I lost it when we equalised. I felt like I was bursting out of my skin. I also knew that

Bayern were broken. They'd been looking at the clock, but were also counting it down and had made a couple of subs to get the game done. Our equaliser broke them. You could see them thinking: "What the hell is going on here?" I wasn't one of these people who thought "we're taking the game to extra-time now". They were at their most vulnerable and we kept on going. Ole scored. I was standing behind him ready to score the perfect winner. I was ready waiting …'

When we put this to Solskjaer, he says: 'Snooze and you lose.' He was alert enough to score.

'What a feeling,' says Stam. 'The pressure vanished; we'd done it. Ten days earlier, we could have lost everything and finished the season with nothing. We knew that everyone who wasn't a United fan wanted us to fail. After all the celebrations, I went into the dressing room and had a couple of glasses of champagne. Then did some press. The party continued on the bus and back at the hotel. I remember saying: "That's me done" and going to bed. I was so tired and ran out of energy, especially after the alcohol kicked in.'

Henning Berg tells his version.

'I'd been injured a month and had tried to get back – even a week before the final. I was nervous like every fan. I thought it was slipping away and Bayern had several chances to score, but United had won so many games in the last ten minutes around that time. We only needed one goal, just one chance. The first goal was great and many teams would have been happy with that. But not United and not Solskjaer. When he received the ball on the left wing, he didn't protect it. He went at the full-back, he wanted to dribble, to go past him. He got a corner. And from that corner he scored. If he and the team had a different mentality, they would have been happy to be back in the game and to organise for extra-time. But no.'

Stam says: 'We didn't need alcohol that night, we floated on adrenaline. All of us. It was an unbelievably nice evening. We were euphoric. Genuinely. We didn't sleep. That feeling was incredible.

It had been such a long season with so much pressure when Fergie had rotated, which is a risk. And then we were set free.

'We went on an open top bus and seeing it turn into Deansgate with all the people waiting for us was one of the most beautiful things I've seen in my life. You could only see red. Everybody was cheering and supporting us, there was no space left for anyone to stand. Year later, I read a piece with Bayern's right-back, Markus Babbel. He said that he felt under such immense pressure and stressed in the last 30 minutes of that game that he just wanted it to be over – regardless of the result. He just wanted it over.

'In 2005, I was on the other side [playing for AC Milan]. Winning 3–0 against Liverpool in the Champions League final in Istanbul, we lost the game after conceding three in six minutes in the second half. When you concede the first, the losing team get their confidence back. And the pressure is even higher now, with all the social media stuff. It's encouraging that there's more attention in the area of mental health.'

United had won the treble but couldn't defend the FA Cup.

'Fergie pulled us into a room at The Cliff and told us we wouldn't be in the cup. It seemed difficult for him to break it to us and that's understandable as we wanted to retain the cup, but instead we were going to Brazil for the new Club World Championship tournament. It was hot out there and we trained at Flamengo's training ground with a stunning backdrop of mountains. You couldn't breathe properly after 20 minutes of training and concentration levels suffered. There were showers and a swimming pool next to the training pitches for Flamengo's players to cool off. We appreciated them and even held a swimming race. Goalkeeper Mark Bosnich organised it. He loved his swimming and was convinced he'd win. He was a proud Australian and they have some of the best swimmers in the world. I joined in a race and was second, which meant I made the final against Mark. Fergie was at the far end of the pool ready to judge and we both went for it. It was close and the gaffer gave the decision to Mark – but all the lads forced him to change his mind. Nicky Butt told him that he might have got the decision wrong and Ryan Giggs agreed. That was about my best moment in Brazil. Us Dutch aren't bad swimmers either.

'The games were awful. In training, at least there was a breeze. There was none in the Maracaná stadium. Some of the lads were desperate to play there but to me it was old and unattractive before it was done up for the World Cup in 2014.'

United drew their first game 1–1 against Mexican side Necaxa. The next match was against one of the five Rio giants, Vasco de Gama.

'The manager said to us: "We've not come halfway around the world and put up with all that shit in the media to go home with our tails between our legs. We are the best team in the world and now is the time to go out and prove it. Let's show everyone here and at home what this club is really about and that is winning matches, no matter who we play or where we play. The prize is there for the taking. Do you want to be champions of the world?"'

United were 3–0 down by the break, torn a new one by legendary strikers Romário and Edmundo, who were assisted by errant back passes from Gary Neville.

'The Brazilian players we were up against were used to the conditions but we actually started well,' says Stam. 'But they scored, and with their manic support, their confidence grew. They started show boating, doing tricks. Our legs were heavy and the competition was over.'

United's final game was a sideshow against a part-time South Melbourne side managed by 34-year-old Ange Postecoglou.

While United's form picked up in the league after the return from Brazil, the team were unable to retain the Champions League.

'We played Real Madrid in the quarter-finals and had an amazing belief that we could win. They weren't playing well, they'd been beaten twice by Bayern Munich in the competition and conceded four each time. We drew 0–0 in Spain, a result we were happy with, although Andy Cole had an excellent chance.' Cole said: 'I also missed the best chance of the game to put us ahead in the Bernabéu, a header which I sent over the bar. I was disappointed but didn't dwell on it. You can't. I waited for my next chance, but it never came.'

'We'd scored eight goals in our two previous games,' recalls Stam. 'We were used to steamrollering teams in the opening quarter with our opponents on the back foot. But our game plan went after Keane scored a freak own goal. He tried to cut out a cross but diverted the ball past Raimond van der Gouw. We then knew that two goals were needed but after Turin the year before, felt we could get them. We were experienced, we'd been there before. We battered away at Madrid but the balls wouldn't drop in the right places. Then, in two minutes, it fell apart. Redondo backheeled the ball and turned past Henning. That left me a bit isolated as I tried to block the angle of Redondo's attack. He threaded a ball to Raúl for a simple finish. An awful goal for us to concede and then Raúl got a second. We were three down but made Casillas work. Beckham scored a beautiful goal after going past three defenders. Scholes got a later penalty after Steve McManaman brought down Keane. Those last few minutes were as exciting and tense as anything I'd known but we were out. I felt like a boxer staggering, having been knocked out. My mind refused to accept that we wouldn't be in the final again. In the dressing room, Gary Neville said: "Have we really just lost to them?" I couldn't believe it either and refused to let go. I told Ole Gunnar that I wanted to replay the game against Madrid.'

Stam played over 50 times in each of his first two seasons for United. In his third, he was injured and missed most of the first half of the 2000–01 season.

'It was my Achilles tendon and I needed an operation. All of the games meant that a small injury got worse and worse to the point that I couldn't warm up before a game. Warming up meant it loosened up a little. I stayed inside where it was warm and even put my ankles in a warm bath in the dressing room. In one game at Leeds, I could barely run. I went to see a doctor and I needed an operation, which I had in Manchester. I was out for four months but I needed the operation.'

He was back ready to play for the 2001–02 season – and he got asked to take on a new responsibility.

'We signed Ruud van Nistelrooy and the manager asked me to look after him and show him around Manchester. I did that, though there was one issue. I took him home after training. I stopped outside and I was still driving a left-hand drive car. He needed to get out of the car into the middle of the street. A big lorry came driving up. He turned around and got close to my car as I drove off ... right over his toes with my big rear tyre. I looked in my mirror and saw him bouncing around in pain. He'd just come back from a serious injury too. We still got on ...'

Not that there would be much time for the previously injured Dutch pair to bond.

'That injury was a factor in me leaving United,' says Stam. 'The manager wasn't sure that I'd ever get back to the same level. That was said internally rather than anyone speaking to me. It was Ferguson talking to the board members within the club. They were making a decision to sell me. A manager needs to make decisions like this and consider whether someone like me could get back to a certain level after an injury and how long it would take to get back to that level. After the operation, we played Fulham in my first League game [the first game of the 2001–02 season, which United won 3–2]. I didn't play that well against Saha, who is quick. He got past me one time and some thought that I'd slowed down. The manager didn't say anything to me, but I felt it a little bit. And before I knew it, I was in Rome [playing for Lazio].

'I don't think it was just the injury. There was the book which came out at the same time and a need for United to raise money.

The message my agent got was that United had sold me and he called me. I need to get the order right and events went like this. My book, *Head To Head* [Collins Willow, 2001] came out in the international break. I didn't think the book was that special but it contains some nice inside information about me and the team. I did it with a journalist, Jeremy Butler. He was good, he didn't write it in a bad way, there were no issues. I didn't do it to slaughter players or people. The book came out on the Monday and it was serialised in the *Mirror*. I was with the national team and on the Monday morning my wife bought the newspaper and called me. The headlines looked bad; they shocked me. They had blown out of proportion what I'd said and twisted it. I called Fergie straight away and said: "I don't like these headlines. I didn't say those things in the book." He told me not to worry about it and said he'd had the same with his book. He said it would blow over and be water under the bridge by the end of the week. I was happy with that phone call.'

Stam stayed with the Dutch national team in London ahead of a game against England.

'On day two there were more headlines from my book. I was confused by what I was seeing and why I was seeing it. I had been told that they had sold a serialisation to the *Mirror* which would run for four days, but the headlines were so strong and I knew there would still be two more days of them. I tried to get a bit more input into the headlines but they basically said: "We don't do that, we do it our own way." On the Wednesday, Fergie's secretary called me and said the manager wanted to talk to me because he was pissed off. I asked why he was pissed off and she said: "Because of the things you've said in the book." I spoke to him and he gave me a bollocking on the phone. There was something about what I'd said about transfer fees and what players were worth. He gave me a hard time on the phone yet I also needed to concentrate on the game. I was worried, I had a bad feeling, I struggled to concentrate during the game. I played and drove back to Manchester and told my wife that I was going to see Fergie first thing in the morning at Carrington to try and sort things out. I did that – and he gave me another bollocking. He was very angry and after that I just went back home. On my way, I got a call from my agent and he asked where I was. I told him that I'd had a conversation with the manager but it didn't go well.

'"They've already sold you," said my agent.

'"What?"

'"United have sold you."

'"What do you mean?"

'"They had a meeting in Monaco with some of the other teams in the Champions League draw and a club put an offer in for you, which was accepted. They are going to call you."

'I was thinking: "What on earth is going on here?"'

Stam's phone went again: Sir Alex Ferguson.

'Where are you?'

'In the car.'

'Where?'

'I told him I was nearly home. He told me to stop and he'd meet me. We agreed to meet near the petrol station in the car park of Tesco's on the A34 bypass, where the manager climbed into my car and said: "We've had an offer from a club. We've accepted the offer. I've brought in a new defender and we are going to play him with Wes Brown. You're going to be on the bench if you stay."'

Stam tried to make sense of what was happening, since he'd just signed a new deal at Manchester United.

'I was on the players' committee and months before we had a meeting with the board. They gave us some inside information about the club and we did the same about the team. They'd said that there was an issue with the budget and Giggsy said: "Just sell one of us then." We all laughed. But that's what happened. I asked Fergie what club and he didn't want to say at first, then he said

Lazio. I told him that I didn't want to go to Italy. He said: "Well, we've accepted the offer." It was clear in that conversation that the trust between us had gone. As he got out of the car, I told him: "I need to think about it."'

Stam drove back to the family home in Bramhall and told his wife, who was in tears. The couple were both settled in Manchester and were renovating the house.

Things moved quickly. Ferguson called Stam again on the morning of an away game at Blackburn. He'd been left out of the squad. Stam said that people would talk even more about the book. It didn't matter.

'We were on a private plane from Manchester to Rome the next day, Ellis and I and people acting as agents who we didn't know. My agent was there but I didn't know who the other people were. There were so many people involved in that transfer. My head was spinning. There were other clubs interested too. Becks called me when I got to Rome. He told me not to leave and that I needed to stay. I told him that I was already in Italy and that the relationship was broken with the manager. I knew I could get back into the team if I'd stayed, but I just wanted to leave with everything that was happening.

'We had a look around Rome, saw the club and said yes to signing but you can see me in the press conference to announce that I'm signing. My face looks like a truck has just run over me. I was still taking in everything that was happening. I think the book was used as an excuse to sell me.'

These were difficult times for the Stams.

'We were a young family. Then we had parents in Holland reading all of this and wondering what was going on. People who we loved and people who we lived among in Manchester. We just walked away in an instant.'

In 2007, Ferguson said: 'At the time he had just come back from an Achilles injury and we thought he had just lost a little bit. We got the offer from Lazio, £16.5m for a centre-back who was 29. It was an offer I couldn't refuse. But in playing terms it was a mistake. He is still playing for Ajax at a really good level.'

Stam had just turned 29. For United that was a last chance of a big fee for him but fans didn't approve. He was considered the best defender in England, if not in the world, a balding man mountain who'd helped improve the team to treble-winning levels. Johnsen and Wes Brown soon picked up injuries.

Stam's direct replacement, Laurent Blanc, was 35 and the Frenchman with the peerless reputation was criticised for his performances and lack of speed. By the start of December, United had lost five league games to Bolton, Liverpool, Arsenal, Newcastle and Chelsea. Or BLANC to use the first letters of those teams. By the time Blanc settled and he and Gary Neville helped seal the defence, the title had been lost to Arsenal.

In his 2013 autobiography, Ferguson again admitted it was a mistake to sell Stam and described the whole move as a 'disastrous episode. Having to tell him at a petrol station was agony because I knew he was a really decent man who loved playing for the club, and who was adored by the fans. It was one of my senior moments.'

Stam and Ferguson spoke properly years later.

'Once my career finished, we met at Old Trafford around a game. He invited me into his office for a glass of wine. He started talking about what happened. He said he'd not made the right decision. He was sincere when he spoke to me and that's how I know him. That was a strength of management: he could admit when he wasn't right.'

And Stam had a fine career.

'I did, but leaving was difficult. We were so happy over there. But it's a great club with great people and I still love it over there. I'm at Old Trafford all the time because of my television work and while I played for many clubs, it's one club that when I go back, I feel respected and welcomed by both the fans and within the club.

'Italy was good, too. I learned a new language, played for Lazio and Milan, lived in Rome and Milan. It's a beautiful life, food and weather. I needed to get used to playing in the sunshine when I first went there. It's positive for a person to experience different cultures. You get wiser, more respectful.'

His family benefitted too.

'My parents would come to Rome. We lived in a gated community and there was an Italian restaurant which my father loved. He would take a package of tobacco from Holland to smoke and would get a really generous measure of alcohol from the waiter back. Dad was really enjoying life after working so hard for all those years. We'd take him to restaurants by the sea and he absolutely loved this idea of ordering a fish straight from the boat. It also helped us when the parents came over because they had the kids.'

In 2005 Stam was involved for Milan when they met United in a Champions League knockout game. Milan won 1–0 home and away en route to a final Carlo Ancelotti's side were favourites to win in Istanbul against Liverpool.

'I went to the first leg at Old Trafford but couldn't play because I was injured,' Stam explains of a game where a Roy Carroll mistake allowed Hernán Crespo to score. 'I didn't speak to Fergie at that time.'

Another Crespo goal in the second leg saw another 1–0 win as United came up against a side also featuring Maldini, Rui Costa, Nesta, Seedorf, Kaka and Gattuso. The 10,500 United following in San Siro's 78,957 crowd to see United lose was the largest of any English club on the continent in the noughties, excluding finals. Again, Stam and Fergie didn't speak.

'The only time in all the years after I left United that I spoke to Fergie – until we had that drink at Old Trafford – was in a pre-season tournament when I'd just joined Ajax in 2006. There was a pre-match press conference where the two managers and captains attended. I was the captain of Ajax. Everybody was waiting in the hotel and you could feel the atmosphere among the journalists and the others in the room. There was tension and the media were enjoying that because we'd not spoken for so long. Fergie came in and we shook hands briefly. The first question was to me and it was to ask me about my relationship with Fergie. I said that these things happen, that it was a long time ago and that I respect the manager who gave me a lot of good things. You could feel the mood relax and we spoke briefly – not properly – after.'

The first time Stam and Ferguson did have more than a few words was at a Legends game at Old Trafford.

'And every time we meet we speak a little bit more. We've had a few glasses of wine too. It was just a shame how it all went at the time. If it had been put to me that United needed the money and that the club weren't sure I was going to get back to being the player that I was and that they were going to sell me, I could have argued my point in an open and fair manner, but that's not how it went.'

Stam's final assessment?

'Manchester United made history when I was there and it's very difficult to repeat that. City have done it – unfortunately for us. I feel blessed to be part of United's legacy. It was only three years, but it was amazing for my wife and I. It's a big club but there's a lot of warmth and a family feel to United.

'I had a good career. I went back to Holland after playing in Italy. I established myself at a high level as one of the best defenders in the world. And all along raised a family of four kids with my wife. We never employed a nanny; my wife did everything. I think I would have accepted all that when I started out over there.'

And with that, he points towards Kampen, beyond the club where he now helps out and where his sons both play.

3

HE MADE THE SCOUSERS CRY

Diego Forlán

'I can be anywhere in the world when I hear it or get told about it,' explains Diego Forlán. 'I've been in Brazil or Uruguay, Japan or Spain watching a United game on television and heard it.'

The Uruguayan striker, who won two European golden boots and was the joint highest scorer in the 2010 World Cup, when he was also named the best player of the tournament, is talking about the song that Reds still sing to this day.

'It goes, "Diego, wooah, Diego, wooah; He came from Uruguay, he made the Scousers cry,"' he laughs. 'I'll be honest, I get goose bumps every time I hear it. It is so flattering. I'm not Ryan Giggs, Paul Scholes or another United legend, nor am I the only player to have scored at Anfield, so it feels a privilege for fans to remember me like this so long after I left.'

It catches him when he least expects it.

'Years after I left, United were playing at Sunderland. I was called away to lend a hand and I missed a couple of minutes of the game. I didn't hear the fans singing my name. Soon after the match ended, I received messages which showed television footage of José Mourinho turning to Michael Carrick to ask who "Diego" was. Fantastic!'

He talks us through how the goals – and thus the song – came about.

'It was December 2002 and I recall how I was getting so few minutes in the team that I didn't even feel like I was a proper footballer before United played at Anfield. I was training but not playing, but something happened that day that would make it one of the greatest moments of my life. I scored two as United beat Liverpool 2–1.

'I started because of injuries. It was not an easy game to start in and the first half was difficult, I didn't see much of the ball and couldn't get it. It was so intense and I thought I was going to be substituted, but it all changed in the second half. The intensity level dropped a little – it would have been impossible to continue as it was – and we started to get chances.

'I saw the ball going to goalkeeper Jerzy Dudek and he missed it. I ran onto it and put the ball into the net. My confidence surged. Yes! For the second, it was a shot from further out.

'This time, I ran to the away end and the fans went crazy. Faces looked like they were going to explode. My teammates were delighted, for the team and for me as they knew I'd had a tough time. Stewards rushed forward to push us away from the fans. Ryan Giggs, who set me up for the goal, told the stewards in bright orange jackets where they should go. I repeated what Giggs said. I knew every bad English word after nearly a year in the United dressing room. Nobody was stopping us enjoying this moment. Nobody. I wanted to jump over that fence and get in with them, which is not responsible, but I was so happy and my adrenaline was pumping.

'I want to go in that away end at Anfield one year. It's on my bucket list. I'll put a hood up and keep my head down – not everyone in Liverpool would be delighted to see me. But I can't sing about myself. Someone else needs to score two that day.'

Back to the game.

'Liverpool did all they could to draw, but we held on. I went into the dressing room and Gary Neville was the first to come up to me as we celebrated. He looked me in the eyes and said: "Maybe you don't realise what you have just done, but they'll never forget you here after that." I always remember that. I knew there was a big rivalry, but I didn't fully understand it. I was a guy from Montevideo, how would I? But I began to understand the importance after that, from the reaction of the players and the travelling fans behind the goal. Gary was right. I've seen Dudek since. He was a good goalkeeper, but we never spoke about that.

'And I should be honest and mention Liverpool fans. In 2010 I played there for Atlético Madrid in the Europa League semi-final. They booed me, which I understood. I scored the goal in the first leg in a 1–0 win and it was 1–0 to Liverpool in the second leg. It went to extra-time. Liverpool scored after 95 minutes. They were going to the final … until I scored in the 102nd minute at the Kop end. I went crazy, but not in an inflammatory way. It was an important goal to score. Fans gave me a lot of abuse but at the end of the game they applauded me. Thousands of them, even though they were hurting. Good football people and a historic club, I respect them.'

Forlán has just returned from an ITF Masters Professional tennis tournament in Lima, Peru, where he reached the quarter-final. Now, he's a 45-year-old father of four married to Paz, a former student of Montevideo's British school, which he also attended. He played tennis to a high level as a kid. Something Sir Alex Ferguson got wind of.

'We were on a pre-season in Portland, Oregon, in 2003. There was a tennis court on the site, the place for Nike elite athletes. David Gill, the former United chairman, was playing tennis against another United director. I asked him for the racquets when they'd finished and Ruud van Nistelrooy asked to play me. He used to play a little bit of tennis.

'All the team started to gather to watch us; they'd just finished training. Sir Alex Ferguson also came to watch. I don't think all of them knew that I used to play tennis at a good level as a junior.

'As an adult, I used to play with Marat Safin and Juan Carlos Ferrero, who were both world number ones in their career. They could easily beat me, but I was good enough to hit the balls back properly to them as they warmed up.

'So it was me against Ruud, who didn't know that I wasn't a beginner. He was surprised when I started serving. Everyone was watching on the side and shouting. Roy Keane, Seba Verón, the gaffer. Suddenly there was an atmosphere. Ruud was really determined and the game was close. I felt the pressure to win because I'd played at a good level. I was not the underdog, I was not in Uruguay any more. I won in the end and that was expected, so nobody really said anything.'

'It was an excellent game of tennis to watch,' confirms David Gill.

Sir Alex Ferguson tells a slightly different story in one of his books. He says that he knew Forlán played tennis well and nobody else did and that he bet money on him.

'That's a better story, but some of the lads definitely knew,' Forlán smiles.

His £7.5 million move to the north of England in January 2002 was a genuine surprise for everyone, not least Forlán himself.

'I was playing for Independiente and knew that Manchester United were interested in me; we'd arranged a meeting. I liked that idea. When I was a kid I dreamed of playing in the first division in Argentina. I achieved that at 18. When I was 19 I started watching English football and saw Manchester United coming back and winning games. I couldn't believe it sometimes, especially in the Champions League final. I started playing as United on computer games. I'd began watching English football as a kid in Uruguay, mainly Nottingham Forest or Liverpool because they were the best teams. The games were broadcast on Saturday morning and the commentator would always talk about "the moustache" – Ian Rush – or "the headband" – Patrick Berger. Italy had a richer league with better players, but it was predictable, all 0–0 or 1–0 games. England was different, more exciting. It still is.'

It wasn't long before he attracted suitors from England's top division.

'Then Middlesbrough approached my agent; they wanted to see me before United. Sir Alex Ferguson found out about this. One day, I got a phone call while I was in the bathroom. My roommate was sleeping on the bed so I was quiet. I could understand English from a very early age, but I could barely understand the man on the phone. He was speaking fast with a very strong accent. I'd been taught English by people who spoke with very clear accents. I made a great effort to understand and worked out that he wanted me to play for him. "We want you," he said. "It's not just interest. We want you. You can be a great player for us. Wait for us. You will play for Manchester United."'

It was Ferguson.

'I didn't say much in reply and I wasn't absolutely convinced that it was him. I called my agent to confirm the caller's identity and he said it was. I thought I knew English but I couldn't understand some of the players,' he laughs. 'It took me one year to understand "meankle". In English, I had learned to say "my ankle".'

Forlán flew to London to sign for United. Though Middlesbrough also thought they had a chance of signing him.

'Ferguson was waiting for me at Old Trafford. My agent and people from Independiente went with the directors to finalise the deal; Ferguson personally took me inside Old Trafford and showed me around the stadium. He knew everything. He showed me the stands, but also inside the stands. Every time he opened a door there was someone there and he knew their name. There were people in kitchens, museums. He introduced me to everyone. I've never had this with another manager since.

'Afterwards, he drove me to Mottram Hall hotel [close to Ferguson's home in Cheshire], where I was going to stay. He spoke all the way about football. A few years later I was playing golf at Mottram Hall when I saw an angry man a couple of holes in front. He was playing badly, the ball was going the opposite direction to where he hoped. Ferguson again, now my boss.

'I hid a little bit because he was angry and I didn't want him to see us. I told him a few days later that I'd seen him and he laughed. He told me that I should have said hello.'

Forlán didn't walk into a United team of champions and also spent plenty of time on the sidelines.

'I wasn't always happy not to be playing, but I understood that he had a lot of players to choose from. And I watched some great football.

'I sat on the bench at Old Trafford when Ronaldo scored a hat-trick for Real Madrid at Old Trafford. Everyone applauded when he was substituted and I was tempted to do so myself, but that wouldn't have been right.'

Forlán would get his chances.

'The Champions League was a huge deal for United, as it is for all the big clubs. I watched it on TV in South America growing up and within a month of arriving in England I played my first game in the competition in Nantes. "This is it," I thought. "I'm here now." I was nervous. I started on the bench but United were losing 1–0. With 11 minutes to go I replaced Phil Neville. We equalised in the last minute when Ruud van Nistelrooy scored a penalty after a handball. The Nantes players were furious, some spat at Ruud in the tunnel after the game.'

There were more snatched minutes in the same competition.

'It was the 2002 semi-final second leg of the Champions League against Leverkusen when I came on after 81 minutes. United were 2–2 from the first leg in Manchester. We were 1–1 in Germany. We were going out on away goals. They'd already knocked Liverpool out. Sir Alex gave me a simple instruction: "Score, son." One goal would have put us through to the final at Hampden Park in the gaffer's – I was calling him gaffer by this stage – home city. We didn't play well, like we had in the previous rounds, but we just needed one goal. With nine minutes left, Wes Brown, who had been our best player marking Ze Roberto, was sacrificed for me. We may as well lose trying to win the game than draw. Ole Gunnar Solskjaer had come off the bench before me and we switched to 4-4-2, the team was now filled with forwards and looking dangerous.

'I was not nervous, despite only being at United three months and having yet to score. With three minutes to play, I saw my chance. I stopped the ball with my chest on the edge of the area, had a great shot, really hard and on target. It beat the goalkeeper, Hans-Jörg Butt. It was going in and was going to be a beautiful goal. My first goal for United was going to get my new team into the final. Except Diego Placente, who I'd played against in Argentina, headed it off the line and Solskjaer hit the follow up over the bar. It was our last chance, we were out. I never saw a United dressing room as silent as that night.'

Things would pick up for Forlán in his first full season for United, 2002–03.

'I scored my first United goal – in the Champions League again. I came on as a substitute, this time for Ryan Giggs against Maccabi Haifa at Old Trafford. I'll never forget the cheer when I came on, I felt that the fans still had faith in me even if some of the journalists didn't. They were saying things like "seven months without a single goal". Of course I should have scored, but I'd played just 14 hours in those seven months. And three of those months were close season!'

United were leading 4–2 when, in the 89th minute, the team got a penalty. The crowd chanted 'Diego! Diego!' It was his 27th appearance in a red shirt, or 789 minutes in Diegospeak.

'David Beckham was captain and told me to take the penalty, which was good of him. I scored. He later said that he would have been hated by 67,000 people if he hadn't asked me to take it.'

Again, it didn't mean Forlán became a starter.

'The standards were high at United. Top players always trying to be better. Juan Sebastián Verón and David Beckham were practising free-kicks after training. They had a mobile wall to wheel into different positions. It didn't jump up and down, but the "players" were taller than normal. For one hour, Seba and Becks hit the ball over it and around it. Their techniques were completely different, but they hit the same part of the goal each time. They would move the ball closer or further from the wall and still strike the same spot. Beckham was clearing the wall and scoring from eight yards, Verón from 16. I thought "Wow!" We were supposed to be tired, but they were in search of perfection. When I saw them repeat this in real games, I knew it was hard work and talent, rather than luck.

'I wasn't a naïve kid watching them, I'd grown up observing professional footballers closely. My dad told me that practice made perfect and advised hitting a tennis ball against a wall with both feet, which I'd do for hours. It's a major reason why I'm completely two-footed. I'd also watched Dad play and have been surrounded by professionals all my life, I knew what dedication it took to be a footballer, the sacrifices which needed to be made. I also knew managers and got a sense of how they worked.

'I should mention one. César Menotti – known as El Flaco ("The slim one") – was the coach at Peñarol, the club I supported in Uruguay, the club my father played for when they were champions of South America in 1966, the club I'd seen become champions again in 1987. Because of my dad, I was in a privileged position and I met various coaches. Menotti stood out. I was ten years old when I met my first great football manager.

'Here was a man who'd led his country Argentina to winning the World Cup in 1978. He'd been at Barcelona and Atlético Madrid, Boca and River. He was the greatest coach in the world in my eyes, more so after I'd met him. He was indeed thin, with long hair and he dressed smartly like a Hollywood actor. He seemed cool. He told me that he wished my father still played and that he hoped I could be a player just like my dad. He told me to work hard and to enjoy my football. It was the normal stuff to tell a ten-year-old, but I was fascinated by him and learned about him. He smoked a lot, which was strange as I'd been told that smoking was bad for you. He was intelligent and read books that made people think he was a philosopher. When he was sacked by Atlético Madrid, he'd likened his axing to being "taken for a drive in a Ferrari and being thrown out at 100mph".

'He was famous for winning the World Cup and for selecting Maradona, but he only got the Argentina job because he'd done so well at Huracán, a small team he took to their only title.

'I next met him again ten years later at Independiente. "Do you remember me?" I asked. "I'm the son of Pablo Forlán." He told me that of course he remembered me and that I'd have every chance under him if I worked hard and listened to him.

'Meeting him again was like a religious experience, it felt such an honour that he was speaking only to me and I listened to every word. He knew exactly how to talk to players. He wasn't patronising, but knowing. I was in awe of him and his presence, probably because of his legend, but also because of the football he encouraged. The crowds loved his intelligent attacking football, his blend of hard and flair players.

'Great managers are leaders who have that presence. They must be the most important person at the club, the man in control of everything. The club president has the real power, but he must pass on all that power to the manager if a club is to do well. Alex Ferguson had it at United. He controlled everything – the players, the media, the staff. He knew everything, his knowledge helped his power. He knew the names of the parents of the 15-year-old players. He knew if a 17-year-old youth player had been drinking alcohol the day before. That power invoked fear, but respect too. And because Ferguson was respected and feared, that added to his presence. But none of that would have meant anything if he wasn't a great coach.

'The best coaches have a mixture of talents. Yes, they need to be good tactically and to know football. They need to make brave decisions when everyone thinks they're wrong. They need to be able to coach personally too, though that's not the most important thing.

'The gaffer took time to learn about his players and their families and that felt great. I always believed that I had his support, that I could go to him.

'I feel privileged to have been part of the United family under Ferguson. I respected his way with people and his knowledge. He knew everything about the opposition. When I played for United against Barcelona in Philadelphia in 2003, he picked Xavi out, told me to get goal side of him when we defended and stay there. "Don't let him get the ball," he'd say. He was right and we won. I scored twice. Whenever I played against Xavi in Spain I'd do the same thing. Xavi used to say: "Again, Diego!" Nobody played him like I did – and that was because of Ferguson.

'I remember that America trip so well. The day before, we were in New York on a pre-season with United. There was a mistake between the keeper and a defender. I jumped because a defender tried to kick me and then came through with the goal open in front of me. The ball didn't move quickly and bounced a little bit. Instead of hitting it with my feet, I hit the ball with the ankle. Unbelievable. I didn't sleep that night, but we travelled to

Philadelphia the next day, where we played Barcelona, I marked Xavi and scored two goals …'

And Ferguson also had great players.

'I first noticed Wayne Rooney while playing for United's reserves at Everton in 2003. Wayne was only 16 but we were told he was going to be a top player, that he was strong with quick feet. Very English in his style, too. Young talents are usually still missing something, Wayne had everything. We shook hands afterwards, but my departure from United in 2004 probably was a factor in Wayne arriving at Old Trafford a few weeks later.

'I can understand why people pick out Paul Scholes for praise, but Roy Keane was also a world-class player at United. He was the captain, the most important person on and off the field. He could be hard on us, a real hard bastard. I don't see players like that now.

'He annoyed his teammates, but maybe some younger players need that aggression from an older player. Keane was intelligent too. He'd give me feedback all the time. He'd comment on my positioning in training and tell me I should or shouldn't do certain movements. He didn't see why I should practise boxes where I had four players to pass to, because he said: "On Saturday, you won't have four players around you running at goal. You'll be alone." He wanted me to be primed to score in matches, not pass the ball around.

'Roy was a great captain and the strongest character but he would still go crazy at me and Ole Gunnar Solskjaer if we didn't train to his standards. Ole told me that I was the hardest trainer he'd ever seen, but that wasn't enough for Roy. He wanted us to be perfect and would give me advice, even on my shooting. He improved me as a player, but he could be too tough.'

When I asked Keane, for *United We Stand*, if he worded players up if he felt they weren't giving their all, he said: 'All the time, especially those who think it will be easy for them. I do it in every game and training session. I can be a very critical person. Critical of myself and particularly of the young lads who I can see have talent. Maybe sometimes I'm a bit harsh and I've left the training field sometimes feeling like I've been a little bit out of order, especially with the younger players.

'But if I wasn't trying to make my point I would feel like I was cheating them. If something needs to be said then I'll say it. I think I've got positive stuff I can pass on to the players from my own experiences. All I ask is that they are focused on what they are trying to do, that's part of my job. And I'm not the only one who does it. Gary [Neville] does it. Giggsy does it.'

But was the criticism personal? I asked Keane.

'No, no chance, but it has cost me certain friendships over the years with players and some can be standoffish with me for United or Ireland. It's just part of my make-up and in the long run I think it's a positive thing. It's a short career and you must be focused on what you do. The last thing I would want to think when I retire is that I hadn't been focused at a certain point in my career. To me that's the biggest crime.'

Proof that Forlán won Keane's respect came when the Irishman became Sunderland's manager in 2006. 'Roy called me and said: "I know you like a beach, Diego. We've got a great one here at Sunderland."'

Forlán was on a more even keel with the lads he became mates with.

'Phil Neville was a friend and made me feel welcome when I moved to Manchester in 2002. Later that year, we played champions Arsenal in a league game. I was disappointed to be dropped to the bench. I'd scored both goals at Anfield the week before and was playing well. I felt I was finding my way in England.

'Phil was named in central midfield to play against Patrick Vieira. Maybe he started because of terrible injuries in our team. Quinton Fortune, who would have been great in an aggressive game, had broken his leg. Roy, the captain, was also out. As were David Beckham, Nicky Butt and Rio Ferdinand.

'Carlos Queiroz, a tactically shrewd coach, told us that the game would be won in the middle. Sir Alex saw it like a chess game and knew Phil wouldn't let him down. He also fired us up like our lives – and the lives of our families – depended on the result.

'We were missing so many players yet Phil was incredible, the outstanding man on the pitch. Arsenal had scored in their 56 previous games but they didn't score that day with Phil intercepting the ball, tackling so hard that the crowd stood up and roared. He was winning the ball from everybody, aggressive, but in a controlled way. When Thierry Henry complained to the referee about Phil, we knew that we had the better of Arsène Wenger's champions.'

United won 2–0 with goals from Verón and Scholes. That result was vital in establishing United as title challengers in a league they would win.

'That was one way you'd see the brilliance of Ferguson. Another was how he realised that individual players were different and wanted them all to be settled. When Cristiano Ronaldo and Kléberson arrived in 2003, he was intelligent with them. He anticipated that as they were young they would be homesick and he tried to give them big holidays back home – maybe ten days in Madeira and Brazil. I was envious of this because I wanted to see my family in Uruguay too, but I wasn't genuinely homesick like they were. In January, the idea of being with my family on the beach in Punta del Este at home in Uruguay appealed, but I never went and Ferguson didn't think I needed to go. I ended up scoring some of my best and most important goals for United when they were over.

'Once, my father came to Manchester. Ferguson knew all about his career and was happy to meet him, two footballers who played in the 60s. My father couldn't speak English and Ferguson couldn't speak Spanish. That did not stop him trying and he had several phrases. My father was impressed.

'Ferguson was unique among the managers I worked for. When we played European away games, he'd get everyone together the night before the games and organise a quiz in the hotel. He took these very seriously and was furious if he lost. It was hilarious. He'd get into arguments with Giggs, Becks, David May and the Neville brothers about events which happened 30 years ago. They accused each other of cheating. I'd sit with Seba Verón and Laurent Blanc and laugh. It was like a family argument, but it added to the spirit at the club.'

The English football calendar also took some getting used to.

'In my first Christmas at United, the team played five games in 13 days and I started four of them. We won the league that season. That's when my family came over. At first it was a strange idea for them. They were used to spending Christmas in the sun and on the beach. Manchester doesn't have either of those in summer, let alone winter. But they did come and they really enjoyed it, even though I couldn't be with them all the time because I was away in hotels. That's the life of a footballer, the decision I made.'

Season 2003–04 was Forlán's most productive, with eight goals and four assists. Nothing compared to the numbers he'd hit after leaving United, but impressive given he was coming off the bench. And he could be a help in other ways.

'Cristiano Ronaldo joined and almost immediately he was taking us by surprise as he shot at goal with both feet throughout training games. He was brilliant and dedicated. Quite often, it would just be him and I alone after training, doing extra sessions on those open training fields at Carrington.

'Even though he wasn't an established player, his arrival lifted the dressing room because he was so talented – he was another weapon to make United better.

'If he saw a player doing a trick that he didn't know then he'd learn it himself and show the player a few days later. His arrival was at the right time too because David Beckham had just left in his position.

'He worked closely with Mike Clegg, the strength and conditioning man. He built himself up with many hours of exercises. Now it's normal, but not many players were training like this then. He used to train with weights around his ankles to make him stronger. His whole life was dedicated to improving his football.

'Not long after Cristiano joined, my father travelled from Uruguay to watch me play. He saw a couple of games at Old Trafford and he was allowed to watch us train at Carrington. Dad remained very interested in how the game was changing. He wanted to watch my progress too and Sir Alex was good with him.

'After a week in Manchester and one training session, he watched some of the best players in the world closely, players like Ryan Giggs, Roy Keane, Rio Ferdinand and Paul Scholes. The one he picked out? Cristiano. My father pointed at him and said: "Diego, when this young guy starts hitting the target, he's not going to stop."

'He couldn't stop watching Cristiano. We were both dedicated to being as good as we could be. That meant shooting practice a lot of the time. Practice makes perfect.

'Ronaldo would hit the ball from distance, but, unusually, he'd hit it upwards into the roof of the net. He didn't curl it around a training wall, but struck the ball true, hard and fast. Most would not go in the goal, but some did. That's what made my father offer his opinion – he picked Cristiano out above all the very good players at the club. And he was right.'

Forlán and Ronaldo became mates.

'He was quiet but friendly. I was asked to translate for Cristiano as he couldn't speak English. He and Kléberson were the new arrivals. Another Brazilian, Ronaldinho, was going to come to Old Trafford too and I would have translated for him, but he went to Barcelona instead and he did OK, didn't he?

'Ronaldo was a nice guy and still is. We've always talked when we've played each other. That early drive he showed at United took him a long way – not many players are considered the best for two different Champions League winning clubs.

'I'd see Cristiano at Mottram Hall where I played golf. He would be there playing pool, usually with his brother who would visit from Madeira. He was very competitive and probably wanted to win at pool, too. That competitive spirit and drive made him the player and person that he is. They took him to the top, to being one of the best two players in the world with Lionel Messi.

'Cristiano's drive, his ego and desire to be the best are not for everyone and not everyone likes him, but they're attributes which have helped him. I'd advise any young player to look at some of his other attributes – his dedication, his professionalism, his eagerness to improve. You don't hear about him away from football for the wrong reasons. He's remained dedicated to the sport he's served so well and never lost focus, never lost his hunger to keep improving, even after all those trophies.'

The pair were playing up front together in 2003 and 2004. Against Glasgow Rangers in a Champions League game, the forward line was Forlán, van Nistelrooy, Ronaldo and Giggs.

'My volley in that game was my best for United. I was on a good run and loved that goal. I scored some other great goals at United. The last-minute winning goal against Chelsea or my first Premier League goal, an equaliser against Aston Villa when I took my shirt off. Or when I scored a winner against Southampton and couldn't get my shirt back on. I'll never forget that noise after that goal. That roar when Manchester United attack is one of the great noises in football.'

But 2003–04 was also when he started to consider his United future.

'When the manager started playing with one striker I knew that it would be difficult for me. Then, when Louis Saha and Alan

Smith signed I realised that I was going to be fourth-choice striker and that I wasn't going to play. I wasn't a young player and I needed to play so it was my decision to leave.

'I did get annoyed if the manager took me out of the team, especially if I had been scoring, but there are many great players at United and the manager did what he thought was right. I spoke to the manager many times; he was good like that.

'I did have one argument with him before I left because he was angry because I was not wearing studs like he wanted. It was at Chelsea, the first game of José Mourinho [in 2004]. I came on for the last 15 minutes and had a chance to score, but I slipped and mis-controlled the ball. We lost 1–0. I knew the gaffer would not be happy and he was not. I went to the dressing room to take my boots off, maybe hoping that he wouldn't see my boots. It was too late. He was shouting and very angry. He picked up my boots and threw them away. He shouted at the kit man too, blaming him for not making me wear the right boots. That was all forgotten when I went in his office to talk about moving to Villarreal. He knew I had to go and was good about it.

'"I wanted to use you more," he explained. He said later said that he regretted letting me go, but we always had excellent relations. He kept in touch with me by text, praising me when I'd played well in games, and he invited me to a dinner for his 25th anniversary at the club. That was my first trip to Manchester after I'd left. Ferguson also wrote in his autobiography that the £2 million fee was too low. "The next thing we knew he was moving on for £15 million." That was some years later.'

First, Forlán had to prove his worth. He wanted to stay in England, but there were only loan offers. Atlético Madrid and Levante were interested, so were Villarreal.

'I knew some Villarreal players from South America, that they had money and ambition. It appealed so I moved. I wish it could have worked out better in Manchester, but I had no regrets.' Nor did his bank manager. Forlán received a pay rise after leaving Old Trafford and he lived by the beach. Some things stuck with him from his move to England.

'I still watched English television because I miss the original films. When you go to see a film here they are dubbed in Spanish. I don't like to see Jack Nicholson talking in Spanish because I know his voice. I miss custard too. I loved English custard. I used to have it all the time with Roy Carroll.'

He also kept in contact with several United players through text messages and he and his sister also keep in touch with Phil Downs, organiser of United's disabled supporters' association, MUDSA. Sister Alejandra is disabled since a car accident when Diego was ten.

'In Spain I played in every game, which is all I ever wanted to do at United,' he goes on. 'When I played for 90 minutes with United I did well. Being a substitute was difficult. Players need a run of games and I've got that now. I was soon playing well and scoring goals. My confidence was high; I was improving as a player and playing in a team with a coach who had confidence in me. That made me feel better.

'Juan Román Riquelme was another reason I moved to Villarreal. We knew each other in Argentina when he played for Boca Juniors and I played for Independiente in Buenos Aires. At 19, I was in Argentina, playing in the same league as Riquelme for Boca, Javier Saviola and Pablo Aimar for River. All were superb footballers and you could see that they wouldn't stay in Argentina long. In a derby, Riquelme backheeled the ball through the legs of Mario Yepes, a top defender, in the Bombonera. Unbelievable. YouTube it.

'We had the same agent too and we got on well. That's important. The group of players at Villarreal are all close. We went out together socially and hung around with each other.

'Of course Villarreal was different to Manchester United but the clubs shared the same ambition. The training ground and stadium were excellent too. The president liked South American players, especially Argentinian ones. We had some very talented ones, so many [South Americans] that we played 11-a-side against the Spanish players in training.'

Manuel Pellegrini was making a name for himself as the manager.

'He loved to coach, to see beautiful football in training and in games. It meant a lot to him that players really enjoyed training each day.'

United did draw Villarreal for the first time ever in 2005 in the Champions League.

'Injury meant I didn't play the United game at Old Trafford, which was a shame as I've still not played back at my old club, but we drew 0–0 and again 0–0 at home. It was nice to see my old teammates and Sir Alex Ferguson got me in the dressing room after the game. I had a lot of friends there.'

As a journalist, I stayed in touch with Forlán after he left United until now and saw him play regularly in Spain, first at Villarreal, then at Atlético. In 2007, a few Reds travelled to the Copa América in Venezuela as fans. Forlán invited us to Uruguay's team hotel in Merida. In 2014, he did the same to the Uruguay's team hotel near Belo Horizonte the day before they played England in São Paulo. The hotel and team security, charged with keeping nosy English journalists out, simply didn't believe that Forlán had invited me. Until he came to meet me and introduce me to his teammates.

Forlán was interested in fans and fan culture and I was interested in his career as he travelled the world. In all, he played professional football at Independiente (Argentina), United, Villarreal and Atlético Madrid (Spain), Inter Milan (Italy), Internacionale (Brazil), Cerezo Osaka (Japan), his beloved Peñarol, Mumbai (India) and finally, Kitchee (Hong Kong) before he retired at 38 after 700 games and 274 goals in club football. Along the way, he played more games (112), and scored more goals (36), than any player in the history of Uruguay's national team at the time, thought the scoring record has since been surpassed by his close friend Luis Suárez.

In 2013 and 2014, we met in Southern Brazil when he was with Internacional in Porto Alegre, my wife's home city. She has little interest in football and the names of the players I interview are just that. But for Forlán, she wanted to come. As did her friend. He has his appeal, Diego.

In 2016, he invited me to his home city of Montevideo, where he was playing for Peñarol at 35. As we spoke, he took sips of *mate* through a thin metal straw. He was now a father of four, who spoke four languages and learned others.

'I've enjoyed many great moments in football,' he reminisced. 'Winning the Premier League and FA Cup with United. Winning the Europa League with Atlético, the Copa América. Being the top scorer and player of the tournament in the 2010 World Cup finals. But, if I had to pick one, I'd say the 2011 Copa América win because it meant that three generations of our family had won the competition. And I've played around the world.

'Good. No regrets. Things happen for a reason. I scored important goals and won titles. I wanted to play more and at times I was frustrated. People were good to me at United. Other players from South America like Kléberson found it far harder to settle as they didn't speak English. They were allowed to go back to South America for holidays. I wasn't!'

Brazilian Kléberson is a good point. He joined United in 2003. The backdrop was that Ferguson wanted to move David Beckham on and United desired an auction situation between his two main suitors, Barcelona and Real Madrid. Barça's prospective presidential candidate Joan Laporta asked Jordi Cruyff to call Beckham and United even put news of a bid on their website in the hope of spooking Real Madrid. Beckham didn't return the call, so Barcelona moved instead for Ronaldinho – United's number one target. Ronaldinho was keen to join United, although the move didn't happen, and even told one compatriot to join him in Manchester.

That man was Kléberson and in 2014 I went to see him in Indianapolis, where he was playing out his career for Indy Eleven – named after a famous Indiana regiment in the American Civil War – in the second tier of US soccer. I sat on a Greyhound bus, one of two white passengers, as it travelled four hours south from Chicago across the plains of Indiana in America's never-ending Midwest.

Kléberson was bought to replace the brilliant but inconsistent Juan Sebastián Verón, who'd departed for Chelsea for a loss in 2003. He arrived on the same day as 18-year-old Ronaldo, not that either signing had been planned.

'Ronaldinho told me he was going to Manchester,' explained Kléberson. 'He kept saying to me, "Come to Manchester!" I wanted to go, but I was reluctant because I didn't speak English and United didn't have any Portuguese speakers. Ronaldinho persuaded me and I went to Manchester. But he didn't!'

Kléberson, full name José Kléberson Pereira, was a 2002 Brazilian World Cup winner, yet his move to Manchester wasn't a success. United fans even sang about compatriot Anderson being superior.

Kléberson was a surprise late inclusion in Luiz Felipe Scolari's Brazil squad before the 2002 World Cup, making a goalscoring debut only five months before the tournament started.

'I was surprised that Felipao [Scolari] selected me then and I'm still surprised now,' he says. 'I was not a big name. The World Cup was a very intense period, but special too. I was playing with so many great players: Roberto Carlos, Cafu, Rivaldo, Ronaldinho and Ronaldo. I'm Brazilian, so to play for my country in a World Cup final felt incredible. The competition is so tough in Brazil. We're a football country of 200 million and to wear the colours of the Seleção in that competition was wonderful. Pressure comes with that because of the expectations. Brazilians expect Brazil to win the World Cup. Not reach the final, win it.'

Scolari felt that his tenacity would help against the high work rate of the England team in the knockout stage. It was a feature of his game which would also attract Ferguson. Kléberson's tackle on his future teammate Paul Scholes led to Brazil's equaliser before they scored again to win 2–1.

Kléberson retained his place in the starting line-up for the rest of the tournament including the final against Germany. Kléberson created a goal for Ronaldo in the 2–0 victory and pushed Ronaldo for man of the match. So, his credibility was decent. He kept his place in the Brazil team for the 2003 Confederations Cup and Leeds United were set to sign him, but it was the United of Manchester who paid £5.93 million for him in 2003. He would become United's first Brazilian.

The midfielder first found out about United's interest when his president at Atlético Paranaense, his club based in Brazil's most European city, Curitiba, told him.

'I couldn't believe it,' he says. 'The red team from Manchester. I looked on the internet and saw Ruud van Nistelrooy and Ryan Giggs. I wanted to come straight away. He also told me about Leeds, but I wasn't so interested in going there.

'Instead of speaking Portuguese with Ronaldinho, I spoke it with Cristiano Ronaldo,' laughed Kléberson. 'I'd never heard of him but when I saw him in training I thought "Wow!" He was so fast, he dribbled. He didn't just do it in training but in games too.

'Diego Forlán spoke Spanish, Quinton Fortune too. I could understand them, but moving from Brazil to Manchester was still very difficult. There were so many differences. The weather and language, of course, and there wasn't so much Brazilian food in Manchester then. I'm told there are three Brazilian restaurants now. I had to drive to London to get Brazilian food, the beans and rice.

My personal circumstances didn't help. My wife was pregnant and I kept getting injured ...'

United weren't oblivious to the problems of a 23-year-old Brazilian moving to the other side of the world with a 16-year-old pregnant wife.

'Sir Alex Ferguson helped me so much,' he explained. 'He actually tried to speak Portuguese with me and learned some key words and phrases. I was so impressed. I should have used his efforts as an example to myself. Instead of speaking as much English as possible I had Brazilian television and I spoke to my wife in Portuguese. I never really learned English like I do now – though I'm not sure I could have understood Ferguson.

'When my son was born, he told me in all seriousness that he had to play for United when he was older. It was light-hearted but it meant so much.'

Klébinho was born on 22 November 2003. It was a day Kléberson would never forget.

'I scored my first United goal and my son was born this day,' he smiled as he recalled becoming the first Brazilian to score for United. The goal, against Blackburn, a spectacular drive from outside the box at the Stretford End, was celebrated by a Bebeto-style 'rocking the baby' celebration, relevant because wife Dayane was about to give birth.

'The baby was due in two weeks, but I had a call on my phone when I got back to the dressing room. My wife had gone into labour. I rushed to Wythenshawe hospital after the game, where my son was born as a Mancunian,' he smiled. 'Every time it is his birthday I tell him that beautiful story of the goal on the day he was born. This day was truly amazing.

'The Premier League is the best in the world, but you have to be so strong to play in it. I had no experience of that. I wanted to pass and move, not fight and kick. With Roy Keane and Nicky Butt in the midfield I was asked to play on the right, which was not my normal position. With the injuries I became frustrated but part of that was because I was young. I should have been patient.'

Again, Ferguson tried to help.

'He told me to relax more in games, that he wanted to support me, but it was still hard because of injuries. If I was out for three weeks then I had to be patient when I returned, but that meant sitting on the bench. Because I wasn't playing I lost my place in the Brazil team, which made the situation even worse.

'Two players stand out in my memory all these years later: Ryan Giggs and Paul Scholes. Giggs made great passes and had great movement. He was a great person too. He also told me to relax and keep going in games when I was afraid because it was too physical. I would control the ball and somebody would foul me. Scholes was different. He didn't speak much to me but I admired his technical level. He played like a Brazilian but he had the toughness to play in England because he was English. He had a great shot but he was intelligent in the way he read the game. Then Ruud was the hero of the fans, the fans used to sing his name: "Ruuud! Ruud! Ruud!" He was deadly inside the box.'

Keane also made a big impression on him.

'He was tough! He would say "Run, run, run" at me. Then "Tackle, tackle, tackle". If I lost the ball then he looked at me like he wanted to fight me. But he was kind too, a nice person. He would ask me how I was after training. He was just tough on the field.'

After 20 league games in two seasons, Kléberson felt his United career was faltering.

'I wasn't playing enough and the injuries were getting me down,' he explains. 'Solskjaer was good with me. He had a bad injury too and tried to raise my spirits, but I'd had enough. I spoke to my family and told them that I was not happy. We decided to change club and I went to see Ferguson. He told me to stay but he said that to all players. I wanted to play. I told him that I was sorry I couldn't help him more, that I was tired mentally and that Besiktas had offered me a contract. I was sorry about the fans too because I wanted to help.'

Forlán wanted to help United too – and he did – and he defends his seemingly unenviable record of 17 goals in 98 United appearances. 'I only played five minutes in some of those games,' he rightly points out to those who mock his record.

He undeniably became a world-class striker and his time at United was an important step in helping his career.

'Playing alongside great players at United gave me knowledge, experience and maturity, which I would use after. However, I wanted to play more and at times I was frustrated so I moved.

'I arrived as a young player in England at a club full of top players. Had I gone back there as a mature player I would have done much better, but I was a better player for my time in England.'

And, as Gary Neville told him, he has passed into United history because two of those goals he scored were at Anfield.

4

HE WOULD RUN 500 MILES

Darren Fletcher

Darren Fletcher signed for Manchester United in January 2000, just as the club moved to the Carrington training ground.

'I was 15 when I signed and quickly started playing for the reserves and doing well,' he explains over a cup of tea at his home. 'I played with Scholesy in midfield on my reserve debut, with Ole, Maysie, Jordi Cruyff, Jonathan Greening and Michael Clegg. Everton had Paul Gascoigne, Michael Ball. I played against Robbie Fowler and Jamie Redknapp a few weeks later. I was slim and had loads to come physically, but I could run all day. And this was also in an era where you were told that doing weights was not good for you – that weights made you bigger, stiffer and slower. I weighed less than 70 kilos.'

There was serious talk about Fletcher making his first-team debut at an age when his peers in Manchester were still in school.

'We played away for the under 21s against Royal Antwerp's first team towards the end of the season in front of a big crowd. I wasn't allowed to go out at night with the others as I was too young. I stayed in with manager Mike Phelan and physio Neil Hough. I had a good game; it felt like a cup final for me.'

Fletcher's reward was to travel with the first team to Villa away for the season's closer. United were champions which opened up a potential opportunity for a young player on the fringes of breaking through.

'I travelled with the first team and was respectful to them. Teddy Sheringham was excellent with me, bantering with me in a welcoming way. Like Coley and David May, he was amazing with young players. Just speaking to us youngsters was greatly appreciated, asking you your name and where you were from. Maysie would give me grief in an endearing way – calling me a lanky Scottish streak of piss – and he'd also kick anyone who dared kick me in games. And Coley's just cool, isn't he?

'I was told that I wasn't eligible to play for United because I was still registered at a school in Scotland and the Premier League forbid players on schoolboy contracts from playing at senior level. To this day I don't know if that's true,' he says. Sheringham scored, United won an 11th consecutive league game and finished with 91 points, 18 clear of Arsenal in second. Fletcher's debut would have to wait.

'I had an amazing childhood in Mayfield, a massive estate just outside Edinburgh,' he recalls, comfortably settled in his house near Altrincham, eight miles or so south of Manchester and pronounced locally with a 'g' in place of the 'c'. His two sets of twins – the eldest two professional footballers at United, the youngest two one-year-old daughters – fill his home with love alongside his wife Hayley and British bulldog, Barney.

'Mayfield was full of kids and you could get a football game anywhere. I'd walk outside my back door and within three or four streets there would be three or four games going on with groups of different ages. Amazing.'

Fletcher's mum is Irish from County Mayo.

'Her family is into agriculture. They moved over to Stranraer in Scotland for work and that's where my dad worked on a farm.

Mum is one of eight, dad one of 13. My background is agricultural. Dad then moved with Mum's family to Edinburgh.

'I feel half Scottish, half Irish. Roy [Keane] was always onto me to play for Ireland. I was around a lot of Irish people as a kid, Irish music, supporting Celtic or Ireland – and Scotland – in Italia '90.'

Fletcher was always obsessed by football.

'I've always been a football nut, obsessed with everything to do with it, from stadiums to strips, fantasy football to computer games. I didn't really like other sports; it was all about football for me. I was obsessed with Spanish football in the 90s and everything associated with that. I'd be an encyclopaedia on World Cups and players. Even to this day. I've tried my hand at golf, but kind of figured out that I'm doing it because it's sociable. I don't really enjoy it.'

He attracted early attention.

'I always played up in age groups and was quickly scouted by Hearts, Rangers, Celtic and then Man United. They all wanted me at different stages. I trained with them all, that meant every night of the week. My dad didn't let me sign with anyone because he wanted me to have lots of different experiences. I did. Rangers had a real influence of Dutch football and passing drills under Dick Advocaat, for example. Dad's family were more Rangers.

'Celtic was more technical with dribbling. They both knew I was training with the others. I was training with all these clubs from the age of 12. United was in the school holidays from 12 to 16. I'd do pre-seasons at The Cliff. Andy Perry was the Scottish scout, Dave Bushell and Les Kershaw were my contacts in Manchester. All top people. I must have done alright in my first trial game at United because I very quickly got to meet Sir Alex, aged 12.

'I was a big Celtic fan. I had a season ticket for when Celtic Park was being rebuilt and expanded. Before that, I stood on the old Jungle terrace. From 11 I would go with my uncle. I'd be at the ground three hours before the game, watching the teams arrive, pitching pennies against the wall outside the famous Celtic bars with drunk fans, soaking it all in around the East End of Glasgow. Just having a Celtic strip on meant that people would give you money. I'd come home with about £20.'

Fletcher was always attracted to midfielders.

'John Collins was a hero, then the three amigos – Pierre van Hooijdonk, Jorge Cadete and Paolo Di Canio. Tommy Burns was the manager and he ended up being my coach. One of the best men I've ever met in football. Celtic finished second to Rangers but played the most exciting football. Yet while I was Celtic, I bought a blue United shirt because I liked it and wore that at the club for my first trial.

'You're allowed to leave school in Scotland at 15 if you have a job so I was going to join United full-time a year early as a schoolboy, but my younger sister was born in the April and I was supposed to leave in June. My mum wanted me to stay at home until Christmas and because I still hadn't signed for anyone as I wasn't 16, Liverpool and Newcastle came in for me. They really pushed to sign me and offered everything to my mum and dad. Newcastle played on the fact that I'd be closer to home, both stressed the age of the United midfield and Sir Alex retiring.

'Newcastle turned my head, I'll admit. They were new and exciting, closer to home and one day I decided to sign for them. They were offering five times as much as Manchester United but I didn't know that. My mum and dad turned it down without me knowing.'

The phone went one day at home. Sir Alex Ferguson was on the other end and he had got wind of the Newcastle interest.

'My sister handed me the phone and said: "It's for you." The manager was going ballistic at me. I was 15. He said he'd been bringing me down to Manchester since the age of 12 and mentioned all the work that Andy Perry, the scout, had put in. I was white.'

Fletcher's mum listened, took over and said: 'I'll stop you there, Mr Ferguson. You do not ring the house and speak to my son like that.' Then she put the phone down on him.

Ferguson called back immediately.

'He said he was sorry and that he was going to come up on the next flight. My mum said no and to be fair, my dad and I did go to Manchester. We were quite direct at this point, talking about my prospects of playing in the first team. Sir Alex was ready to retire at this point so that was a worry for us, but he was amazing. He talked about doing the best for Man United right up until the last moment. He told me that if you are going for an apprenticeship for any job in the world then you should go to the best – and that United was the best. Maybe there was a little bit of love missing for me that I needed to sign for United, it's hard to explain. It's difficult when you're so young and you have lots of people offering you different things. I'm not saying that United didn't, but maybe they thought me signing was a formality when it wasn't. And forever after, Sir Alex always asked about my mum. I think she impressed him – and she certainly impressed me as a mother. She was big on principle and always said to me: "Remember everyone on the way up as you'll meet them again on the way back down."'

The trips down to Manchester continued.

'I did pre-season in 1999 when we'd run around Heaton Park in north Manchester. I was told to bring my trainers so I did, my adidas shell toes. The rest of the lads had Asics or running trainers, but I wasn't used to a full-time pre-season environment. I was running around in shell toes, which isn't ideal. Everyone must have been looking at me, thinking: "What is he doing?". But I was still comfortable in the middle of the group.'

Ah, shell toes, like the ones Wes Brown had cut in half but was never certain of the culprit.

'That was me and Wazza,' admits Fletch. 'We cut them with the chef's sharpest knife. It was the cleanest cut, almost surgical. Then we put them back together, waiting and watched Wes put them on and then they pulled apart.'

Fletcher eventually signed for United in the first month of the 2000s. Unlike other new players, he could understand the manager's accent perfectly.

'Other players swore on the training ground but if I ever swore, he told me off. Every single time. My relationship with him was not what people think – and I don't mean that in a bad way. The manager was the manager, my relationship with him was the same as others. I probably had fewer interactions with him because he knew I was low-maintenance and I was – I wasn't in too much trouble off the pitch. I just got on with it and did whatever he said. A "well done" was all I needed from him and I'd get that. People have this perception that he and I used to talk about Scotland and the Loch Ness monster or whatever, but him picking me was enough. Deep down I knew that he believed me, trusted me and valued me and on the rare occasion I went to see him, he'd keep my spirits up, lift me, send me home to Scotland. He was a great manager.'

Fletcher's first team United debut didn't come until 2003.

'If we go back to the summer of 2000 when I nearly made my first-team debut, I was on top of the world that summer. Aged 16, playing for United's reserves, training odd days with the first team. Then I went away with Scotland's under 17s and we played in the Faroe Islands on astroturf. That's when I broke my fifth metatarsal, before such an injury was a thing. I'd never been injured in my life before. The worst thing is that they told me I had a hairline fracture and not a clean break. I was looking at the X-ray, thinking, "It's not even broke, it's just a little thing." Because of that, I didn't rest enough and tried to come back too quickly. I wanted to play League Cup games for United because that's where we got a chance. Me, I was young, naïve and stupid. I refractured the injury twice. I had it pinned and then I played. I got a double hernia, had ankle injuries and didn't play for two years from the age of 16 to 18. And when everyone else was doing driving lessons, I couldn't because I had a broken foot, so I'd get taxis. I was ahead of my time – I had a chauffeur, a Scottish taxi driver from Urmston!

'I played the back end of the Youth Cup and had six months in the reserves under Choccy [Brian McClair]. He was brilliant, ahead of his time. We all thought he was mad. He was dry, he was funny. He'd do things like walk into the dressing room before a game, point to a player and say: "You're in charge of set pieces today." At the time we wondered what he was doing … which was giving us responsibility and taking ownership. Another thing Choccy did was hold training sessions where you weren't allowed to speak so that you had to increase your awareness – since nobody was saying "man on" or "turn". You had to figure it out yourself. That was smart thinking. Then he'd do the opposite and say that every time you made a pass, you had to speak with information where the pass was going. If you didn't, it was a foul. That taught you to give the right instructions. There was a freeness with Choccy, you were free to express yourself. I enjoyed his calm demeanour and him giving us a platform to express ourselves.'

Fletcher won the reserve player of the year in 2002–03.

'The highlight was Choccy getting on stage and telling jokes which only four people in the room would get. You'd have 50 people utterly baffled and four people crying with laughter, including me. Choccy loved the awkwardness of the situation and the fact that only four people found him funny.'

Fletcher's debut finally came against Basel in the Champions League in March 2003, the competition in which he also played his second game, against Deportivo La Coruña.

'One of the best moments ever. The sacrifice that you have put in your whole life to get to that stage. I didn't go out when I was a kid. My parents said: "You have been given a great opportunity here, don't do anything which will affect it." We'd already qualified. I played right wing against Basel at home, first touch was a back heel, Gary Neville scored and we drew 1–1. David Beckham came on for me. We lost at Deportivo. I was into Spanish football and could name their whole team then – and now. They had all their big names; we had a young team. I wasn't one for swapping shirts but I made sure I did with Juan Carlos Valerón because he was unplayable. He was so smooth and my first experience of taking on a top player outside my own teammates in training. Valerón's balance, touch, his glide. A beautiful footballer. After those two games I was in and around the squad for the rest of the season.'

Roy Carroll from Northern Ireland was United's goalkeeper for Fletcher's debut and went on to appear 72 times for United between 2001 and 2005.

'A big personality with a big hearty laugh. He was well liked in the squad and was good with me as a young player. Roy was a hard-working and solid goalkeeper.'

Fletcher was on the bench at the Bernabéu in the next Champions League game, a quarter-final against Real Madrid.

'That's still one of my best memories in football. My best mate Damian, my cousin, travelled to the game and told me later that he'd slept on a bench in Madrid because he didn't have enough money. That and Damian liked to save a bit of money. I got him a ticket. It was his dream to visit the Bernabéu. I'd long been fascinated by Madrid and players like Fernando Redondo. I was only about ten for the 1994 World Cup and was starting to understand football. I remember this long-haired Argentinian holding their midfield, spraying passes around. In '96 Sky started showing Spanish football and I began watching it, especially Real Madrid. There wasn't the internet around then so I couldn't check, but I spotted Redondo playing for them.

'He's remembered around these parts for that back heel at Old Trafford in 2000, but I was following him long before then – the classic Argentinian number five holding midfielder. I read a lot about him in *FourFourTwo* and always followed his career.'

In 2003, Vicente del Bosque's side won the first leg 3–1 with goals from Figo and two from Raúl within 49 minutes. Ruud van Nistelrooy pulled a goal back after 52.

'Madrid, with Raúl, Zidane, Roberto Carlos and Figo, were on another level to our lads and ours were at a very high level – the best players in Premier League history. Yet Madrid were passing the ball around Becks and Roy and the rest.

'I couldn't believe how quick the pitch was and struggled to control the ball in the warm-up because it was so wet and hard. Old Trafford wasn't that sort of pitch then. In Madrid, I was thinking "I'm not ready for this" and I've never felt that before or since. Yet we played well, as we did in the second leg when we won 4–3.'

Fletcher's breakthrough season came in 2003–04 when he made 35 United appearances, including in the FA Cup semi-final against Arsenal and final against Millwall.

'Arsenal were The Invincibles, unbeaten all season and favourites to do us. We were out of the title race by that time, despite being top of the league at the start of the year. The semi was a massive game for us and the crowd responded. I'd played well at Highbury so maybe that's why I started the semi. I got direct instructions from Sir Alex to help Gaz Neville with the overloads on the left with Robert Pires and Henry. I was also told not to let Cristiano get pegged back, so I played centre mid and press against Vieira, then get over and help Gary and Cristiano, who we wanted to stay forward and not have to defend.

'Arsenal played 4-4-2, so we put in an extra midfielder and my job was to overload the midfield, running Vieira away to create space for Keane to control the game. We did a number on them and it was one of my best games of the season, a big moment too. I'd gone from being right wing at the start of the season, which was difficult as it wasn't my natural position, to having the chance to play central midfield and show what I could do. I was also unique in the squad at that time because of my legs and running power. I had to show that I could complement Roy and Scholesy and help Cristiano – and the team. I was 20 years old and had to build towards being a starter.'

Fletcher was still living in digs with fellow youth players Colin Heath and David Fox, where he returned to after winning the FA Cup. Fox was seeing the girl across the street and one of her friends was Hayley – who became Fletcher's girlfriend and then wife.

'I was super professional, I'm rare – a non-drinking Scotsman. I've tried beer and don't like the taste. I wasn't around alcohol as a kid. Mum doesn't drink, Dad was a decent footballer and everyone talks about him in Stranraer, where he played junior football and one game for Stranraer's first team at 16. Dad would have a couple of drinks having worked hard all week, that's all. He'd go to the pub, put his £5 on his teams on the football coupon. Dad's the best grandad now – and he was also the best dad. People don't appreciate how much parents help footballers. I was playing four games per weekend and Dad was taking me to them.'

Fletcher became established in arguably the best midfield in football, following the 35 games in 2003–04, with 30, 41 and 40 games over the ensuing seasons. In 2007–08, that was down to 24.

That was down to 'injuries and form of other midfielders,' he says. 'I missed two chunks of that season. A ligament problem in the last minute of a Scotland game against Croatia.'

But by that time, United were back winning titles. Champions of England, Europe and the world in 2008. Liverpool was the European city of culture that year, Manchester, according to the flag hung at Old Trafford, European capital of trophies. Fletcher scored against Gamba Osaka in Yokohama.

'We took the Club World Cup seriously, especially the South American lads. It's massive for them. The jet lag was hard on that trip and we didn't see Berbatov for a week, I think he got sick and was stuck in his room. We beat Liga de Quito and celebrated, though not like winning the Champions League. Because by that time the winning had become expected, yet I think we could have celebrated more. And we always followed Giggs and Scholes for the standards.'

It was Fletcher's close mate Wayne Rooney who scored the goal that made United world champions.

'Wayne helped me a lot in the dressing room when he arrived. I was quiet, I'd listen and learn from all these amazing characters and leaders. Wayne was younger than me but way more confident. He'd say stuff to the older players with no fear. He'd start conversations or shout at them on the pitch. Wayne and I clicked straight away. He's witty, but angry. Everyone feared him at Everton because he was so aggressive and snappy and determined and a superstar. When he first came to United he was immediately unbelievable as a player, but he couldn't take a bit of banter. Rio would kick me under the table and tell me to wind him up, so I'd give him some because I could. Maybe I was a calming influence on him, someone to say "Wazza, come on". And he was an influence on me. It was a relationship which worked.

'Physically, Wayne was a man and I was a boy. Cristiano started to develop. They were strong, aggressive and quick. Wayne had a superb football brain and IQ, he knew positions even as a young player. Tactically, he'd drop into what people call half spaces right from the beginning. He was an unselfish team player with moments of genius and instinct that you couldn't practice. He'd sense it, felt it, executed it.

'Cristiano was also unbelievable from day one. His talent, ability and what he could do as a player. Some lads had doubts about him and wondered if he was a show pony. Honestly, I never did. He was a young boy who'd come from a different culture and country at a young age. He learned English quickly, he was good with people. And he did all that while having a tough time. He'd have lumps kicked out of him in training, we all did, but he did things that got you having lumps kicked out of you more and he wasn't happy about it, but he took it and was like "Give me the ball again".

'I thought Walter Smith was a massive influence on Cristiano, even though he was only at the club for six months.'

Nicky Butt left the club in 2004.

'[He was] one of the biggest characters in the dressing room and I thought he was a great player. I almost became the Butty in the team because Roy's Roy and Scholesy was Scholesy. Specialists. How Scholesy was never nominated for European or World Player of the Year is beyond me, especially when he was scoring 20-odd goals a year from midfield when he was among the very best. He probably didn't get those awards because he disappeared straight after training and didn't do any interviews.

'Look at the foreign players after the European games – they all wanted to swap shirts with Giggs and Scholes. It was funny watching [Iván] de la Peña before the Espanyol game [Solskjaer's testimonial]. He was in awe of Scholesy and looking up to him as if he was a god. He arranged for shirts to be swapped before the game. Scholesy seemed a bit embarrassed. Good players know great players and they respect them. I'd train with Scholesy every day and knew how good he was. It was hard to get near him.

'Butty was a proper midfielder who did a lot of everything, box to box, can head it, get a goal, tackle, can play around the corner first time. Could do everything at a high level. I was really surprised when he left.'

Another midfielder, Liam Miller, arrived from Celtic in 2004.

'Being a Celtic fan I know how highly he was rated but it was a big jump up from Celtic. A lovely, quiet lad who found it hard at Old Trafford.'

In 2005, Roy Keane would move to Celtic. Keane had spoken to me in 2004 when he said: 'I really get a buzz out of pre-season training, I really do. I never take my place in the team for granted and really enjoy working with Mickey Phelan, Carlos and the gaffer. Working with players like young Fletcher too. I try not to harp on about a player but he impressed me from the very first moment I saw him. He has got the potential to be outstanding. He's got unbelievable talent but he's got a good head on him and that's what I like about Fletch. He could be up there.'

'Roy Keane was the biggest influence on me day to day in the whole club,' says Fletcher. 'He let me know what it meant to be a Manchester United player every day. He was tough on me, brutal and hard on me, but I had that much respect for him that I saw it as "this is what you need to be a United player". Roy offered to help me do my contracts as a young player, his standards were the highest you could get. I had high standards, but Roy's were on another level. In training, he would ping the ball to the strikers with such accuracy and if they didn't control it, he would tell them to sort their touch out. He'd test you every day in passing exercises. If he was passing the ball to you then you knew that he would fire the ball at you and that your touch had to be right. You always had to be 100 per cent with Keano. If you were not 100 per cent right on a Wednesday, then you would not be 100 per cent right going into the game on the Saturday. That was his ethos.

'I'm so glad that he helped me become a better player and leader to get to the level I needed to get to. And while people focus on the time he was hammering me, 95 per cent of the time he was giving me confidence. And I probably became a nightmare for the other lads because I treated every training session like the World Cup final. I had to – look who I was up against, better players. I loved training with them but I had to show them I could play and pass to a high standard. I had to get in their face, press them and tackle them with high energy. Them kicking lumps out of me meant I had to move the ball quicker. Roy once said to me in training after I switched sides midway through – and this is a huge compliment and put down: "Fletch, will you fuck off. You're like Zidane playing against me, but when you're on my team you're useless." He had a point, we were winning when I'd swapped to Roy's side.

'Roy had a good dressing room dynamic with Butty, then there was the Gary and Phil dynamic, where they'd both come in and say "Morning, Gary!", "Morning, Philip!"'

Something Phil Neville said stuck with Fletcher.

'Phil came up to me before the FA Cup in 2004 and said: "Well done, Fletch, you earned your place in the team." When he said it, I didn't think much about it, then I thought, "He's on the bench and he's taken the time to say that." It helped me, that comment. I took that comment with me and used it myself if it was true.'

Fletcher scored 24 times for United.

'It should have been more. I was more worried doing other people's running defensively when I got into the team. I knew that Giggsy, Scholesy or Cristiano could win the game for us, so I wanted to help them. Had I ran more into the box, the law of averages would mean I'd have scored more.'

Fletcher was one of those supposedly on the end of Keane's infamous comments on that video from 2005.

'I saw the video and didn't have a problem with it. It's such an iconic moment. As time has gone on, Roy has alluded to the fact that there was much more going on – that I was completely unaware of. The perception off the back of it is that Roy had a go at me and that he and I had an issue. That couldn't be further from the truth. And also, in the meeting, I'm one of the few that he compliments. We all watched the video and nobody said anything until Gary Neville said: "I think you were a bit harsh on Fletch." So then I had Roy and the gaffer looking at me, the two most important people to me at United, and in my head I was thinking: "For fuck's sake, Gaz, I'm fine!"

'I was asked if I had a problem with what Keano said and I said, "No, that's what Roy is like with me and I'm used to him being really direct with me." Then Roy said something like "The reason

I'm harsh on Fletch is because I like him and I want him to do well. If I don't speak to you then I have a problem." He also referenced Sheasy in a complimentary way.

'The thing about the video is that Roy watched a clip of me in an action which maybe resulted in a Middlesbrough goal. I didn't do well in that action.'

Keane left in 2005, new players continued to arrive, sometimes in Fletcher's position(s). In 2006, for instance, it was Michael Carrick. In 2007, Anderson and Owen Hargreaves.

'I'll go back to the Verón signing and me being a young player in the physio's room and hearing Roy say: "United should be signing top players, we need to get better. It's my job to be better than them and stay in the team." I remembered that whenever new players came. I was sure of what I was as a player. I didn't verbalise it but I had a lot of confidence in myself. I knew what the lads and the manager thought of me.

'I'd played against Carra [Michael Carrick] just before he signed. He never tackled me but he never let me pass the ball where I wanted to pass it. So I had to go sideways because his angles in blocking off my passes were effective. He stopped me doing what he knew I was trying to do. Sir Alex was big on us passing the ball forward and breaking lines.

'Owen Hargreaves was a nice lad who knew a lot of the lads from the England national team. I could see his professionalism. Good player, great lad who fitted into the dressing room.

'Ando made me laugh and still makes me laugh. What a player he was. A powerful and strong personality who wanted the ball. He was so good at stopping then quickly accelerating. He was dynamic, a bundle of energy on and off the pitch, who was sure of himself. Ando was obsessed with the letter "W". He'd put a "w" at the end of his name and sign it "Andow". The manager loved Anderson. When I played with him against Arsenal, who he loved playing against, I'd say, "I'll get Cesc (and I once did that to the detriment of a red card), so wherever I go, you go opposite." Ando could do that for 70 minutes and he'd have some excellent games against Arsenal. Anderson stood up for himself.'

Fletcher is now a sensible, popular and highly regarded coach of United's first team, one still fit enough to join in training to help improve the team. He doesn't do the pranks that he did in the noughties.

'The one I'm most proud of is putting red food dye in Wes's new adidas Predators. My mate Damian, who'd slept on the bench in Madrid, played junior football and told me about a prank they'd done in their team where they laced a boot in red food dye and once they started training and sweating, their feet became bright red. So he gave me an idea. I went to Tesco in Altrincham and went to the section which sold food dye. I took it into training the next day and poured it into Wes's boots, allowing the dye to dry overnight. He came in, trained and took his boots off. His feet were bright red. The best thing was that he got on the phone to his agent, who started complaining to adidas about his new boots. This prank was going far better than I expected. Wes then received a new pair of boots and I waited for them to arrive and laced them with dye again. This time, I told the rest of the lads, so everyone was waiting. Again, his feet were bright red when he took them out of the boots, red for a week in the shower. This time, he clocked me, Wazza and Rio laughing and realised that he'd been done.

'Wes did me once. Stirred a spoon in his tea and put it on my neck. It hurt and I had a red teaspoon mark for months. But we did some other funny ones. Gerard Piqué loved his clothes. Most of us had a different style to him. We'd hang his clothes up in the dressing room, but on one occasion I tied them to the security barrier when you leave Carrington. So he couldn't find his clothes, but he – and the rest of the lads – saw them going up and down on the barrier as they left training. Wayne and I were the main culprits. Gerard was raging.

'I had Rio's passport for about a week one pre-season. He left it on the side. Big mistake. We were away and didn't need our passports but were still travelling. I got a bit paranoid as I was carrying two passports and if I lost Rio's passport then it would be a big issue. When we finally came to passport control, I went through and watched Rio checking his bag to find his passport. The lads were in on it. We stood watching him. The gaffer started to ask what the hold-up was. We let him sweat for five or ten minutes. He was really panicked and didn't even think that the lads would have it. He couldn't even see us waving his passport.'

And there were more pranks.

'We travelled in suits to game, but you would put on your pyjamas or tracksuit for any long flights. We hid – me and Rio hid – Wazza's trousers on one such flight to the USA. The flight was coming to an end and everyone started to put their suits on. Wazza was standing with his shirt, his tie, boxers and socks. No trousers. But he's staying calm because he knows they've not disappeared and someone will show them eventually. The plane landed. Wazza is still in his boxers. He's trying to show that he's still not bothered – he's an experienced joker himself, remember. But time is running out as the plane arrives at the terminal and the seat belt sign comes off. Wazza then runs to the front of the plane in front of the directors, Sir Bobby and Sir Alex and all, and he stands in front of everyone, holds his hands up and says that nobody is getting off the plane until his trousers have been found.'

Wayne Rooney was a global superstar. The idea of him leaving the plane and walking through an airport where fans and media were waiting, wearing boxer shorts, was inconceivable, but also one which Ferguson smiled at.

'Finally, someone threw his pants towards him and we disembarked,' laughs Fletcher. 'We'd only do tricks on the lads who were a similar age to us. Giggsy, who was ten years older, for example, was off limits.

'For away trips, I was the man who had to get the crisps, sweets, biscuits, magazines like *World Soccer*, *FourFourTwo*, *FHM*, *Nuts* and *Zoo*. I was the supply. The rest of them wouldn't even go into a garage because they'd get mithered more than me. I could walk around the Trafford Centre unnoticed; I didn't even put a hat on, just wore a tracksuit most of the time and no flash gear. I was never mobbed. The odd person recognised you and if you stop for a photo that's when people started to take notice. Without being rude, I just told people to be quick.

'It was totally different for Wazza, Giggsy, Rio and Scholesy. So that's why I was sent out to get stuff. That and the other players were all pretty tight. Wayne Rooney owes me a lot of money from sweets and crisps over the years. And for controls he's broken while playing *FIFA* because he's been angry after I've beaten him.

'Anyway, *FHM* magazine had a blow-up beer bin for the summer. We played a card game with silly rules. Lose two in a row and you weren't allowed to speak, that kind of thing. We played it on the bus to games. As Wazza got older he started to think he was a bit more mature and that he should be sitting with Giggsy and Scholesy on trains to game and not with us, his mates. So, we needed to get him back. On one train to London, Rio sneaked up to him and acted like he was having a chat, but he was secretly filming Wazza. We sneaked up to him and put the blow-up bin over his head and started jabbing him in it. We knew how he reacted so we were expecting fireworks. The manager was in another coach, so we were safe. Wazza's head was bobbing around everywhere inside an inflatable beer bin, but he tried to play it cool and refused to take it off. Eventually he took it off. Then he picked up a cup from the table and we thought he was going to throw it, but he said: "You're all lucky lads. I've been told to count to ten when I'm angry." This was the new, mature Wayne.

'Our forwards were spectacular. Carlos Tevez wore shorts and flip-flops to training every day, even in winter, walked in, grunted at us all apart from Evra and Ji, who he spoke to. Hardly trained, loved the second day recovery when he played two touch with Patrice and Ji. Then, when the game came, he ran more than anyone else and was like a Tasmanian Devil who was brilliant. Carlos was Carlos, fine with everyone, fine being who he was. Ji was quiet, humble. We did no tricks on Ji. Same with Vida. The consequences would have been too severe, yet he played computer games with us. Most of us would play and it helped us young lads to communicate. We'd invite in younger players to join us, like Tom Heaton, Darron Gibson and Jonny Evans. We'd play poker nights at my house on a Wednesday or Thursday night. Order a Chinese, football on the TV, £30 maximum all in. Loads would come: Wes, Sheasy, Rafa, Fabio, Chris Eagles, Gibbo, Jonny Evans, Wazza and Rod Thornley, the physio.'

Towards the end of the decade, academy graduates Gibson and Evans played first team football. Heaton would wait until 2021 to make his United debut.

'Gibbo was a great lad. When you're young you're usually quiet in the dressing room. Looking at Gibbo, you'd think he was serious and angry. He wasn't, that was Gibbo. Gaz Nev would probe him to get a reaction and it became a funny dynamic as Gibbo started giving him a bit back, which helped him because he became accepted in the dressing room. He was an underrated player who could run, shoot, pass and deal with the ball. Injuries and other bits and pieces probably stopped him getting to the level he should have got to. He was good mates with Jonny Evans, who was rated by everyone and was good with everyone. He was respected by Rio and Vida, the best two central defenders in the world. As soon as one didn't play, they wouldn't be worried if Jonny played. Jonny was smart, a grade A student – not that I knew that when he played because he liked to hide it. But I had a hint of it from Dave Bushell and Jonny had to lower his intelligence level when he was around us. But he couldn't hide his intelligence in his play. Everyone talked about Michael Carrick not making tackles but stopping opponents doing what they wanted to do, but Jonny was the same. Like Rio, he didn't need to make a last-ditch challenge because he'd already read the situation. He did a lot of defending, which isn't appreciated visually. People like last-minute challenges and blocks, but that usually means you've made a couple of mistakes before it. Jonny had solved the problem by intercepting or reading it beforehand, by stepping up to play offside. He was in the school of intelligent defenders that stats don't lend themselves to, super smart and two-footed.'

There was a flag which read: 'Darren Fletcher, football genius'. A song, too.

'I liked it. My mate texted me from a game to tell me about the flag. I was watching the game on television and thought that I'd seen it. So I rewound the Sky+ to appreciate it in all its glory.

'Maybe it came out of a joke and its sarcasm used to wind up opposition fans, but I quite liked it. United fans do it a lot: they're serious, yet take the piss and laugh at themselves. And some of the terrace humour was funny.

'I played in front of some incredible atmospheres with United: Celtic Park, Ibrox and the grounds in Turkey. San Siro on the night they beat us in 2007. I couldn't hear them when I was on the pitch. The game started and I blanked the noise of the crowd out. When the ball goes out for a throw-in then maybe you hear something, but it was a blur.'

In December 2005, United had failed to get out of the weakest Champions League for the first time in a decade, losing in Stade de France to Lille and defeated by a Benfica side who were sixth in Portugal and missing three of their best players. Several times Ferguson claimed that it was the media who are responsible for the negative stories surrounding the club and that fans were showing no such alarm, but fans were alarmed at the end of a grim year for United. Keane had gone, George Best died. Fletcher's goal in a surprise win against Chelsea which ended their 40-match unbeaten run in the Premier League did lift spirits. And then things turned around remarkably quickly.

'2006–07 was a good season for me. Won the league. I was confident. I love challenging myself against all the best players and a lot of them play in the Premier League. I watched how good they are, but I relished the challenge playing against them and testing myself. Mentally, you've got to prepare yourself to play these people. I'd hype myself up, but I loved the challenge of playing against the best players in the world. Lampard was the one. His movement was outstanding for such a big lad. He was fit, ran all day, but if you turn your back and he gets blindside of you, he's gone. You had to be so aware of him for the whole game, concentrating 100 per cent. You can't watch the ball; you have to watch the player. Lose your concentration and switch off and he'd punish you. When we play against Chelsea, the manager asks me to get against him and stop him. Stop those runs into the box. I've managed to do that.

'We reached the Champions League semi. Smashed Roma 7–1. Scholesy was suspended and I'd just become a dad to twins – for the first time. I was getting up every night and I was up the night before the game feeding the babies at 3 a.m. and thinking: "I've got a Champions League quarter-final later on today." But having kids helped me, it relaxed me. I was a bit too intense with football and it gave me a distraction, a maturity.'

The lack of sleep didn't seem to hinder Fletcher.

'Everything just clicked. The energy was right, the crowd, it was amazing. Milan were next in the semi and we won 3–2. Kaká was unplayable and scored two, but the goals we conceded were soft goals. We battered Milan and should've won by more. We lost 3–0 away and they deserved it. They came out full of energy. Gennaro Gattuso ran out before the game and the place exploded. That action didn't intimidate us, but it lifted Milan. Kaká was the best player in the world and the best one I played against. It was the first time I'd played in midfield against someone I felt was better than us and made a big difference to their team. Kaká was lightning quick, six foot two, he could score, dribble and head it. And good-looking too! I remember me and Carra just chasing him. We always felt good together. Not that night.

'We've learned as a team how to play in Europe. Experience gave us that. You got a totally different game in the Champions League compared to the Premier League. It was a lot more about keeping your shape and keeping disciplined. You could throw players forward in the Premier League and the game will have more movement and be a bit more free-flowing, but not away in Europe.

'In Europe, you had to be strong when you haven't got the ball, but when we won possession we were capable of hitting any team on the counter-attack and creating goalscoring opportunities. The most important thing for us was to control the home fans and make sure that we are solid defensively and that we get back into shape when we don't have the ball. That made us hard to beat. We'd made a jump: we'd gone from not qualifying from the Champions League group stage in 2005–06 to the semi a season later. We had to see where we could go the next season.'

The 2008–09 season was trying for Fletcher and, rarely, he had some self-doubts.

'In 2008 I had a year left on my contract and we'd just won the Champions League. Michael Carrick had signed and I had started about five Premier League games in the previous season when we won the league. I had come on lots of times for the last ten minutes when it was a bit tight, usually as a replacement for Cristiano and with the instruction to "get on the right and be solid in midfield".

'I had been injured a few times, including playing for Scotland against France when Patrick Vieira fractured my leg in Paris. There were over 20,000 Scotland fans there that night, more than home fans, and I went to close Vieira down in midfield and take the ball. He just took me out.

'At United, Carra and Scholesy were frightening in midfield. It was Ando's first season and he was a revelation too. When I came in, I actually did really well, but the other lads were doing the same regularly. Owen Hargreaves had signed and I wasn't sure about my future.

'I went to see the manager and said: "I've hardly played, boss." He told me about my injuries, pointing out that when I had got in the team, I had then got injured for Scotland. "These things affect what happens to you here," he said.

'"Boss," I said, "I've got a year left on my contract. I know the club have offered me a new four-year contract, but that can work against me because the club can ask for any fee for me and other teams might not pay it. I'm in a good position now because I only have a year left on my contract."

'I was being a little bit selfish and thinking about myself, but sometimes you have to do that. The boss said, "Well, what are you thinking?"

'"Boss, I don't want to leave the club, but I don't want not to be playing next season."

'He looked at me and laughed, and said: "I'm not letting you go. I need you. You are staying."

'"Boss, OK, we'll see how it goes this season."

'A few of the lads picked up injuries and I started to get in the team. I stayed there most of the season and enjoyed one of my most successful seasons at United. I really enjoyed it and signed a new contract halfway through.'

Fletcher started against Arsenal on 5 May 2009 and what happened there was a personal catastrophe.

'I try not to dwell on it and it made me more determined to get to a final again. When I got sent off at Arsenal, I had my little sisters and mum crying on the phone. I had to be strong for them. They were not at the game, but I called them straight after. I saw the missed calls on my phone. Mum and Dad and my three little sisters. They were distraught. They were ten, 16 and a year younger than me. Mum is emotional and can't watch football, she's never really been to a game. She sits in the kitchen at home, Irish, Catholic and prays.

'They thought I would be distraught but I had to put a brave face on it and promised that I would drag the lads to another Champions League final. I said, "What's meant to be will be. If God doesn't want me there then it's not meant to be." And then I decided to concentrate on winning the league with United. I had to take it on the chin and not let it affect me. I didn't want to go into every game with a chip on my shoulder so I didn't.

'The best person I spoke to was Dad. There was talk of an appeal [United's appeal on compassionate grounds was rejected] but Dad just said: "Darren, you're not playing in the Champions League final, you'll get there again." Dad was my biggest fan – but he'd also tell me when I wasn't doing stuff which wasn't right, attitude or work rate. His words helped me. Then he said: "Now your job is to help United win the league." I did and I felt I had my best season the following year.'

But the red card stung.

'I'd given a good account of myself in those two games. I'd won the ball. Everyone says should I have let them score? Sometimes I still think about that, but we'd worked on staying with Arsenal's one-twos. That was the focus of our preparation and for that split second, I didn't stay with my players in the game and had to make a recovery tackle.

'One of the things I take from that is that Giggsy had just come on. He might not have started the final, had I not been sent off. He could have been thinking "I'm in the final here", yet Giggsy was the first person to go to the ref to plead with him, asking why he sent me off. That showed me what the team and he was about. I loved Giggsy to bits and his evolution as a player. I think Giggsy is United's greatest ever player. When he hadn't been in the team for a few weeks and had a point to prove with a bit of edge, he was unplayable. And he was the only person who Scholesy never tackled. He'd kick everyone apart from Giggsy.

'But it was all very frustrating. I have been a fan of football since I've been a young kid. I've loved the Champions League, the music before games and everything about a big match. It's like you know that you are on the big stage and you really get up for it.

'To miss out on the final after working so hard to get us there was disappointing, but I wasn't going to sit out and moan about it. I still had a league title to win for United and had to concentrate on that.'

Then Internazionale coach José Mourinho said: 'Fletcher is more important than people think … he eats opponents in defensive transition. I believe Xavi and Andrés Iniesta are happy Fletcher is not playing.'

Fletcher watched from the sides in Rome as United took on Barcelona.

'I hoped that we would win in Rome and I turned into a supporter for the night. I sat just behind the bench with Gary Neville and a few of the lads who were not in the squad. I was shouting and encouraging the lads. We are a team. We got there as a team and I wanted to win it as a team. The 11 on the pitch would have taken the plaudits had we won, but it was a squad effort to get there and players including myself made sacrifices to help us get there.

'We started well and I thought we were going to win two or three nil. But we never recovered from the goal from Eto'o after ten minutes and Barcelona kept the ball as they did. I don't think that it was as one-sided as people have suggested. Barcelona didn't create too many chances and we did create one or two. If one of those half chances would have gone in then you never know. But when Messi scored, it was game over.

'It wasn't just him. Iniesta – I remember watching the 2006 Champions League final and he came off the bench and changed the game. Everyone thought that Henrik [Larsson] changed the game, which he did to an extent, but Iniesta came on before him and changed everything. If he's asked to play on the left wing, he plays there. If he plays in the middle, he's exceptional there. He was humble, the anti-Galáctico as the Barça fans liked to say. Wazza said after the final that we'd just witnessed the best player in the world and he had a point.

'Iniesta and Xavi were fantastic. Xavi was better in possession, but Iniesta gave Barça a little more creativity going forward.

Then Cristiano left.

'Any team in the world would miss him. He was a fantastic player and a great goalscorer. He adapted so much when he was here. He went from being a silky winger to being a goalscoring winger and the best player in the world.

'Teams adapt when players leave. Much as Cristiano was brilliant for us, the team sacrificed a lot for him too. As a midfielder, I knew that I couldn't go bombing forward because Cristiano had gone forward. I knew that I had to cover on the right so that the left-back and left-midfielder couldn't double up on our full-back. We became a more rigid 4-4-2, with everyone knowing their role. There were more opportunities for midfielders to get in the box and get goals and we needed more goals from midfield and more goals from all the players. Others stepped up. Wazza was in the shadow of Cristiano and often sacrificed himself for the greater need of the team. It was his time to become a bit more selfish and score the winners. Giggsy was fantastic and reinvented himself as an inside forward who is going to create goals for everyone.'

Michael Owen arrived in 2009. Did the United players wind him up because of his Liverpool background?

'It was never a problem. He came in and we saw straight away that he was a nice lad. The fact that he came to United given his Liverpool history shows a lot of character. He was a winner. He wanted to win trophies so he came to Manchester United. He'd achieved a little bit of success at Liverpool, but he didn't win the league and he did that at United.'

If the noughties were when Fletcher made his name and established his reputation, the following decade was more problematic.

'In 2011 the illness kicked in and that's when I had my first extended period of stopping playing to see if the medication would help. I'd played all season up until the quarter-finals. I felt like I was in my prime after a very good couple of seasons, I was more or less always playing in the big games and a leader in the dressing room. I was in the PFA team of the season, I felt invincible, then I get shut down with ulcerative colitis and didn't know the road I had ahead. I did come back for the last league game of 2010–11 and was on the bench for the final at Wembley against Barcelona. I was very calm about it, but the illness was brutal. I was always thinking, "I'll get some medication and I'll be well", but it ended up being a two- to three-year illness.'

Fletcher went from a 40-game-a-season stalwart to one who could only manage 10, 10, 18 and 12 games over a four-year period.

'I was really ill: it was like a blur. Doctors were trying to get me right. They were trying to work out if playing was making me worse. I had a bowel disease. I had symptoms of blood and mucus, needing to go to the toilet 30 to 40 times per day.

'The only time I didn't was when I played football. I was still at a decent level, but I was ill and sick, losing weight, looking ill without much of a life. I couldn't leave the house to go to the park with the kids or to a restaurant, as I'd need to rush to the toilet. My wife was amazing throughout all of this.

'I was told that I would never play again when I was 29, 30, by multiple surgeons. I went to a doctor in Harley Street in London. He looked me up and down and said nothing. I went back to Carrington and the United doctor asked me how it had gone with the specialist. I told him that it was strange as he'd barely said anything to me.

'"Well, he's just sent me an email absolutely raving about you," said United's doctor. "He can't believe that you're not in hospital or how you are still playing. He can't get his head around how you are training and playing and not on an IV drip in hospital. His recommendation to me is that I take you to hospital right now and put you on a drip."'

Fletcher changed.

'I became a different person in the dressing room. Medication was changing me. I was in my own world, whey-faced, head spinning, always waiting to go to the toilet. Straight home from training to crash on the couch. One day, Hayley called the doc and said: "Come and have a look at him." He did and took me straight to hospital. I had surgeons tell me that I wouldn't play again and needed four operations in a year, including taking out my large intestine and reconstructing my small intestine. I was 30 and, all along, said: "I'm not stopping playing." I refused an epidural before the operation because there could be complications. The doctors suggested otherwise, they even told my mum that I should have one, but I was ready to handle the pain and I did.'

United stood by him.

'The club were brilliant with my contracts. I'd signed a big new contract before I got ill. I went to see Fergie and said I'm being paid and I'm not playing. He said I'd earned it and not to worry. He was all about me getting my health back. He'd call my wife and I ended up having a closer relationship with him, and an even better one since I stopped playing. To this day I can call him whenever I want and I love seeing him at games.

'I had operations and came back and under David Moyes played seven weeks after my last. I played well, even as the other lads were on a downer. I was running on adrenaline, like a man possessed. I did a good pre-season under Louis van Gaal. My personality was still there to play for Man United, I was good in the dressing room, leading and challenging the lads, but my physical power was not.

I was no longer at the level of being a Man United player and didn't want to be a cheerleader, known for being a good lad but nothing else.'

So Fletcher left United in 2015.

'I went to West Brom and played every game. Great club, loved it. I was probably entitled to a United testimonial and I didn't want it. I left through the back door in the January transfer window.

'I was happy with my career at United and I'm still proud of it, but illness took me in my prime. I watched as Michael Carrick ran the midfield and part of me wanted to be out there with him every week. I love Carra and was delighted when his football went to another level. Gary Neville used to say: "Lads, when your time is up at United it's up, the club doesn't owe you anything." He was right.'

Fletcher made a full recovery. He looks healthy now and happy as a coach at United, where his two sons play. I think he'd make a top manager, but not for the first time, real life has intervened.

'I could do with some help,' says Hayley as we can hear the youngest twins cry.

'We've seen a completely different side to Dad with the girls,' says his son Jack as we both smile.

5

THE HARDEST MAN IN ALL THE TOWN

Wes Brown

'Wes, you need to come around to my house,' said Anderson.

'I've got things on today, Ando.'

'No, you have to come.'

Wes Brown went round to Ando's house.

'There was loads of food out on tables for us – for like five people. He said some people were also coming over, but first he needed to show me something.'

Anderson walked his visitor to his garage.

'The door opened and three beautiful dogs rushed out.'

'Ez Brown!' shouted Anderson to one of the dogs. 'Sit.'

'This dog sat down as I tried to work out what was going on. Ando told me that the dog was me – he was called Ez Brown. Ez was how he said Wes. I loved Ando to bits and still do. He's fun and he was passionate on the pitch. He'd play well against the big teams. He had so much ability and made people smile. He had his own version of English so instead of saying "Wes, do you want to come to my house for lunch?" he'd say, "Ez, my house lunch." We had good times.'

A decade earlier in 1998 Wes Brown was 18, living at home in Longsight with his family, taking the bus to Old Trafford.

'I didn't drive because I couldn't afford a car – I was on £250 per week. So, I'd get the bus with my boots in a bag because I wasn't yet a first team regular with boots in the boot room. I'd keep my head down and wasn't really recognised. I was on the bus one day and two lads, probably City lads, started to say things about me. I could hear it. They were saying I was shit, they were taking the piss out of me. My dad had taught me to defend myself. One of the lads turned around and said: "United wanker." I replied: "Mate, if I didn't play for United and I'm sitting on this bus, you wouldn't even be saying this." They were chirping up a bit and one of them came over aggressively and went for me, so I elbowed him in his head. The other one came over to attack me so I gave him a little left hook. He went straight down. I'm not proud of that but I had to defend myself. I can have banter all day but they were in my face.

'Anyway, Fergie found out – I've no idea how as there were no cameras then – and got me in his office. He asked me for my version and then shouted: "What the fuck are you doing, fighting on a bus?" I couldn't get a word in, but he told me to start getting taxis. I wasn't good at arguing with the manager – I could freeze like most of us – but for some reason I thought: "This is my chance."

'"I have to get the bus because I've always got the bus and it's all I can afford," I said. "I have to pay my mum £90 a week. I'm buying snide Ralph Lauren clothes to wear because I can't afford the real ones. What do you want me to do?"

'Sir Alex Ferguson paused and started to think. "We're going to get you a new contract, son," he said.

'That new contract was all down to a fight on the bus!

'I grew up in Longsight. Mum is English, but her mum is Austrian. She once shook hands with Hitler before she moved to Manchester. Dad, who was from Manchester, Jamaica, was strict. Everyone knew my dad; he was well respected. Older, tougher lads would come up to me when I was ten. I was a bit scared, then they'd say: "Your dad got us off the streets", which they loved as he was keeping them out of trouble.

'From the age of eight, I went to karate at Withington leisure centre. I was energetic and always playing football on the street. Happy and giddy too. And Dad thought: "I need to do something with him, he's got too much energy." I was doing hundreds of press ups and sit ups every day. I was ripped as a ten-year-old, when I took my black belt. I failed that twice. That's when my friend Leon Mills said: "Never mind karate, come with us to football. Fletcher Moss Rangers." I'd never played for a team before, only street football. I was pretty good, but the idea of joining a structured team had never been part of my life. I didn't know if my parents could afford it, for example. My life was centred around the streets that I lived in.'

Brown did join Fletcher Moss Rangers.

'I loved it and got straight in the team on the right wing, then the school team, then I got into Manchester Boys under 11s side, all within a year. That was when I met the best kid footballers in Manchester.'

Brown's move to centre-back came when he was 11.

'A player was ill and he asked me. I thought: "I can do that, it's a game of two." I must have done well because when I went to get my number 7 at the next game the coach said: "Stay at the back." I didn't argue, but I was sulking a bit. And, after a few weeks, I loved it. I realised that nobody could run past me because of my pace, then I'd bring out a few tricks to get out of trouble like a little Cruyff turn as I was running back towards the goalkeeper. It made me feel good.

'I also remembered my first proper 50/50 where I went through a lad – and was hurt a little – but I still jumped up and thought: "I want to do that again." The adrenaline had got me.'

Brown stayed at the back.

'Players around me were getting selected for different clubs. I wasn't, maybe because some people still saw me as a right winger – a tall, skinny, fast winger. Aged 12, Dad told me that Oldham Athletic wanted to sign me, but he said: "You've only just started playing, I'm not sure it is the right thing for you." I didn't go.

'At 13, Manchester City asked me for a trial, but I wasn't selected, nor was I bothered. A week later, I heard my mum talking in a posh accent on the phone so I knew it was important as she is not posh. Dad told me it was Nobby Stiles and that I was going to United.'

United's 1966 World Cup winning midfielder was waiting for Brown at The Cliff.

'Where have you been before this, son? Because you are here now and you are going absolutely nowhere from here.'

Brown trained once a week indoors at The Cliff.

'That's where I met Richie Wellens, Alex Notman, Adam Sadler and players like that. I was nervous for the first time. And my mate Leon Mills, who'd got me into Fletcher Moss, was also there. But things went well and before long I was at trials for the National Centre of Excellence at Lilleshall, where I was selected. My mind was never on schoolwork. I was a United fan too but none of us went to games. That wasn't something people where I lived do, though we once roamed the streets and ended up at Maine Road when City were playing – we rushed the door when the game was on. I left straight away, I was nervous. I was in Moss Side but I'm not from Moss Side – not that I was in any gang. I would see lads who were and they would call me "The baller". They loved that someone from their community was doing well at football, they wanted me to do well. But my dad wouldn't have been happy about that because roaming the streets brings trouble.'

Brown would only occasionally do that.

'I was living at Lilleshall aged 14 and came home one weekend. I decided to visit the Grand Central complex in Stockport and jumped on the 192 bus. I was messing about in an arcade, looking for girls, bored and doing what you don't want your kids to do. We saw some of the naughty lads there from Longsight and they said: "Yes, lads, what you doing?" They were fine with us, but I wanted to get back home. We started walking and the other lads were nearby. Suddenly there was a police helicopter and armed police. I had no idea what was going on, but the police grabbed me and put me in a cell. I'd done nothing. My mum and dad came to the police station and told me to tell the truth, but I'd done absolutely nothing wrong. The accusation was that a man had been held up by a gun. There were five black guys, two white guys and two mixed-race guys in the vicinity. Most were locked up and the description of the guy who'd pulled the gun was that he was mixed race. I was the only mixed-race boy in custody. It was mistaken identity, but I had to do an identification parade.'

Manchester United found out about the incident.

'The problem went away. I don't know if that's because I'd not been picked up in the ID parade. But I was allowed to continue my football career and did well at Lilleshall. I had to mark Michael Owen every day – that was brilliant for both of us.

'When I'd finished at Lilleshall, United wanted me to go into digs close to the training ground, but I'd not lived at home for two years and wanted to live at home. United backed down, but then I got a call off Dave Bushell [a widely respected long-time employee who still helps the young players], who said: "Wes, we've had a call from one of the landladies who said that you're in the digs where your teammates are every day, eating the same food as them, but she's not getting paid for any of this."'

At United, Brown's central defensive partner was Alan Griffin. In his 23 years at the club, Paul McGuinness, the youth coach, said Griffin and Ravel Morrison were the two players who lost their way and that United didn't sign Jonathan Woodgate, later with Real Madrid, because they had Griffin.

'Alan was absolutely brilliant and reminded me of Ronald Koeman,' says Brown. 'I was more athletic; he was more advanced as a player technically. He was from Ancoats in Manchester. He just didn't come to training and eventually the club let him go. I'd see him around every now and then, we'd been close mates, but it was a big shame that things didn't work out for him. I'm sure he had regrets.'

Brown's career took a different direction.

'I was in the B and A team, then the reserves quickly, before the manager, when I was 17 said: "You're training with the first team now." It was horrible. I was used to dominating my age group, then I was up against the first team. As a 16-year-old I'd marked Mark Hughes in training and couldn't get near him, but the manager had still said: "Well done." I was baffled because I hadn't done anything well.'

Brown was twice awarded United's young player of the year award, something only Ryan Giggs and Mark Hughes had also achieved.

'It wasn't actually a big thing,' said Brown. 'And I didn't get an award until someone from the club called me in 2023 and said they had it for me.'

He would still be on the bus – two across Manchester to The Cliff.

'The 192 to Piccadilly and M10. But when we trained on a Sunday I'd have to do a run from Piccadilly – about three miles. That was my warm-up before the warm-up.'

The first inkling that Brown might play first team football came when Gary Pallister told him that he was playing against Leeds, in May 1998.

'I completely shit myself,' says Brown. 'Pally was a joker but he wasn't joking when he said I was starting. I was in my bedroom in Longsight wondering if I should tell anyone that I was playing. I did tell my mum and dad that I might play. I was excited, panicking and, soon, exhausted mentally. I hardly slept.'

Brown was named as a sub the following day.

'People often ask me for my favourite United memory but they don't expect the answer I give: that day when I made my debut. Nobody saw all the shit I went through to get to that stage. I also played well. I was shattered but full of adrenaline. I was up against Jimmy Floyd Hasselbaink, one of the best, fastest strikers in the league. I kept beating him to the ball as it was played over the top. At one point, he said: "Wes, slow down, please." I didn't even know that he knew my name. I was buzzing and told all my mates what Jimmy had said. That made me feel good more than anything else. We won 3–0.

'Danny Higginbotham, Jonathan Greening and Marc Wilson played at Barnsley a week later when Arsenal had won the league. We won 2–0, but then it was summer. I didn't want summer to come.

'Gary Pallister left that summer, Jaap Stam came in. I was told that I figured in the manager's plans so it was a positive thing that new defenders like Jaap were joining. Stam was brilliant; I've never seen a stronger defender. He suited English football.'

Brown played 21 times in the treble season.

'I was suddenly playing against Barcelona and Bayern Munich. Your concentration levels were off the scale. I won a header against Effenberg of Bayern. He was massive but my header was clean and powerful. I was buzzing with myself because I still didn't know if I could do it.'

After the highs came the crushing low. Brown didn't play at all in 1999–2000.

'I did my ACL pre-season at The Cliff in a two v two session. Coley went to shoot with his right foot, I put my foot out. I landed to a pain like I've never felt in my life. I fell to the floor. Steve McClaren told me to get up. After about 40 seconds I looked at my knee and it had ballooned. I was taken straight to get it scanned, where I was told I'd done my ACL or "the thing that

Gazza did". My first thought was: "Well, Gazza came back and played again."

'It was all horrible, especially after '99. I remember going to have the operation – and I'd never had an operation before – and being asked to sign something which basically said: "If this goes wrong then it's nobody's fault." I looked at the doctor after reading it. He said nothing.

'I really struggled. I was told to sit down for a month – that would be different now. I was told it would take seven months to a year, but I'd never had an injury longer than the six weeks I was out with a double hernia. With the ACL, it was three months before I could try and get into any rhythm. My head went a bit and you feel like you are by yourself. I put weight on – not much – for the first time in my life. I was still in Longsight.'

Longsight was also becoming synonymous with gang violence, with shootings and jail sentences. Did Brown know some of those involved?

'Yes. And people who lost their lives too. Looking back, it wasn't the best environment but it wasn't a problem for me. I wasn't in a gang. I was not involved. And my journey changed from going to The Cliff to Carrington to do my rehabilitation. It was horrible seeing the lads playing, especially as I kept getting setbacks. Every setback was my fault. Instead of doing the right exercises I'd been told to do, I'd do 12 and, because I felt good after ten, carried on. Then things started to hurt. It was a year of frustration.'

We're talking sitting at a table outside Eastern Bloc records in Manchester. Brown insists that he wants his back to the wall as he doesn't like sitting 'with his back to play' – the street activity in Stevenson Square behind. His instincts on the football pitch carry him through his life, though he wears a hoodie. His mother doesn't approve, but while he probably spends more time interacting with fans than any other former United player around Manchester, he could do without being stopped every five metres.

'After a year I came back in a reserve game. I knew that a 50/50 challenge was going to come at some point and kept saying: "Don't think about it." And then it happened. I went into the challenge full-on … then I stood up after it and felt fine. I didn't think about my ACL from that point again.'

Life was changing off the pitch, too.

'I moved to Bramhall, I had my own car, a Subaru Impreza. It cost £24,000. I didn't think about how much the insurance would be – it was £10,000, which I couldn't afford. I became named driver on my sister's insurance for £3,000.'

The football went well.

'I was more determined than ever to show people I could play at the top level. I was thinking: "If I carry on like this then I can get a good ten years as a footballer." The World Cup would be in 2002. I'd made my debut for England aged 18 at right-back – a position I'd not played regularly, only when Gaz was injured. Gaz Neville was the best right-back I've ever seen. It's a completely different game there. You can relax more at centre-back, at right-back you go forward a lot more. I played right-back against Wimbledon and did well. I nearly scored having cut in. I'd run up the pitch and looked for the pass. It didn't come so I carried on forward towards the 18-yard box. I laid a pass off for Coley. After the game, the gaffer said: "Well done, son." I thought he wanted me to go forward more until he said: "Never do that again, son." His point was that I was to win the ball and then pass it to the players to score – and there were better scorers than me.'

The mood was good in the dressing room.

'Butty, Maysie, Anderson and Quinton were the main jokers. I think I only ever saw Quinton angry once, he was calm. And Wayne or Fletch cut my shoes one day, which was very funny but I was going to a meeting after training. They cut the shoes right across the top and I only realised when I put them on and my shoes split into two. I had to go to a meeting wearing old running trainers. I got angry about that and snapped within myself. You couldn't show your anger, so I was talking to myself and that made it worse because they were all laughing at me. I was normally the guy who was giggling.

'Fletch and Wazza were complete jokers. Fletch used to come for me because I got him with a teaspoon once – a hot teaspoon which I put on his neck. He jumped up and screamed, proper lost the plot. I was running around the canteen being chased by Darren Fletcher.

'I never burned anyone's trainers but I saw pairs on fire just outside the boot room.

'We played a game online called *SOCOM* on every trip, eight of us playing four v four in the army. We'd play it on the bus or in hotels in adjacent bedrooms. You didn't need team bonding sessions when you played *SOCOM* because it was all about looking after your teammates. We had the same mentality in *SOCOM* that we had in games, like a Band of Brothers. Occasionally, the manager would tell us to calm down, but I think he knew it was good for his team. I was close mates with these lads and still am – Wazza, Fletch, Ando, Sheasy.'

Brown was called up for England for the 2002 World Cup, though he didn't play.

'Then I broke my ankle in a Champions League qualifier against Zalaegerszeg at the start of 2002–03,' he says. 'Ninety seconds into a game and two of us chased a ball that was going out of play. I took him out, broke my ankle and that was me out for five months. I'm strong mentally, but it was frustrating, another step back. There was another issue – your knees start to hurt.'

Other centre-halves and defenders arrived. Laurent Blanc had signed in 2001.

'I loved Laurent. He'd been unbelievable when he'd been younger, but he was older when he came to Old Trafford and his legs had gone a little bit. He just couldn't run as fast, yet he performed because he read the game so well. He'd pull me and say:

"You should be doing better than what you are, you have all the attributes but sometimes you're too chilled." Laurent would tell me to make noises when I was defending. I asked him what type of noises and he said: "Anything, whistles, shouts, to put the attackers off." I never did.

'We played Charlton and Laurent went to clear a ball on the goal line and Cruyff'd it out to clear it. I was impressed but the manager said after: "Did anyone see Laurent do that? Well, only he is allowed to do that, not the rest of you." He was so experienced but by the time he was 36 his game was changing. A game against Craig Bellamy, one of the fastest players in the league, killed him. I hate that day because people remember it for Laurent and I hate it because I should have helped him.'

Rio Ferdinand was signed in 2002.

'I was fine with that. We'd lost Yip Jaap. I was very surprised when he's left at the time, we all were, but I was a kid and didn't want to ask too many questions. Jaap wasn't getting old, he'd go on to have a great career. But Rio had been flying at Leeds. I knew him because we'd gone to Vegas after the World Cup – me, Rio, Ashley Cole and our mates. Rio was the calmest I've ever seen on the ball, a good leader too. He could be nasty if he wanted to be, but later he left a lot of that to Vida, the best player I've ever seen head a ball. He would never lose a ball in the air.

'I felt that if the camp was well, then things went well. It was a blow for the team when we missed Rio [because he missed a drugs test] as he was our best defender.

'That meant I played with Mikaël [Silvestre].' The Frenchman played 361 times for the club between the European Cup winning years of 1999–2008, he also played 40 times for France.

Gabriel Heinze was another top defender that Wes played along-side.

'Ultra focused. Great player. Battler. Then Patrice joined and Gabby looked elsewhere. What hurt him in the dressing room was when he said he was going to Liverpool. I was like: "What, we're trying to build something here", but I'm saying that as a Manchester lad. Why should someone who wasn't feel like I do? He's from Argentina, he's not a United fan. And he ended up at Real Madrid with Ruud van Nistelrooy. Ruud was a prime-time finisher, up there with Ole Gunnar. He only needed one chance.'

The 2007–08 season was spectacular for Brown, who played 52 United games, usually at right-back.

'That season was the best I ever had. I didn't feel any pain. My only regret was being knocked out of the FA Cup by Portsmouth. We battered them but the ball wouldn't go in the net. I still tell Jamo [Portsmouth goalkeeper David James] that it pisses me off all the time because we could have won another treble, but I was also pleased that Portsmouth won the cup and you can't win everything.

'Our defence was usually me, Vida, Rio and Patrice, with Edwin behind. The trust was complete with Edwin. If he called it then you knew you could give it to him. He didn't panic, but while teams still had chances, Edwin would save them. All the defenders bonded. We knew what we could do and what we were capable of. Our mentality that season was crazy. We thought: "We're not messing about this season." In front, Cristiano could win you a game out of the blue. If everyone was having an average day, he'd take it upon himself to do something special. Very special. The header in Rome [in 2008] was a joke, the long-range strike in Porto the next season. Big Champions League games away from home against top sides and we'd win. His ball skills were there from the minute he arrived, but he was nowhere near as big as he became. He worked on everything; he's the only player I've seen work that hard in the gym every day. He was that good that I started to think: "'What are we going to do with Wazza?' He'd been the main man centrally." I'd played against Wazza when he was at Everton. He was 16 yet built like a fully grown man. He had one of the best techniques I'd seen. He could finish from anywhere. I'm still close mates with Wayne but even Wazza knew that Cristiano was the main man that season. He adjusted his game, went wider and became an even better player. Have you seen some of his assists from that season?'

And Tevez?

'Horrible to play against. I'd watch him in training and think: "He's not really doing it", then I'd watch him run all day in games. He'd spring towards opponents, even in training. He'd be running in circles because players would pass the ball beyond him, but when he did it in games, when he hunted down defenders, it put so much pressure on them. Carlos kept himself to himself, hanging out with his mates, Patrice and Ji. In the middle, we still had Giggs and Scholes. Giggsy was the same. I hated marking him in training. He's one of the fittest lads I've ever met. Keano set such high standards at the club that he influenced Manchester United long after he'd left. He trained every day like it was the Champions League final against Liverpool.'

Alan Smith was the player Brown knew better than most. He signed for United from Yorkshire rivals Leeds United.

'I'd been at Lilleshall with him, he was my boy. He was a year below and I used to look after him. Then he scored a header for Leeds against us when I was marking him. Football can be weird, I knew he'd scored that before he did, despite me being in the right position to mark him. He just ran in behind me and I joked with him that he was a little bastard after the game.

'Smithy was brilliant when he joined us. A lot of people will remember him for doing his ankle at Liverpool in an FA Cup game [in January 2006]. I was one of the first players there and his face looked like all the blood had drained from it. He was just looking at me going: "Wes, my ankle." He was trying to get up and I told him to stay where he was. I felt so sorry for him and his game did change a little after that injury.'

* * *

In 2015, I went to see Smith's new house overlooking the rolling hills at the southern fringes of Derbyshire's beautiful Peak District. The Smiths were playing on a loop in his kitchen. BMX, Motocross and Moto GP memorabilia adorn one room. He'd been a BMX national champion aged eight.

'Most mates wanted to be a footballer, I wanted to race bikes,' he said before adding: 'I'm not really one for interviews,' in a distinct Leeds accent. Ninety minutes and another cup of tea later, he was still talking about a superb career at Leeds United, Manchester United, Newcastle United, MK Dons and then the world's oldest club, Notts County. Oh, and he played 19 times for England.

'There were better teams than us, great sides like Man United and Arsenal with more experience and world-class players,' he said of his time at Leeds. 'We never had the expectation of having to win like there is at Man United. You can't buy that, but we didn't have it at Leeds. We had young lads who'd come through together and maybe we needed a little bit of help.

'Being local and knowing the club as I did, I realised that everything wasn't right and heard grumblings that players needed to be sold. We sold Rio to Man United in 2002 for £30 million. Leeds couldn't turn that down and it made me think that we weren't as close to bridging the gap as I'd thought. We were attracting attention from massive clubs. We finished fifth, fourth and third. David O'Leary got sacked for finishing fifth – ridiculous.

'There was then a bigger turnover of managers, but I didn't want to see any bad in Leeds. I only really realised there were problems when I came back pre-season in 2003 and we had eight or nine players. We went down that year but I was blind to it. James Milner and Aaron Lennon played at 16, we had lads from France who'd never played in England. I still thought we'd stay up, right up until it was mathematically impossible.

'Relegation was tough, the worst feeling ever. We'd failed. I blamed myself, but I don't think I could have done any more.

My last memory of playing for my hometown club was relegation. Horrible.'

Signing for Manchester United was not something he could have ever envisaged and Smith once promised Leeds fans that he'd never join their red rivals across the Pennines in Lancashire.

'That's not a myth; I did say it,' he laughed. 'I've also learned to never say never in football. When I said it I was young and naïve and never thought that a) Man United would ever want me and b) Leeds would ever sell me. Look how silly I was.

'I also didn't envisage Leeds getting relegated. I would probably have never left if we hadn't gone down but Leeds were trying to sell me to the highest bidder. It was a free-for-all and I didn't like it.

'I'd been at Leeds when Eric left to go to Old Trafford. I was ball boy the day he came back and scored at the Kop and saw the feelings that day.

'I spoke to Sir Alex and he said: "I never thought you'd be brave enough to make that decision." But the Leeds I left wasn't the Leeds I knew. There were people in charge of the club who I didn't like. I went to meetings and saw some bizarre things, with me being touted about to the highest bidder.

'I had the chance to go from a team who'd been relegated to the champions of the country. Arguably the greatest club manager ever wanted me. How could I turn that down? What I found at Old Trafford was a club who wanted Leeds back up because they loved those games.

'As for waiving the transfer fee. I had five years left on my contract. I was entitled to money but the last thing I wanted was to see Leeds go bankrupt. I've never spoken about it because I don't want to speak badly about my club. I've been back once and most people were pleasant with me. With hindsight, I think people realise there were serious problems.'

Of the injury at Anfield which an appalled Brown witnessed, he said: 'Liverpool's medical staff were great with me. They tried and failed to put my leg back in place. They were worried that because there was no blood flowing that I could have had a club foot. The dislocated ankle was worse than the leg break because I snapped all the ligaments and there were complications. I knew that I was never going to be the same player again.

'I've appreciated every single game I've played since that injury because I know how close I was to being finished, but I couldn't have been at a better club to recuperate. I never felt pushed aside.

'When the lads won the Carling Cup they wore t-shirts for me. I'd been in hospital for a week and got back to my flat in Manchester alone. I watched the game on television then saw my teammates wear t-shirts with my name on. That meant more to me that I have ever let on. I had no idea they'd planned that. It's a proper football club.'

Smith's versatility had attracted Ferguson.

'People said I was going to Man United to take Roy Keane's place. Nonsense! Most of my games there were in a three-man midfield with Roy and Scholesy. Roy had such high standards and would always be on at me for flying into tackles. In one game at Liverpool, I left my position and went flying into a tackle. Roy was shouting at me to stay on my feet. Two minutes later he went after a ball and smashed a player. He got up and laughed at me, but he was the captain, he was allowed! And he was an immense captain. I spent a lot of time with him. He's a good lad.'

Following Keane's infamous MUTV interview in 2005, Smith was one of the players that are thought to have been criticised.

'If you're captain of a football club you're entitled to say what you want. Roy never said anything in that video that he wouldn't have said to us as players. He was probably calmer in that video than he was in the dressing room. I had a great relationship with Roy. I read his book, enjoyed it and appreciated what he said about me.'

United fans respected Smith but tried to wind him up, singing 'Smithy – kiss the badge' at a European game in Prague in 2004.

'It's because I'd kissed the Leeds badge, the badge of my club. The Man United fans were having a laugh, but it was quite intimidating, seeing 5,000 of them steaming in Prague and singing at me. I was a football fan and I still am. I'm a normal lad who ended up playing football, so I could see where they were coming from. I didn't kiss it and they probably respected me more for that.

'I hope that fans of all the clubs I played for think that I was a player who has always tried his best. I've never shirked a tackle.'

Despite falling one game short of the ten appearances needed to qualify for a Premiership winner's medal in 2006–07, the league granted special dispensation for Smith to receive a medal on the last day of the season.

'That meant an awful lot. A lot better players than me never won a title medal and I really appreciated it. We went through a lot together and even though I didn't come back until March 2007, I played in some of the biggest games of my career that season. I played against Roma in the quarter-final of the Champions League. I was fresh and hungry and told the manager to use me in every game. I had 12 months of frustration to take out in nine games! I played in the Manchester derby. I'd been sent off in my first one so I needed to make up for that …'

It was pleasing that Smith mentioned the Roma game, where he scored the second goal to help United on their way to the memorable 7–1 victory.

'It was incredible and Old Trafford is at its best for a Champions League game. We came back from 1–2 in the first leg and Totti had a chance of putting them ahead, but I don't think of standout memories. I tend to think of how I enjoyed my time at a club and I loved it at Man United and living in Manchester, even when I was injured. That time made me appreciate how much I loved football.

'Even though I was injured, I always felt included in what was going on. I tried to get to as many games as possible, trying to watch and learn and staying in a football environment.'

Wes Brown saw players come and go all the time. He fondly recalls the few goals he scored at United.

'I didn't score enough goals, it was never my thing,' he says. '[Man United coach] Eric Harrison used to say to me to get five goals per season because it would make me a better recognised player. I told him I was more about stopping goals, but my first goal, in the Champions League, gave me one of the greatest feelings of my life. It was against Juventus at home, a cross from Beckham. I didn't panic, didn't think too much about it because I would have fluffed it. Buzzing.'

Brown was celebrated as being a hard player in fan songs.

'My first was "We've got Wesley Brown" [to the tune of "Knees Up Mother Brown"]. That one was: "He's big, he's bad, he's Wesley Brown. The hardest man in all the town. With orange hair beware, come and have a go if you dare."

'I was laughing when one of my mates told me about that, I thought it was brilliant from the fans. I played for the fans; I was a fan. I hurt when we had a bad day – and we had plenty.'

He came up against plenty of players who were hard to mark.

'Duncan Ferguson was tough and I realised, like with Mark Hughes, that you couldn't fight him to the ball. You had to let him do his own thing, he was always going to hold you and not let you get to the ball. I'd let him feel me and then move away and try and nick the ball.

'John Hartson was tough at Coventry City. I tried to be aggressive and bully him, but he bullied me all over the pitch. I was young, I learned a lot from him. It took me time to learn that you could play opponents in different ways.

'Craig Bellamy did me once. I didn't mind people trying to run me down the line, that's when I got my tackles in, but he took me by surprise and cut across me. That was the only time I can remember that happening and I played well against the better players like Shearer, Agüero, Henry or Drogba. Mentally, I'd step up my game, not that it made it any easier against R9 or Zidane. It was horrible playing against them. I played against Ronaldo in the Bernabéu where he did that move going left, then right. I knew it was coming and fouled him, but the ref didn't give it. I was thinking: "I know what he's going to do but I still can't stop him." He'd had his injuries but he was still unbelievable. I marked him again at Old Trafford when he scored a hat-trick. Maybe we gave him too much respect in the sense we gave him a lot of time, but when he shot he scored. Our fans cheered him off that night. I could understand why.

'Zidane – you couldn't get a tackle in on him. He'd flick it, pass it quickly, he was clever. I was right-back and he was on the left side of midfield. I couldn't get near him because I didn't know what position he was supposed to be in. I'd go to make a challenge and he'd one touch the ball out to Roberto Carlos, who'd then run past me. They were so good; there was no point me even playing. And I marked Messi. Once he picks the ball up and starts running, you're in trouble. Somehow, you've got to stop that. You can do that just by being close to him, so he must pass it, but you don't want him getting it, turning and running at you at full pace. He is very hard to tackle. Not only that, he will bring you out of position to make space for other people to run into.

'I remember those words going round and round in my head before we played Barcelona in the Champions League semi-finals [in 2008]. I'd had it drilled into me by the gaffer. Often, it would be my job to keep an eye on Lionel Messi, and the instructions were simple: "Don't. Dive. In". Repeatedly, that was the message.

'Messi was only 20 at the time, but he was already one of the best players in the world. Everybody knew all about him. He and

Ronaldo were only young, but they'd both just finished in the top three for the Ballon d'Or. Obviously, we trained with Ronny every day, but this was the first time we were coming up against Messi and it was something we were excited about. Carlos Queiroz drummed the tactics into us before those games and we got it right.'

Queiroz, the assistant manager, was twice number two to Ferguson between 2002–03 (when he left to manage Real Madrid) and 2004–08. They won leagues and the European Cup. Ferguson sought Queiroz's advice daily, consulting his insight and wisdom about players in areas of the globe with which he wasn't familiar. Born in Mozambique, Queiroz is a polyglot who's worked all over the world at the highest level.

Queiroz boasted a peerless knowledge, whether it was advising Ferguson how to deal with one of his former students, José Mourinho, recommending players and being instrumental in the development of Cristiano Ronaldo from emerging talent to the best in Europe.

I had met Queiroz informally because Quinton Fortune played for South Africa and United. In 2014, I went to Tehran to meet Queiroz, where he was coaching the Iran national team. Getting an Iranian visa as a British journalist to visit Iran was extremely complicated and took six months, even with the support of the national team coach, who was very popular among Iranians.

'Quinny was getting a lot of injuries so Sir Alex and I used to talk about why,' explained Queiroz of how his move to United came about. 'I learned later that he was looking for an assistant manager and that he'd asked Quinny about me. He also asked [Scottish UEFA boss] Andy Roxburgh. Fortunately, they spoke about me in a positive way and I was delighted to be offered the opportunity. It was a great opportunity to work at one of the best clubs in the world with some of the best players. And with one of the best managers in the world. Even better, they were going to offer me a salary to do this.

'On my first day, I went early to Alex's office at Carrington. I'd been a manager for 16 years and now I was an assistant. I knew my position. I asked for the training programme. Alex asked me what I meant. Then he said: "I brought you here to be responsible for the training and the preparation. I want you to express yourself."

'"Yes, but you're the manager," I replied.

'"If you have any doubts, my door is always open," Alex said. I was a little confused. I felt like he'd given me the keys to the Ferrari on my first day – and one with tyres! I went quickly to my office and prepared training. I hope the lads didn't notice that I hadn't prepared training that day.

'After a week or two we played a friendly in Ireland. Roy [Keane] had come from a problem in the World Cup [in 2002] so there was a lot of attention. The manager said that he had a presentation in Glasgow. I was to be manager. I thought Alex was crazy, but he was intelligent. He trusted me and he wanted the boys to see that he trusted me. I learned that day that if I was ever manager again, I should trust my staff and let them express themselves. That and never to panic.'

Queiroz was essential to the development of Ronaldo.

'I was once in my office at Manchester United's training complex at Carrington and saw something moving in the trees far away,' he explained. 'Maybe it was a spy,' was Queiroz's first thought. 'We used to have them. I called security and they went to check the suspicious figure out. Their answer? "It's Cristiano Ronaldo. He's training alone." He was unique.

'I worked with some outstanding young Portuguese players like Rui Costa, Jorge Costa, Luís Figo, João Pinto and Paulo Sousa. I worked with very good players at Manchester United and Real Madrid, but when I saw the young Cristiano, I could tell his potential was the best I'd ever seen in a player.

'You'll have to ask Cristiano if he thinks I was important in his development but from my perspective, after a couple of weeks at the start of the 2003–04 season, I called him to my office and said: "Look, this is very simple. You were born to be the best player in the world. This is a gift you have; it could be your destiny. It's up to you to commit yourself to become the best player in the world. If you are ready to reach that goal, we start working towards it tomorrow and you'll have my full support because it's not enough for you to be a great player. You need to understand that God gave you the skills and opportunity to be the best, but if you want to be only one more player, I'll treat you like I treat the others."'

There was a knock at Queiroz's Carrington office the following morning.

'It was Cristiano. He simply said: "I'm ready." He started that very day. It was very rare to see in a young player so much talent and such a strong personality, purpose, persistence and commitment. I read about Arnold Schwarzenegger learning to dance the tango. He was obsessed to be a perfectionist. Cristiano is the same.'

Countless former United players have their own stories about Ronaldo's dedication.

'He was always the best at step overs, but he started doing them with weights strapped to his ankles so that it would be easier in a real game,' recalled former teammate Quinton Fortune. 'He would practise even when training finished. He would practise a trick slowly by himself. Then he'd try it in training games. Finally, he'd do it in a real game. If he saw someone do a new trick he would ask them how they did it. Then he'd teach himself until he was the best. I used to balance the ball on my forehead and roll it onto the crown of my head. Cristiano asked me about it. Three days later he was better than me at it and he goaded me to say that he was better.'

Queiroz left to manage Portugal in 2008.

'Leaving United for a second time was tough,' Queiroz admitted. 'It's hard to decide between two lovers. My soul and heart didn't allow me to see in a clear way, so I made the decision blind to go to manage Portugal. I wanted to finish what I'd failed to finish in 1994 [when he left Portugal as manager first time round]. There was a beauty in that Portugal team and I wanted to make them queen of the beauties. There was a World Cup in Africa, where I was born.'

Sir Alex Ferguson described him as 'brilliant, just brilliant. Outstanding. An intelligent, meticulous man. He was the closest you could be to being the Manchester United manager without actually holding the title.'

I asked Queiroz why United won season after season.

'One example,' he said. 'I sat in the dressing room at Anfield. We'd played a Champions League game midweek and the boys were very tired. I didn't think we had a chance. The boys were quiet, but then something magical happened in the tunnel at Anfield, near that "This Is Anfield" sign. The boys were transformed as they walked onto the pitch. I couldn't believe it. They walked out and looked at the away fans to their left and then to the Kop singing "You'll Never Walk Alone".

'The United players knew they couldn't be beaten. They had so much enthusiasm and pride in playing for United they won the game. They knew they couldn't lose, that it was in the DNA of a United player to be at his best against Liverpool. I've worked in football around the world, in Spain, Portugal, Africa, America, Japan and now Iran. And I've never seen footballers with that focus like at United.'

Brown was one of them, though Ferguson used to prod him about his concentration.

'We played Leeds and were 1–0 up at half-time,' he says. 'I thought I'd played well at a tough place to go. Leeds fans had thrown all sorts at us on the way into the ground. I loved that. Even when people shouted: "You ginger bastard", it didn't bother me. I'd laugh at them and use their abuse to motivate me.

'But at half-time, the gaffer just went for me and I looked up as if to say, "Me?" I didn't reply to him, we won the game. Mark Wilson, who didn't get out of his suit that day, saw what happened at half-time. But he also said to me: "When you'd left, Fergie said to the coaches that Wes will play even better now." He got me angry and I did play well. I concentrated more and if the gaffer had one issue with me, it was my concentration. He thought I cruised too much and nearly let players in. Nearly. They never did get in.'

Socially, Brown was a regular at the poker nights at Darren Fletcher's house.

'We paid £30 each maximum stakes. It was never about money, more about being with your teammates – the ones who were a similar age to me. There were groups within the group and always new players joining. Tomasz Kuszczak was the goalkeeper from Poland. He'd say "Good morning" to everyone each day in a funny accent. Great guy, shocking clothes – although we can hardly talk given that photo of us walking down a street in Manchester in baggy clothes. What on earth were we thinking?'

Moscow topped off Brown's best season for United.

'The manager gave the best speech where he picked us all out and said a few things about us. "Wes is a local lad who would die for you," he said. "He could have got himself arrested as a kid." The result was that we walked onto the pitch and I didn't feel any nerves, only that: "The boys are here. We are Man United." We battered Chelsea for the first 20 minutes. We just needed the second goal but credit to Chelsea for getting back into the game. And when they did, it was a proper battle. The biggest was between Vidić and Drogba. Vida used to give me a nod before a game. We were similar – if there's a tackle to be made, we'll make it. We'd fly into tackles without any concerns for our own life.

'I came off the pitch with 20 seconds to go so that Anderson could take a penalty. I felt such relief coming off, but also worry for the lads. The party wasn't like '99 because everything was so late there, but, as usual, I was the last one standing, Michael Carrick and I dancing. I was so tired that I got drunk quick, but we'd done it, we were champions of Europe.'

Brown's friends and family were proud.

'My dad, who has passed away, came to every game, my mum never really came to matches. Grandad took me to Lilleshall but died in '97. My brother Reece played at different clubs but didn't really get a run anywhere. He was a good player who could pass better than me. He didn't have my aggression or speed though. My best attributes were that I was a team guy, someone who could calm conflicts between teammates if need be. So, if two teammates weren't speaking, I'd tell one that the other wanted to speak to him when he didn't because ultimately you must try and get in the flow. I spoke to every single player, both when we played and since. The only player I've not seen since I stopped playing is Gabby Heinze. I've even spoke to Carlito [Tevez], despite him elbowing me – properly in the face – when he was at City. When he did that, I said: "I'm going to fucking smash you." Carlos said: "I didn't mean to do that, Wes, sorry" in his broken English.'

Brown left United in 2011.

'I knew when I played Bolton at Old Trafford that it was my last game for United. It wasn't that I was shit, I just knew that I wasn't the same player I'd been and that was because of my knees. I was the sort of player who was on you. If you received the ball then I was there. If you want to try and turn me then I'll square up, spin and race with you. But I couldn't do that anymore, not after I turned 30.

'It was a bit like Nev's last game at West Brom, I felt I was letting the lads down because I couldn't get there anymore and was dropping off. My knees were sore too. I had a year left on my contract, but we had Rafa, Fabio, Phil Jones and Chris Smalling. On a bus to a game, the gaffer said: "You're not going to play as much, Wes. I'm more than happy for you to stay but I must push the young lads on, like we did with you."

'I'd been in the first team for 12 years, been in three squads and won lots of trophies along the way. I was there for eight Premier Leagues but only got five medals from playing enough games. The rules have changed since. I was gutted when I left because I didn't see anyone to say goodbye to properly. I only saw people when I came back to Old Trafford. My trips back didn't always go well with Sunderland – I scored an own goal in my first trip back, which we lost 1–0 in 2011, and I was sent off in another. But we also won twice, including the League Cup semi-final on penalties.'

Brown was not short of offers. His situation was like that of John O'Shea.

'Sheasy said to me that Sunderland had made him an offer and I told him they'd made me one too. I called Steve Bruce, Sunderland's manager. He didn't know who I was. He was on holiday and thought it was a prank call before he finally believed me. He said we should speak the next day. Everton offered me a three-year deal, Stoke City too. They were closer to Manchester. I called Sheasy and said: "What do you think about Sunderland?" We both liked the idea. But, because I didn't get back to Steve Bruce straight away, Sunderland came back and offered me – and Sheasy – a four-year deal. We agreed our decision to go to Sunderland and play together.'

Brown travelled to the north east.

'I called Sheasy but he didn't pick up. When he did, he explained that something else had come up and he nearly took it, but that he was going to sign for Sunderland the next day – a great club, but not Man United. We both learned a lot about the other side of football. I was there for five years and learned what it was like to be in a relegation battle. It's horrible.

'I look back with pride on my time at United and have no regrets apart from that tackle when I did my ankle,' says Brown, as we get up to walk through Manchester, Brown's city, among his people.

1. Ole Gunnar Solskjaer during the Champions League quarter final against Real Madrid, 23 April 2003. Adam Davy / PA Images via Alamy Stock Photo

2. Jaap Stam in action in the Premier League against Newcastle United, 20 August 2000. Matthew Ashton / PA Images via Alamy Stock Photo

3. Ole now © Andy Mitten

4. Jaap now © Andy Mitten

5. Diego Forlán celebrates his first goal against Liverpool during a Premier League match at Anfield, 1 December 2002. John Giles / PA Images via Alamy Stock Photo

6. Darren Fletcher against Manchester City in the Premier League, 23 October 2011. Simon Bellis / Associated Press via Alamy Stock Photo

7. Real Madrid's Ronaldo scores his hat-trick goal against Manchester United as Wes Brown slides into a tackle, 23 April 2003. Neal Simpson / PA Images via Alamy Stock Photo

8. John O'Shea celebrates scoring a late winner in front of Liverpool fans during a Premier League match at Anfield on 3 March 2007. Peter Byrne / PA Images via Alamy Stock Photo

9. Diego now © Andy Mitten

11. Darren now © Andy Mitten

11. Wes now © Andy Mitten

12. John now © Andy Mitten

13. Chelsea's Joe Cole and Patrice Evra at Old Trafford, 23 September 2007.
Michael Rickett / PA Images via Alamy Stock Photo

14. Patrice now. Abaca Press / Alamy Stock Photo   15. Dimitar now © Andy Mitten

16. Dimitar Berbatov at Old Trafford during United's 3–0 win over Chelsea in January 2009.
Allstar Picture Library Ltd / Alamy Stock Photo

17. United's captain Gary Neville celebrates victory against Bolton Wanderers in the Premier League, 1 April 2006. John Walton / PA Images via Alamy Stock Photo

18. Gary selling United We Stand © Andy Mitten

19. Nemanja Vidić celebrates a goal against Everton at Goodison Park, 15 September 2007.
Allstar Picture Library Ltd via Alamy Stock Photo

20. Nemanja now with former Yugoslavia international
Budimir Vujačić (and the author) © Andy Mitten

21. Ryan Giggs celebrates after levelling the scores in a Champions League tie against Celtic at Celtic Park, 5 November 2008. Nigel French / PA Images via Alamy Stock Photo

22. Ryan now © Ryan Giggs

6

UNCLE PAT

Patrice Evra

In 2014, I was asked if I was interested in working on a book with a former Manchester United player. As I didn't know him, I wondered if it was a good idea. I sounded out Gary Neville.

'No!' was his advice. 'You should get Patrice. Now he's got a story.'

Patrice Evra? I hadn't spoken to him beyond a few brief questions and answers in the journalists' mixed zone.

Rio Ferdinand, I was told, would definitely know his number and the player offered to track it down. Nothing happened and, with a new daughter born that year and a lot on my plate with work, I didn't chase it up. Then in September 2015, quite by chance, a United staff member suggested, 'You'd be really interested in Patrice. He's great.' She offered to ask him if he wanted to do his autobiography and get back to me. 'Patrice will be in touch!' Silence.

By this time I wasn't going to give up on the idea. While planning a trip to Italy to interview some players in October 2015 I saw that Juventus, for whom Evra was now playing, were playing Sassuolo in Reggio Emilia, close to where I was writing a piece on the resurgence of Parma. I have friends from Reggio who I used to play football with, except they'd both left the city. Their ex-girlfriends hadn't though, and I knew them too.

I got a press ticket for the game at Sassuolo, checked into a hotel and wrote a handwritten letter to Evra, outlining why I thought his life story would be compelling. I put the letter in a hotel issue envelope and accepted a lift from the two girls to the stadium, which was on the outskirts of the city up a single-track road. It was raining heavily and security tried to turn the car back as we had no passes. When the window came down and two beautiful Italian girls smiled back, we were miraculously waved through.

Sassuolo beat Juventus; Evra didn't play. I waited in the mixed zone after the game. It was packed and nobody seemed to speak English. Why should they? After an hour, the Juventus players started coming through in their immaculately cut Trussardi suits including Paul Pogba, with his designer pants tucked into socks and trainers. Barely covered from the rain, the zone was also full of local big hitters and their families who wanted selfies with Juventus players. It was chaos. The last player to come out was Evra. I knew I had to take my chance, pushed through the melee and shouted: 'Patrice, Andy Mitten.' Then I thrust him my letter in a Novotel envelope.

'Andy,' he said. 'I'm sorry I didn't call you. Come over here.' He beckoned me towards the end of the zone by the Juventus bus and we talked in the rain. And talked.

He was weighing me up and I was weighing up whether he was serious about telling his life story or not. I didn't want to waste any more time. He said he was and felt that United had been the high point of his career and he preferred to collaborate with an English writer. London is also a capital of book publishing, where the most prestigious publishers are based. I'd written ten books and wasn't naïve about how the market works.

'I wanted to do a book,' he says. 'I just wasn't sure how. People didn't know the real me. They thought they did because of what they saw of me playing football, but they knew very little about me. I had a lot of things that I wanted to explain so that people could understand me better, things which I'd told nobody about.'

At the end of the chat I tweeted a photo of Evra, with a message saying that he missed Manchester. It went viral. I was struck by how popular he was. Evra wasn't on social media himself at the time, surprising given how central it is to his life now.

We left that meeting with Evra saying I should call his agent. The Juventus team bus sped off flanked by police outriders and I stood in an empty car park at midnight with no taxis anywhere.

I called his agent and, a month later, he called me back, stating that he'd been doing background checks on me. 'And who did you ask?' His reply was that the first person was another player, who I'd long got on with. The agent suggested that we meet in London the following Wednesday.

'But I'm in Italy next Wednesday.'

'Where?'

'I'm going to Modena to see Hernán Crespo.'

'I live close to Modena,' he replied. 'Come to see me.'

A train ride later, the agent and I walked and talked around his city. The book was agreed in principle, the next stage involved getting enough quality material from Evra to shape a 10,000-word synopsis – so that any potential publishers knew what they were bidding for. The minimal involvement of some players in their autobiographies is notorious. And a cliché-ridden book saying nothing – and several United players have put their names to such books, damaging the sports publishing market – would be of no interest, particularly not to me.

I started to go back to Italy to see Evra. He was a key player for Juventus, but he was correct when he said: 'Every time you came to see me play, I didn't play.'

Evra was on the bench for one game against Verona when I was there. I waited for him in the players' lounge afterwards as Pogba and his family sat at the next table. Then I walked out of the ground with Pat, gaining a few small insights into the life of a professional footballer as little kids ran up to his car at the traffic lights near the stadium and screamed 'Evra!' The window came down and he posed for selfies, earning beeps from the cars behind. We were supposed to go to a restaurant but it was closed, so we sat talking in a layby by Turin Airport for two hours. One of Pat's questions was about social media. This was January 2016. I told him the pros and the cons. Four months later, Pogba was clearly more persuasive in getting him to join up and since then he has accrued 14 million followers on Instagram alone.

I began to go to Turin regularly. We'd talk for hours (and I'd estimate that a book of the quality Evra deserved took 800 hours of work, plus travel), he was completely engaged in the idea.

His feelings for United clearly ran deep. During Euro 2016, he messaged me to say that he could help any fans out with complimentary tickets for France matches, but they had to be for 'proper Man United fans'.

Patrice moved from Turin to Marseille in 2017 and I began to travel to the French city. He was excellent to deal with. Always honest and frank. I'd laugh and shake my head in astonishment as he told me his life story at a rate of knots, laced with his quickfire wit. But he also discussed many serious issues and I began to realise that there was a real depth to his character. He was prepared to put in the hours but my idea of leisurely three-hour chats after training in the Provence summer went out of the window when Pat said he wanted to speak after games at night, when he struggled to sleep. The late shift it was then, until three or four in the morning. I'd fly to Marseille or take trains. It was time-consuming and one train was so delayed it meant an overnight stop in Montpellier. I texted the man I'd been to see: 'I don't love this train.'

Pat was carrying a knock so I'd watch games with him in his box at the Vélodrome, just me and him in a 16-seater box. Actually, me, him and a giant stuffed panda, which appeared for the Toulouse game. As we got deeper and deeper into his life, I said it would help if I met those nearest to him. For the PSG game in October, his close friends and family came along. They couldn't have been more helpful.

Once, I arrived in Marseille and met Patrice at his hotel and it was clear that he had something big to share. 'I have to tell you something,' he began and revealed the sexual abuse he'd suffered as a child. It was horrific. I recorded everything and just listened. He said he hadn't told anyone and I didn't tell anyone, but he wanted it in the book.

I sat there angry and upset. We'd taken a couple of years to get to this point – not that I knew it was coming. I thought him brave to tell me, astonished that he had. I knew he had a good life story but I expected it to be mostly football-related. There were long pauses before the conversation would continue or we just didn't continue and he'd say: 'I had to tell you. I want it in the book.'

Asking about a game against Portsmouth didn't seem to matter after that.

I left the hotel the next morning and walked around Marseille in a daze at what I'd heard. The more I thought about it, the more I began to think that the book was part of a process for Patrice, that he wanted to get things off his chest, that he wanted some good to come from the bad he'd suffered.

A few months later, my wife called me and said that I should look online. Patrice had kicked a fan while playing for Marseille in Portugal.

My first reaction was 'Oh fuck.' Selfishly, I was deep into the book and wondered whether it would be put in jeopardy. What if he was jailed, what if, whatever …

I didn't know the circumstances. I messaged him to ask if he was OK. He said he was. He'd reacted because he'd been racially abused and, like Cantona, had no regrets about attacking the fan. No regrets, but he becomes absolutely serious when he speaks about it.

'I do not condone violence,' he says, but then goes on to say that he was not going to take the abuse and the threats – towards his family. 'I am like Cantona,' he says. 'We both kicked the fan. Cantona told me he respects me for that. My respect for him is total.' And he is especially vehement about what he calls 'toxic masculinity', which he no longer has time for.

The publishers left us alone, they trusted us to produce a quality book and never once asked us to include or not include anything. And all along, I watched Patrice's profile rise among a demographic who knew him more for being happy on Instagram than for playing football.

My favourite post was Pat and his friends upon hearing that Gonzalo Higuaín was signing for Juventus in a record Italian deal. They started dancing and singing around a table tennis table.

He laughs about it later. 'I was on holiday and celebrated the news in a video by dancing around the table with my agent's son and Tshimen's [his childhood friend] son to "My Boo" [by Ghost Town DJs] and shouting "Forza Juve!" I was really happy. I'd had a great connection with every Argentinian I'd played with. Higuaín was one of the best strikers in the world and he was coming to play with me. Why not celebrate with a little dance? When he arrived at Juve, he came straight over to me and thanked me for the video. He said he felt that the club wanted him.'

Patrice's posts were getting hundreds of thousands of views; the kick was back-page news in the UK, mentioned on the BBC six o'clock news and was front-page news in France. Publishers talk and I started getting calls about Pat the following day, including several from French journalists. I couldn't see how me saying anything could help his situation, so I didn't. Ironically, the kick was having the opposite effect to what I'd feared.

I've also had British journalists asking me if I could put them in touch with Pat. They hadn't seen the efforts I'd gone to, to get in touch with him myself, and I was hardly predisposed to hand over details. Besides, players don't like it.

Marseille became London when he joined West Ham and I'd sit in his bedroom taking notes about his life. Once, I started to feel sick and rushed to the toilet by his bedroom and vomited. I don't think a journalist had spewed up in his presence before, let alone in his bedroom. He took it all in his stride.

Some of his stories were hilarious, such as how he learned to drive in Nice.

'I should have had problems with the police because I spent most of my time in Nice driving without a licence. It wasn't that I had failed my driving test, but that I had never taken it. According to my mind, I knew how to drive and so didn't need a piece of paper to tell me that I could. I'd managed to buy my first car by bluffing that I'd left my licence at home in Paris and would send it on later.'

His car?

'I bought an Audi A8 but, in true Les Ulis [where he grew up] style, I didn't like the wheels on it because I considered them too small. Some friends in the quartier managed to get me bigger wheels from another car, which naturally didn't fit and so the car didn't drive well. So I took it to the Audi showroom to get it sorted out and when they asked for my papers I gave them my friend Tshimen's driving licence – two black men, who could tell the difference? They didn't spot the fraud, but they did say that the wheels made the car too dangerous to drive. I told the man at Audi that the wheels were perfect and I wasn't going to change them.'

Then there was his driving test.

'The 18 hours of driving lessons were a complete pain in the ass because I already knew how to drive, which the driving instructor recognised immediately. I was soon booked in for my test and was so confident that I reclined my seat, unclipped my seat belt and reverse parked with only one hand on the wheel – at speed. I was so competent at driving that I could do that, but the examiner looked shocked. The two other students in the car who were also taking their tests took a different approach. They put both hands on the wheel and had the driving seat upright, which didn't make them look relaxed at all. In Les Ulis, you can't drive like that – you have to put the seat down and chill. You're not cool otherwise.

'The examiner passed the other two students and I waited for him to do the same for me. "You are a danger to other road users," he said. "You are too confident and I know you've been driving without a licence. And I thought I had seen everything in this job …"'

Evra booked the test again and promised himself that he'd be a model student and not a street gangster. This time he passed – no problem.

He was a normal driver by the time he drove me from his last game, an awful match against Manchester United for West Ham. After that game, he took me to his flat overlooking the Thames as his former United teammates like Paul Pogba called him to discuss happenings at United. They spoke in English. Why?

I went to Les Ulis, a banlieue of only 24,000 people where he and many other players grew up, to meet his old friends. Pat was always ready to speak about Les Ulis, although he doesn't sugar-coat it and always prefaces any discussion of his childhood home by stressing that football saved him from prison or worse and that its streets could turn dangerous in an instant.

'Les Ulis is a football factory,' he said proudly. 'Thierry Henry, Anthony Martial, Yaya Sanogo, Moussa Marega and I all grew up there. We are probably the only town in the world with players that have won every major trophy in football – the World Cup, Champions League, Europa League. All of them. I myself have won more trophies than Manchester City. That is the truth.'

Or it was then.

'Why are there so many top footballers from my home? It's no mystery. First of all, the kids are outside playing football all the time. Second, it's an escape from violence and crime. It was for me. When they opened a synthetic pitch near my school we hung around there and played football rather than go to Carrefour to steal things. Third, the immigration. There are big players from Africa. Not me! Small Arab players from Morocco. Fourth, from the age of six, there are great teachers in the school and qualified coaches – like my friends Tshimen and Mahamadou. They are brilliant coaches who both coach in my old quartier. They try to support and develop the whole child, not just his football.'

They couldn't have done more for me on that cloudy day in Paris.

I'd cross check as much as I could from the stories he told me – the fights with former United players in training, for example, and then tell him. He does an interesting impression of Gary Neville which, a few years later when we did a Q&A event at the Lowry theatre in Salford, was met with howls of laughter.

'What did Gary say?' asked Patrice of a story he describes thus: 'In training soon after I'd arrived at Manchester, Gary went for me. He touched the ball but he hit my legs too. I felt pain, I was on the floor. I looked at him, expecting him to say sorry. He looked straight at me and said: "Fuck off, I took the ball."

'"Really?" I said, "really?"

'I got up but I was in pain. The ball came to Gary, who jumped to chest it. I saw my chance. I did a kung-fu kick to get the ball and hit Gary. I nearly broke his shoulder. The other players were angry and crowded around me. Wayne Rooney said: "Are you crazy, Patrice? You could have broken his neck."

'"Yes, but next time Gary will say sorry."

'Ferguson and his assistant Carlos Queiroz stopped training and shouted: "Everyone inside." They were the teachers telling off the naughty children. I was still in pain and putting ice on my leg inside when Gary came to me and shouted: "You're fucking crazy, Patrice."

'Gary didn't like fakes or guys who weren't team players. In return you could always count on him.' And the upshot? 'The rest of the dressing room knew that I was not a pushover,' except that he didn't say pushover, but he reminds me that he doesn't condone swearing either, except when 'I have to be real'. 'Being real' is something Patrice says again and again. Which is why he was prepared to reveal some of his closely guarded secrets in the book.

The people I checked with would confirm that they were true. We finished the book in 2018 and there was a photo shoot for the cover. It was a difficult time. My father was dying of cancer, Patrice's football career was ending, his marriage too.

We held the book back for far longer than I expected and then started on it again in 2020. I reminded Patrice about this and he told me that the time had to be right. In 2020, he was very happy with his new partner, Margaux; his smile had come back. I was set up to speak to Margaux over Zoom and corroborated what Patrice told me about when they first met in a chicken takeaway in Chelsea.

Evra's name comes up frequently among his former teammates and it was at United where he became one of the best full-backs on the planet. It wasn't like that at the start after he joined from Monaco in January 2006.

'My debut was a disaster,' he said. 'United had a great record against City under Ferguson, but City had grown more confident at home against us. From the start, Trevor Sinclair kept running past me and leaving me on my ass. He knocked my eye with his elbow after two minutes. I also banged my head and couldn't see properly five minutes into the game. I was in shock, asking myself: "Patrice, what the hell are you doing here? The football is so quick and so strong." After all, I was a top player who'd been at Monaco and reached the Champions League final and played for France, and there I was on my backside. Now my head was spinning.'

Trevor Sinclair scored after half an hour and played a part in a second goal just before half-time.

'I was being targeted by City because they knew it was my first game. They hit long diagonal balls to Sinclair and he would run aggressively straight at me and get behind the defence.

'I was taken off at half-time when United were 2–0 down. Ferguson was shouting at everyone. I barely understood him because I couldn't speak English, but I didn't need to know the language to appreciate how furious he was. He looked at me and bellowed: "Evra! That's enough! Now you can sit down, watch the game and start to learn to play English football in another game!"'

Queiroz, who spoke several languages, translated Ferguson's words into French, tapping Evra on the shoulder as he did so.

'I asked him again what Ferguson meant. "It means that you don't go back on," was the reply. I couldn't believe what was happening to me. We lost 3–1. My agent Luca had travelled to watch the game with his wife. For him, it was supposed to be a proud moment. I was the boy he'd rescued from the Italian third division and now I was playing for Manchester United. Luca came to see me at the hotel. I opened the door and he nearly cried when he saw me. Even his wife looked sad for me. I didn't feel sad, I felt empty, like shit, especially after the way Ferguson had talked to me. Luca told me that he thought he'd made a huge mistake bringing me to Manchester, that he didn't think I would make it at United, that he thought the jersey, like my coat, was too big for me. It was painful, but he motivated me to prove him wrong.' The coat was an outsize designer affair which Patrice claimed looked great in Italy but tragic in Manchester.

But things would pick up as Evra immersed himself in his new city, even if it was a struggle to live in a hotel in a country where he and his family didn't speak the language, one which was a little different from his previous homes by the coast in the South of France as he played for Nice and Monaco.

'Slowly, I began to fall in love with Mancunians and Manchester United,' he said. 'Every time I pulled on that red shirt I felt I was pulling on history. I'd spend time reading about the history of the club and watching DVDs. I was very emotional and felt pain when I read all about the Munich air disaster and the Busby Babes, the great young players who died. I read about the crazy fans in the 1970s, the wingers, the promotion of young players from the academy. Cantona, George Best, Denis Law and his legendary teammates like Sir Bobby Charlton, who I still saw around the club and whose hand I could shake. The legends like Giggs and Scholes, who I played with every single day. And Alex Ferguson. I was living history every day of my life.

'Before every game Ferguson would tell us a little story and as my English started to improve, I began to understand. Sometimes he'd tell us about when he'd been Aberdeen manager. Other times, he'd walk around the dressing room and tell us how proud he was to have all these boys assembled from around the world, the sacrifices and obstacles we'd had to overcome to get there. He was so inspiring.'

Evra was learning about his new environment. And making mistakes in it.

'I did one interview where I said living in Manchester was difficult because of the rain and the lack of quality restaurants. It was the truth, but the newspapers killed me for that, and Diana Law, who dealt with the media for United, came to see me.

'"You're in trouble for saying this, Patrice," she said.

'Ferguson was angry and demanded: "What is this you are saying about Manchester?"

'I explained that I didn't mean to say it in a bad way, more being honest when I was asked for the difference between Manchester and Monaco. From that moment I realised that I had to be careful with the words I said to the English newspapers because they could twist them. I didn't want to offend the people who paid my wages, the people who had made me feel so welcome in their city.'

Evra's second game, against Liverpool, went better.

'I won a free-kick that led to Rio Ferdinand scoring. I also went into a tackle with Steven Gerrard that made people see that I was capable of being tough when needed. We won 1–0 at home and I heard how loud the United crowd could be. It was the first time that I thought: "I can do this in England. I can play for a Man United team that beats Liverpool."'

Games against Blackburn followed.

'We were winning but I was not performing at my best. We lost the league game 4–3 and those three goals led Ferguson to say to me: "You're playing well, Patrice, but we're conceding goals with you." He was right. It would take some time for me to adjust my game and to win his full trust.'

Then United met Liverpool away in the cup.

'When Ferguson told me I was only on the bench I was disappointed, especially as it was an important game that was being televised live in France and I knew my friends and family would be watching, but I understood. I put my kit on and started warming up with the players. When I went back to the dressing room, Carlos Queiroz said: "Why are you warming up? You are not on the bench, you're in the stand."

'I hadn't understood the manager properly. I felt embarrassed and said to Queiroz: "Can I please keep the tracksuit on and sit on the bench to pretend that I am a substitute?" I was so ashamed, my ego was bruised. My name would not have even been listed on French television. I told people that I'd picked up a knock in the warm-up and couldn't play. I was allowed to sit on the bench. Not for the first time, Queiroz was the one who was calm with me, the good cop to Fergie being the bad cop who shouted at me and told me that I had to improve.

'I was in and out of the team, which was hard to accept after what I'd done at Monaco, but I was in competition with Mikaël Silvestre, a beast of a player. The French media was saying that I was going to take his place and I don't think he was happy with that, but that meant he trained harder. He warned me, "You're my friend but you're not taking my place." And that's how it should be.

'And even though I was in competition with him, he was giving me advice and trying to help me settle in Manchester. He invited me to his house to eat, he showed me around and introduced me to Wings, my favourite restaurant in Manchester. There are plenty of assholes in football, but Silvestre is not one of them. As my career went on I learned from him how to treat players in the same position.'

Three months after signing, Evra came on for the last seven minutes in the League Cup final victory over Wigan Athletic in Cardiff's Millennium Stadium.

'I only got on the pitch because Ruud van Nistelrooy refused to go on. He wasn't happy because Louis Saha was selected and, when United were winning 4–0, Ferguson told van Nistelrooy to warm up. He said no and told the manager to fuck off. I had to ask for clarification of what I'd just heard and then I thought, "Whoa." Ruud was a big name and personality in the team, the top scorer and popular with fans. Ferguson's face was red with anger and Queiroz had a go at Ruud.

'I knew that the sentence was going to be a severe one for Ruud, but I just wanted to get on the pitch. Ferguson sent Nemanja and me to warm up instead. The Serb's fortunes were similar to mine – he was starting to settle. I played the last few minutes and said to the boss in the dressing room at the end: "It's so easy to play for Man United. Three months and I already have a trophy."

'"You fucking French!" he said, laughing. I was so happy and so was the manager, who I was really starting to respect. He later explained that he'd brought Vida and me on because he wanted us to experience what it was like winning with Manchester United.

But what are Patrice's thoughts on van Nistelrooy?

'Ruud? In my very first training session he fouled Ronaldo, and Queiroz who was refereeing awarded a foul. Ruud disputed it. Ronaldo had just lost his father and he was emotional. Ruud said: "Queiroz is your dad! Go and cry to your dad!" Ronaldo started to cry. Things were misunderstood. Ruud wasn't nasty, he was a good guy, but he wasn't happy either.'

In the summer of 2006 United toured South Africa, where Evra met one of his heroes, Nelson Mandela. As he went to shake his hand, the mobile of Albert Morgan the kit man went off and his theme tune was 'The Great Escape'. Morgan struggled to turn his phone off.

'Albert was the right man to have around in the dressing room, discreet and reliable at his job but also a man to raise a smile, even if he didn't mean to do that most of the time. We visited a wildlife park on that trip, where there were signs telling us not to touch the electric fences. In front of a reclining rhino, Albert got out his old camera from the 1990s and set his zoom off – into the electric wire. Albert was soon dancing like a popcorn with his hair standing on end. Someone in our party was concerned, shouting a warning that Albert had a heart problem, but even that couldn't calm the laughter.'

It was on that tour where assistant manager Mike Phelan had a word with Evra. 'You're looking like a United player now, Patrice.' Evra played in the first league game of the season against Fulham and United won 5–1.

'I felt amazing, physically stronger, fitter and more confident,' he recalls. But despite playing 36 games in 2006–07, Evra was still not first choice all the time. 'Gabriel Heinze, by then my main competition for left-back, played 38 games, but he was used also as a centre-back. Gabby and I didn't really work together on the pitch. He attacked the ball like I did, so maybe we were too similar to play in the same team.'

Michael Carrick joined in 2006, a year after Park Ji-sung.

'Carrick would make strong and accurate passes from midfield forward to the striker – a quick transition from defence to midfield then to the forwards. He was very effective and improved our team, but he lost some form after three years and Ferguson wasn't happy. Maybe injury was to blame, but then Carra became very important again and spent more than ten years at the club. He's a United legend.

'I'd become good friends with Park Ji-sung. We spoke in English – Ji spoke it better than me but he was really shy so people often didn't hear him. I'm intrigued by shy people, I wonder if I can get to know them. I see it as a challenge. I became close to Ji, especially when he was injured, because I was his nurse. I'd go to his house and we'd switch on the PlayStation after training. His leg was suspended in the air as it had to be elevated. Ji's parents also lived in Manchester and his mum would make soup and rice or a Korean barbecue. Amazing food. I've never seen two people play badminton as fast as Ji's mum and dad. I'd watch them in the garden, smashing this little shuttlecock at each other. I played against them and they beat me really easily. I told Ji that I thought his parents were on performance-enhancing drugs for badminton. He told them and they laughed – and still treated me like a son. They were the nicest family.'

And what of Gary Neville?

'[He] was my captain. United was the most important thing in his life and he was Ferguson's man to maintain standards among the players. One day, Ravel Morrison, a very talented youth player, took Wayne's phone off charge and plugged in his own one. Gary went mad at him for coming into the first-team dressing room and charging his phone. He picked up Ravel's phone and threw it on the floor. Wazza hadn't been the slightest bit bothered and I thought Gary's reaction was a bit too strong. But Gary's point was that young players needed to learn what they should and shouldn't do.'

Apart from the argument described earlier in this chapter, Gary and Evra never had another one. 'He was very good to me. He'd shown me around houses when I first arrived in Manchester. When I wanted to see a priest, I expected to be taken to a church. Instead, he brought a priest to Carrington.'

Evra won the Premier League for the first time in 2007, but he didn't make the line-up in the FA Cup final. That the memory is still bitter is very apparent.

'On the morning of the final I ordered breakfast in my room. I was dancing with music on. It was a beautiful day and I was going to play in the FA Cup final. There was a knock at the door. I thought it was my breakfast but, no, Alex Ferguson was standing in front of me. "Patrice," he said, as he walked in and sat on a sofa in my luxury hotel room, "what is this noise? Do you think you have a nightclub here?"

'He was nice to me at the beginning, but he hadn't come to talk to me about music. I turned the music off, some R&B. His expression changed. "Son, I will play Gabby," he said.

'My face dropped. I respected Gabriel Heinze, my rival, and we got on well. He'd helped me when I arrived in Manchester, even though I was direct competition for him. I spoke French with him as he'd played for PSG. We also spoke some Spanish. I don't know how the Spanish language came into my head; it just did when I was at Monaco because we had several Spanish speakers.

'So Heinze started the final. Heinze had been angry with Ferguson because they bought me when he was injured. Ferguson told him that he was still first choice – which was probably right because Heinze had been one of United's best players in 2005, the year before I joined. But I had been playing so well that Ferguson had no choice but to start me – except that now, in the Cup final, he was dropping me. And right now, with Ferguson standing in front of me, I was angry.

"'I know you are upset and you are right to be upset, but I will tell you why," he continued. "The pitch is heavy. It's better suited to him. You are quick, fresh and fast. You are going to come on and win the game for us."

"'Boss, I'm really disappointed," I said. He left the room. The one-man Patrice Evra party was over.' Evra didn't get off the bench in 120 minutes of a game United lost.

'In the dressing room Ferguson tried to shake my hand, but I refused. I wanted to leave the club and told my agent. He told me to calm down but I didn't listen. I couldn't get beyond it being my first time at Wembley, my first big game since joining the club. And the manager didn't start me.

'There was a party afterwards in London, even after the team lost. Guests, including other players, were asking me: "Why didn't you play? Are you injured?" I was still blazing. I again called my agent Luca, who is Italian, and said: "I don't want to play for Manchester United any more. Get me a club in Italy!"

'He told me to calm down once more, saying that I'd just finished a really good season. He was being sensible.

"'No, it's over," I said. "I've done everything I can do for this team and it's not good enough. They didn't start me in the Cup final. Then the manager told me that I'd come on and win the game. Then he was asking me to warm up after 20 minutes. He lied to me. Lied!"'

The pair never spoke about it again, but Evra's fortunes would dramatically improve at United. In the following pre-season, Heinze told the players that he was going to join Liverpool. The case went to a Premier League tribunal, where Liverpool claimed they should be able to buy him and United alleged that he'd been illegally approached by Liverpool. For a month Heinze did nothing, until the ruling was given in favour of United and the next thing the players knew was that Heinze had joined Real Madrid. United barely missed a player who'd been so influential two years earlier.

'The standard of the training was getting better and better. Ronaldo was doing stuff none of us had seen before. Ferguson changed the way Ronaldo thought about football. Before, Ronaldo had been all about numbers, about goals and assists, but Ferguson made him think more about the team. I remember Ferguson telling him in one team meeting to stop the circus tricks. He told him that he had the ability to score in every game if he cut the tricks out. Ferguson made him a killer, made him a man.

'I was tackling everything in training, Vida was a rock and Rio was his partner and equal in defence. Giggs was flying around like he had been 15 years earlier, Rooney was a machine and Scholes was just being Scholes. We'd play nine versus nine in training on a Friday and it was more competitive than some of the Premier League games, with the winners hammering the losing players in the dressing room afterwards.'

There were more new signings.

'Anderson was a big deal in his first season at the club. The Brazilian was wild – and I mean that as a compliment. I loved him. My mum is from Cape Verde so I could speak to him in Portuguese, which I was also improving by talking with Ronaldo. Ando was only 18 and he was the type of guy who would say to Ferguson: "How much do you earn?" The manager had never before been asked that by any player and didn't know what to say. One day before training, the manager asked me: "Patrice, has Anderson put weight on?" Then he called Ando over, who replied: "Boss, easy. Give me the ball. Bam! Bam! I win all the games for you."'

And United did win, even the difficult ones.

'We went to Lyon away in the Champions League last 16 [in 2008]. As I knew only too well, they'd won every Ligue 1 title since their first one in 2002 – a French record – and there were hopes that they could become the first French team to win the European Cup since Marseille in 1993. With a team containing Juninho, Hatem Ben Arfa, Sidney Govou and Jérémy Toulalan, Lyon were strong and Karim Benzema, still only 20, scored. Carlos Tevez equalised with three minutes left, giving us a crucial away goal. Carlos was like a lion. Carlito could change a game. He would give blood for a team, he was always angry and fired up. He always gave 100 per cent, yet as a professional he didn't train hard. He was lazy, he didn't care, he couldn't even be bothered to tie his boots properly. You didn't want him in your team in training, but he did also train at home alone, and when you saw him on the day of the game he was a completely different person.'

There's one game which still annoys Evra from 2007–08.

'Portsmouth knocked us out of the FA Cup with a 1–0 win at Old Trafford in March 2008. Tomasz Kuszczak, who replaced Edwin van der Sar at half-time, was sent off and Rio Ferdinand took over in goal. I was furious, and not only because I hit the post. I know the lads found Lassana Diarra hard to play against in midfield, but he kicked Ronaldo in the neck and didn't get sent off. We should never have been knocked out of the FA Cup that day. That defeat came a few days after we'd beaten Lyon 1–0 to reach the last eight in Europe.

'Ronaldo was having his best season so far and when we travelled to Italy to play Roma, the travelling United fans sang their new song "Viva Ronaldo!" really loud. Cristiano scored a magnificent header and Rooney made it 2–0. My old Monaco captain Ludovic Giuly came off the bench to try to help his team in vain. I felt like I was playing for the best team in the world and people were starting to compare us to United's treble winners. Ferguson was not having that and warned us: "You've won nothing yet." But I knew he was excited by us, especially when he said: "You will be the worst team in the world if you don't win this competition." We beat Roma 1–0 at home, thanks to another goal from Carlito.

'Manchester United were so strong all over. Rio and Vida at the back gave us the perfect platform. Rio was like a number 10 who played in defence, Vida was a warrior, and they complemented each other perfectly. Rio would finish the game with no blood on his shirt because he'd read everything so well. Vida would be covered in blood because he put his head in where it hurt. He'd smash a striker, as if to say: "You can't go into that space." Ferguson always compared them to Gary Pallister and Steve Bruce, with Vida as Bruce.

'Wes Brown, who also featured at centre-half, played at right-back because Neville was injured, and he was our Mancunian warrior, a local boy. I loved playing with them all. They'd say: "Go forward – we'll take care of everything behind you." They were so comfortable and confident even when playing one against one. Ferguson always urged us to stay calm and not be too confident, but he also said: "If any of you can't take one player, you shouldn't be in this team." Vidić never asked for support with a striker because a one-against-one was a challenge, a talking point in the dressing room afterwards. If a rival striker got a shot on goal, we'd kill the defenders for letting it happen. We could win 4–0 but if Nemanja or Rio had let one player shoot, we'd destroy them for it rather than talk about winning 4–0.

'We stood in the tunnel before a game and knew we were going to win. My France teammate William Gallas told me what it was like for an opposing player. He said they'd look at all these tall United players and admit: "These guys are something special." We felt invincible, and our opponents knew it and expected to lose against us.'

United were going to win the league again.

'The Champions League became a bigger focus,' says Evra. 'Barcelona in the semi-final, with the first leg at the Camp Nou.

We were not scared of them and felt relaxed as we stayed in our hotel on the outskirts of the city. The manager didn't want us to be seduced by the sea and sun and the beauty in the centre of the city.

'Barcelona's Camp Nou is so big that you feel like you are in a spaceship or Rome's Colosseum, so big that it's not noisy or intimidating. I was told that I was to mark Lionel Messi and follow him everywhere. The gaffer said to Cristiano in the dressing room: "Messi is the best player in the world right now" to motivate him. "Patrice, I don't care about Messi because you are going to keep him quiet. And if you don't keep him quiet the team will lose this game. If you don't do your job then the team will lose this game. But I know you will do your job." I was nodding in agreement, but deep inside I was thinking: "If I fuck this up, I'm going to lose the confidence of my teammates and my manager."'

Cristiano Ronaldo missed a penalty after two minutes.

'My focus was Messi. We had about 20 one-against-ones, but he only took advantage once when he passed the ball over my head and the crowd roared. But we drew 0–0 and I had done what was asked of me. Messi and I shook hands at the end. He'd played well, but I was like a Pitbull always on his toes and maybe that surprised him. "Well done, son," the boss congratulated me back in the dressing room. Marking Messi that day gave me a lot of confidence.

'We'd done half the job, but there was always the risk Barcelona could get an away goal. Nil-nil is a risky scoreline in Europe, but a Scholesy strike won the second leg at Old Trafford. It was the loudest I heard the stadium in all my time at United. I wish Old Trafford could be like that more often, but it's not every game you beat Barcelona in the semi-final. I felt the pressure during that match more than any other game. All Barcelona needed to do was equalise and they'd be through, and I kept saying to myself: "If they score, we're fucked." I had a knock on the head at the end of the game and felt dizzy but we survived until the whistle when Old Trafford roared so loud you could feel the noise in your chest. I was going to a second Champions League final and this time I was confident that I was playing for the best team in the world.'

Chelsea were the opponents in the Moscow final.

'We'd beaten Chelsea 2–0 at Old Trafford in September in the league but our away league game against them came in between those two Champions League semi-finals. Even though I didn't play, I made headlines because I got into a fight with the ground-staff afterwards, which I regret.'

Evra had a visitor in Moscow the day before the game: Sir Alex Ferguson. This time the bad news was not for Evra.

'He knew I had become close friends with Park Ji-sung. Ji and I had such a strong connection and we still have it. He's the best friend that I've ever had in football, a man I have so much respect for that I travelled to South Korea for the funeral of his mother.

'Ferguson could not understand our connection. He asked, puzzled: "Which language are you speaking?" Carlos Tevez was friends with us too. Ferguson would say: "You're French from Senegal, you're from South Korea and you're from Argentina. How do you communicate?" But we just did using a hybrid of languages and we had so many laughs. Ferguson called us "The good, the bad and the ugly". I think I was the bad. We spoke a little English, a little Spanish. Ji spoke English.

'In Moscow, Ferguson told me to explain to Ji that he was not going to play in the European Cup final and that he wouldn't even be in the squad. That was difficult, especially as Ji's parents had flown from South Korea to see him play. Ferguson told me that he felt terrible, that it was one of the three most difficult decisions of his career. Ji's parents gave Ferguson a present after the game so that probably made him feel even worse. They wanted to thank him for looking after their son so well. I told Ferguson that he was asking me to do a difficult thing, but he said: "I know, but I know how close you are to Ji. When I speak to him, he's so respectful that I don't know what his expressions mean."

'I learned a lot from Ji about humility and respect, which is important in Korean culture. I went to see Ji in the hotel after training the day before the game. He said: "Don't worry, Patrice, just focus on the final and win for United." But I knew he was hurting, and he told me later that he was hurting a lot and had cried alone in his room. I'd never seen him show his emotions before.

'Ji was right to be disappointed, especially as he'd been one of our best players in the semi-final against Barcelona, both home and away. Even Xavi Hernández later said: "Wow, that Korean never stopped running." He didn't. Louis Saha also didn't make the team. He cried too, but we had to focus on the game.

'Ferguson was inspired in his pre-match talk. He told us that his greatest achievement that season was not any trophy, but bringing 21 of us together from all around the world. He was so proud of that. He picked us out individually, saying: "Can you imagine what it was like for Patrice fighting for food with his many brothers and sisters? Can you imagine Rooney on the streets of Liverpool having a tough time? Or Carlos in the estates of Buenos Aires? Or Vida when bombs were landing on his home town in the war?" It was emotional and we left the dressing room feeling like we could beat anyone. Fergie had barely spoken about the game, but he'd stressed to us throughout the season that if we wanted to be champions, then we had to do better than Chelsea. And we had only beaten Chelsea to win the league by two points, thanks to Giggs' goal at Wigan Athletic in the final game of the season. There wasn't a lot between us and Chelsea.

'In our Moscow hotel, we watched a video about the treble in the run-up to the final – 1999 was in our head and was one of our motivations. I was feeling confident before the game, and then more so when Cristiano Ronaldo put us ahead. Then Lampard equalised to make it all square. There were battles all over the pitch. Drogba came close to scoring in extra-time and it was clear that one action was going to win the game. In extra-time I went through with the ball and crossed to Ryan Giggs. He shot but John Terry blocked it, meaning that the game went to penalties.

'I can't understand how anyone can miss a penalty, yet I am talking from a position of trauma. When I'd played for France Under 21s against Portugal, I missed a penalty. I didn't think you could – or should – miss a penalty and vowed never to take one again, and I have been true to my word.

'In Moscow, Queiroz asked me out on the pitch as we prepared for the shoot-out: "Patrice, do you want a penalty?" I shook my head. He was surprised because I was an important player who should have taken some responsibility. But I feared missing again. The kids like Anderson had no such fear. Giggs had reminded the manager that Ando was good at penalties, and Ferguson had brought him on as substitute in the last minute of extra-time. His first touch of the ball that night would be when he took his penalty.

'Edwin van der Sar had no choice but to face the penalties, but there was no better goalkeeper to do that. Ed was our brain at the back. A complete gentleman, he was always calm, even if we didn't protect him enough. He'd always shout encouragement or try and help – "Patrice, look on your left!" I could hear him in the loudest stadiums. He was like a manager on the pitch. He could also hit a very accurate long ball that could kill the line of strikers or even the midfield line too. Sometimes that ball came to me and I'd play it forwards. We were on the attack in only three passes.

'I also saw John Terry's tears on the pitch and I felt genuinely sad for him. Unlike my teammates, I had been a loser in a European final too. That image of Terry stays with me. Chelsea were a great team and we pushed each other so hard that we were the best two teams in the world, but they'd lost the league to us and now they'd lost the Champions League.

'After a long celebration in the dressing room, we were taken back to the team hotel. All the players were drinking alcohol except me. It was so late that it was getting light, maybe three in the morning. If you look at the photos I'm the only one not smiling. I regret that, but I think I know why. I was disappointed that we hadn't won the treble, that we'd lost in the FA Cup to Portsmouth at home. As I said before, we should have never lost that.

'This was what I told my brother Dominique, who was back at the hotel for the party. "Patrice, you're crazy; you've won the Premier League and the Champions League," he said. "You have a problem. You have issues." But that's how I felt. I didn't really celebrate so much. Instead, I danced with Ji's father. He was disappointed about his son, but decided the best way to feel happy was to dance. A kung-fu dance! I joined in with him, and he could kick really high. Wonderful.

'My family and agent drank champagne. Everyone thought I was miserable because I didn't join in. The players said: "Get Patrice a hot chocolate or a water because he's boring." It's true, I should have been happier, but I had the medal around my neck and I was kung-fu dancing with Ji's dad at five in the morning, which I think deserves some credit.

'Unlike every other player, I felt quite fresh the next day. I decided to play some music on the plane, "American Boy" by Estelle with Kanye West. None of the other players wanted to hear my music because they were all hungover. Giggsy moaned: "Patrice, turn the volume down, we need to sleep."

'"No way," I said. "Patrice's party carries on." I needed Ji's dad to dance with, but his parents were flying back to South Korea.'

Evra was disappointed when he landed back in Manchester.

'I expected thousands of fans to meet us. I'd seen the images from 1999 and the treble, when they said half a million people were on the streets of Manchester celebrating. As we landed I looked out of the window. There was only a man with two ping-pong bats to guide the plane. We got on a bus from the plane and left the airport. There were a few hundred people at the airport. I was thinking: "This can't finish here, this is so disappointing."

'Ferguson took hold of the bus's microphone. "Well done," he said. "Congratulations. But if I don't see you work as hard next year to win it again then I'll tear up your contract. Have a good time with your national teams and see you next season."

'There was no victory parade. The police decided it would be dangerous and a risk to public safety and would cause major disruption to people on a normal working day. Rubbish. They'd had parades before and they've held them since, for United and for City. Rubbish.'

7

WHEN JOHNNY GOES
MARCHING DOWN THE WING

John O'Shea

My head feels like it's going to explode. Barely ten yards in front, John O'Shea is wheeling away in celebration and the stunned Scouse silence means the joyous screams of the Manchester United players are audible. United have beaten arch rivals Liverpool in dramatic and many will say undeserved circumstances: 1–0, at Anfield, with a killer injury time goal after defending for much of the game. Sir Alex Ferguson's side have gone 12 clear in the race for a 2006–07 Premier League title most fans considered out of reach the previous August.

Ten yards is a long way. While the players can holler and hug, I must contain the euphoria of this perfect, body-tingling, buzz without showing the slightest sign of positive emotion. If I do, my safety will be seriously compromised because I'm standing on the Kop, a lone Mancunian in a mass of 12,000 furious Liverpool fans.

After glancing one last time at the ecstatic United players and 3,000 delirious travelling fans in the Anfield Road stand, I jog back to the car through the streets of dilapidated and boarded-up Victorian terraces which surround Anfield. Past Liverpool's pubs, some tourist haunts, others where time-served Scousers drink.

Not unlike Old Trafford then. Finally, in the relative safety of the car I let my emotions go and punch the air repeatedly, before looking to see a man staring at me from his front room. He raises his two fingers. It's no 'V' for victory and you don't need to be a lip reader to understand that he has said something that rhymes with Manc runt. It's time to get on the East Lancs Road and back to Manchester.

My mood before the match was in sharp contrast as I queued to get in the Kop for the first time. I'd not seen a United fan all day, save for the Mancunian ticket touts working the streets alongside their Scouse counterparts behind the famous terrace. 'We're in the same game and we all know each other,' explained one. Whether you're at the Winter Olympics in Japan or Glastonbury, most spivs will be Mancunian or Scouse, an unholy alliance of wily, street-wise grafters.

They, like me, and 95 per cent of the United fans at Anfield, wore no colours, but paranoia crept in as I took my seat. It would take just one person to suss I wasn't a Liverpool fan and trouble would ensue. I wasn't going to attempt a Scouse accent or call anyone 'wack' but I wasn't going to advertise my allegiances either.

There's not a chance I'd get away with it now in the social media age where your face is a quick search away and even then I was getting odd stares – and a message three days later to say I'd been spotted but I did get away with it. I've reported from Sinaloa, Mexico, and from standing with Lazio's ultras for the Rome derby, but never felt as nervous as in the Kop that day in 2007.

Then, in 2015, I asked Jamie Carragher to talk us through O'Shea's goal. He replied: 'No! That was Steve Finnan's fault, that. Good player but his fault. It was right in front of me at the Kop. He switched off.'

I'm telling John O'Shea this story for the first time in 2024 in a restaurant near Manchester Airport and, by chance, Liverpool's goalkeeper, the Brazilian Álisson Becker, is on an adjacent table.

'No way,' says O'Shea about my tale, shaking his head but smiling, and he proceeds to tell me his story of the day.

'I had come on in the game for Wayne. He was fuming that he had to come off, but he'd hurt his foot bad. He went straight to the dressing room to ice it up. Scholesy gave [Xabi] Alonso a little backhander and got himself sent off so we were down to ten men when we won a free-kick. Giggsy dived a little bit. Then Ronaldo took the free-kick. I'd seen him play for years and knew that when he got a certain distance, he wasn't going to cross it but go for goal. And that's because he's good enough to. I was just trying to anticipate where and if it would drop and moved around. Jamie Carragher and Peter Crouch were trying to mark me and I was trying to evade the two of them.'

O'Shea read the situation well.

'Pep Reina spilled Ronnie's free-kick and I thought, "If I go low here, he might save it with his foot." So I went for the roof of the net. Bang! Goal! Get in! I was so close to the Kop and coins flew my way. You sure you didn't throw one to make yourself look like a local? They battered us then for the final minutes but we held out. It was a massive goal, not just because we won at Anfield but because for what it did for us in the league. Chelsea and Arsenal would have been watching and expecting us not to beat Liverpool, so it was a big three points.'

O'Shea and the victorious players returned to Manchester.

'One of our mates was having a birthday party that evening and he asked me for my shirt from Anfield,' he says. 'Not a chance I was giving away that shirt.'

A few weeks later, O'Shea went back to Merseyside and scored again at Everton against the home team who'd gone 2–0 up.

'A bit of anticipation again,' he says of the 61st-minute strike. 'Goodison was one of my favourite grounds, a tough spot where the fans are right on top of you. We'd won the league there in 2003 so I had happy memories. But for that game in 2007, we started slowly before Giggsy took a corner and the young keeper Iain Turner, in the only league game he'd played that season, spilled it out and I just got in and tucked it away. A Phil Neville own goal made it 2–2, then I clipped one in for Wayne to dummy and score. Chris Eagles – Bambi Legs, good lad – got the last one in the final minute: 4–2.'

These are some of O'Shea's high points in a United career which took in 393 games between 1999–2011. No other player's career in this noughties book quite bookends the decade as well as O'Shea's. He also played 118 times for the Republic of Ireland in a 20-year professional career that took in a staggering 802 games for clubs and country. He did so while performing in almost every position including goalkeeper. Not that Association Football was the natural path for boys growing up around Waterford, the Republic's fifth biggest city.

'I had a very good childhood,' he explains. 'Dad was a master cutter at Waterford Crystal, a source of local pride. They were the biggest employer in the city during my childhood. My uncle Jimmy was the head designer. He'd go to New York every New Year to see the lights switched on and I thought that was just so cool.

'My dad was involved in Ferrybank, the local football club in the little town just outside Waterford. There's a local joke that Ferrybank is in Kilkenny, but it's Waterford. Kilkenny, where Dad is from, is more hurling territory. My older brother Alan played football and I played constantly with him and his mates, plus my own mates. Alan still tells me that he has a better left foot than me and I'd possibly agree since he was six foot seven and used to take the corners. He's a detective now. Alan's mates realised I wasn't bad when I was about ten and could cope physically.'

O'Shea supported Celtic and Liverpool as a kid.

'My dad and brother were big United fans and I always loved Paul McGrath. There are pictures of me in a Liverpool kit from when I'm younger. That picture did the rounds as I was supposedly a Liverpool fan. But there's a photo of me wearing a beautiful blue Man United away kit with Sharp on the front too. Maybe Dad made me wear it. Dad would often say "Watch how United play" in the early 90s. He passed away a few years ago. Mum is still alive and well. She's been a constant, calm, solid person in my life. She'd still have me in Ireland now and if she'd had her way, she wouldn't have let me go to England. My dad was different. He said: "Let him have a shot at it."'

O'Shea played hurling for a couple of years before concluding that 'it's organised madness. I loved Gaelic football and enjoyed playing it until I was 16. Ireland in the 90s was still a time of significant emigration. A good few of my friends headed to Australia or America or Canada in search of a better life. That was totally normal, though a lot came back as the Irish economy started to do well.'

His family stayed. Interest in John would start to come from a long way outside Waterford – the city's football team ironically one of only two Irish teams ever to play Manchester United in a competitive game, during the 1968–69 European Cup.

'At 14 I played in a national tournament, the Kennedy Cup. I played for Waterford and we got to the final four with two Dublin teams and Galway. We had a weekend in Athlone and word filtered in that the Irish under 15s team was going to get picked from those four teams. I was centre midfield and we were beaten by the North Dublin team – almost all of those players had signed to an English club. Ritchie Partridge went to Liverpool, where he was blighted by injuries. But not so many of the Waterford lads had been signed.

'There had been word that I was in the Irish 15s squad – and then uproar when I wasn't. Some said it was political and favoured the big city boys – or maybe I wasn't good enough. That was when my dad said: "I'm never telling you anything again until it's absolutely concrete."'

An administrative twist meant he'd have another shot.

'The dates changed which meant I could qualify for the under 15s the following year, when I made the squad. After that, I got a trial for QPR for two weeks. QPR were in the Premier League. I'd been there a week in London and they offered me a four-year deal – two-year YTS, two-year pro. I was thinking, "I'm off as a footballer! I'm on my way to QPR!"'

He wasn't.

'I did well in my exams – honours in nine subjects. Economics was my best. I could have gone to UCD, an amazing college in Dublin. My mam pushed for that but my dad said: "Let's take some advice." He called a man who knew Kevin Moran [the former United and Republic of Ireland legend]. Well, Kevin Moran had done a prize draw at a local football club and someone had his number.

'Dad asked Kevin: "What would you do?" Kevin said: "It depends on how he's doing in school. If he likes it and thinks he'll do OK, then he should continue because if QPR are offering a four-year contract after only one week, there will be more teams in for him in a year's time."

'So, I stayed and played for the school team. We did well. We got to an all-Ireland semi-final, where we got knocked out on penalties – I missed a penalty. John Mullane, a famous hurler in Waterford, was on the team that day as he was also a good footballer. He never lets me forget that penalty.'

Moran's advice proved correct.

'Dad counted 17 different teams trying to sign me, most in England and Scotland, though PSV Eindhoven also came for me. They'd seen me playing for Ireland's under 16s when we won the Euros. Liam Miller, Andy Reid, Tommy Butler were in the team. We beat Italy in Scotland in the final in front of a 10,000 sell out at St Johnstone. Two months later, the same manager, Brian Kerr, led Ireland to be under 18 European champions.'

O'Shea was lauded back in Waterford.

'I was put on the back of a van by myself and driven around the area. It was very embarrassing but I had no choice. I was driven slowly around Ferrybank for people to see me to an area where there was a little reception and a man on a microphone saying: "Welcome back to our European champion: Johnny!" There's a few pictures floating around of me on the back of the van by myself.'

The O'Sheas continued to speak to Moran and whittled the clubs down.

'Liverpool wanted me and they asked for me to fly over every weekend, but I said no. I had exams to study for. I felt they should either want me and wait – or not. Celtic – I took that seriously. Newcastle United made me a great offer, from a financial perspective too. After thinking everything through, I was just about to sign for Celtic and my mind was made up ... but Manchester United came in at the last minute. They'd watched me in the Euros, the club's Scottish scout and Martin Ferguson, the manager's brother. Martin Ferguson had managed Waterford so he had a few connections – enough to do background checks on me and my family. The feedback was that I was a good, solid citizen.'

A call came to go to Manchester and meet United's chief scout, Les Kershaw, and it was explained that Sir Alex Ferguson would also be there. O'Shea had not even needed a trial.

'I went to a hotel in Castlefield and Darren Fletcher was also there with his family. Sir Alex came in and said: "OK, son, we'll give you a six-month trial." When you think that I'd had four-year offers, I was a bit surprised and said so to my parents. This was not good. But Les Kershaw intervened and said: "John will be coming on a three-year professional deal, Alex."'

'"Ah, welcome to the club, big man!" said Ferguson, as a relieved O'Shea shook his hand again.

'We went to The Cliff training ground in Salford for a look around and I joined as a second-year Youth Training Scheme player. Michael Stewart, Paul Rachubka, Wayne Evans, Paul Wheatcroft, Ged Gaff, Steven Cosgrove, a Glaswegian who I was in digs with, were in my group. Ben Muirhead, from Doncaster, was in digs too. This was the end of 1999 and the club were changing from The Cliff in Salford to Carrington in south Manchester. People were telling me that I was lucky as I'd be living in Sale and not Salford. I moved to Cecil Avenue with John and Carol Daniels, lovely people. Bojan Djordjic came to our digs a year later, a character.' Djordjic and his family had escaped war in Yugoslavia to start a new life in Sweden.

For these young players, the format was training each day, college on a Thursday and a youth team game on the Saturday. There was also time to relax.

'We'd always go out on a Saturday night to Piccadilly 21s or Discotheque Royale. During the week we'd go to the legendary Love Train at Royale's, then the Ritz, where Brutus Gold was the DJ. What a man! He'd walk out with his Afro, medallions, a gold suit and platform shoes. The music, disco from the 60s and 70s, was superb. We'd have a few drinks on the Wednesday but not too many. We'd have a few more on a Saturday night. We'd get attention but there were good people around us. Wes Brown was a year above us and could guide us where to go or not to go, what to do or not to do. We'd go to the press club, which was supposed to be for journalists, later for a drink.'

By joining in the second year, O'Shea missed out on the 'football educations' dished out to young players by first-teamers.

'The lads my age had to get drinks for the first team and they messed up one afternoon. The solution was for two of the players from Scotland to have a boxing fight, with gloves and everything. The manager wasn't happy when he found out so things changed and were calmer when I joined. All these tough rituals, dished out to young players if boots weren't cleaned properly, stopped. The initiations became things like singing a song. Some lads loved it and thrived but for others you just had to close your eyes in embarrassment for them.'

O'Shea made his United debut at Villa Park in a League Cup game in 1999. Richard Wellens and Luke Chadwick also made their debuts in a rare defeat, 0–3.

'That was the first time I saw the manager lose it,' recalls O'Shea. 'Chaddy and I were sat next to each other at half-time, keeping our heads down, and lads slightly older like Ronnie Wallwork and Danny Higginbotham were taken to task.'

The Irishman had his own task of marking experienced Premier League players Julian Joachim and Dion Dublin.

'It was a serious level,' he remembers. 'I was doing OK but was never comfortable. They were fast and physical and I was thinking: "This is the level I have to get to." I was also pleased that the manager trusted me to play that level, though he explained to me a few weeks later that he didn't trust me enough yet to play in the first team proper. That was when the idea of a loan came about.'

O'Shea didn't want to give up his studies.

'I was about to embark on an Open University degree in Social Science and I should have, but Fergie called me in and said: "I need you to go on loan, you're finding the reserve games too easy." He wanted me to get a few black eyes, to toughen up. His suggestion was Bournemouth in the third tier. I had a think about it overnight and agreed. Going on loan is a good idea if you find the right club. Mel Machin, who'd been Manchester City manager, was in charge at Bournemouth, with Sean O'Driscoll his assistant. Two good football men.'

It all made sense, yet football often doesn't.

'There were people in the football world thinking "he's going to Bournemouth, that's John done at United" but I never felt that because in a 30-minute chat with Sir Alex he said that the loan would make me more physical and learn. I trusted that.'

O'Shea moved 200 miles south and into digs with Audrey and Ken 'Nimbus' Sullivan.

'Rio Ferdinand and Jermaine Defoe stayed in the same house, before and after. Amazing experience, lovely people. I went in mid-January and my first night out with the players and staff was Mark Stein's 40th. I was 19. I'd played the first game that day. Steve Fletcher, a Bournemouth hero who still works for the club, explained that he was the main man and that if I had any issues then I should see him. Eddie Howe and Jason Tindall were players. I played ten games and had my loan extended.'

O'Shea was back at United for pre-season in 2000–01.

'I felt I was doing well in training but the manager told me that he didn't think I was ready. I trusted him.'

In 1998, United started a link up with Belgium's oldest professional club, Royal Antwerp, the theory being that United would send talented youngsters to Antwerp to get valuable playing time, but the Old Trafford club would benefit from Belgium's looser labour laws, which could allow players from outside the European Union to get an EU passport via Belgian citizenship. While Antwerp had a fantastic club secretary, Paul Bistaux, who cared for the United players, the club were cash-strapped, played in a dilapidated stadium and the idea didn't fully work out. The irony was that across Belgium's second biggest city, the far smaller club Beerschot were bringing through Thomas Vermaelen, Jan Vertonghen, Moussa Dembélé, Toby Alderweireld and Radja Nainggolan.

Yet players who'd be proven in the Premier League including Jonny Evans, Danny Higginbotham and O'Shea were all sent to Antwerp.

'Antwerp was a proper life experience for me,' recalls O'Shea. 'Beautiful city – my mates who came over loved it. I had an apartment in a high-rise block overlooking the city. I was there with Jimmy Davis, who drove. I didn't drive, which I was gutted about, because you got a free club car. Jimmy suggested that he'd give me a driving lesson in a big car park between the stadium and the training pitches. He started off by trying to teach me reverse parking. I put the car in gear, looked behind me and thought I was all cool reversing. In fact I saw no reason why I couldn't drive backwards a little faster. Then I heard a bang and Jimmy was shouting "Stop!" I hadn't been reversing but going forward and crashed into a fence of the training pitch. We, or rather I, damaged the fence.

'At training the next morning, the other players were asking "What has happened to the fence?" Jimmy and I said nothing. Thankfully there were no cameras at the time.'

Royal Antwerp had fallen far from being the club which had reached the 1993 Cup Winners' Cup final.

'My first game was Anderlecht away in January 2001. They had Jan Koller and Tomasz Radzinski, who later did well in the Premier League with Everton and Fulham. Luke Chadwick had gone over there the previous year and got them promoted. Chaddy was a god over there, but it was tougher in the top flight and we were just above the relegation zone. We just about managed to stay up and I played 14 games. Sir Alex came over to watch me in one of the games towards the end of the season. He told me that I did well and in the next pre-season, he told me that he thought I was ready.'

United spent that 2001 pre-season in Malaysia, Singapore and Thailand, with optimism high around new signings Juan Sebastián Verón and Ruud van Nistelrooy. In one 8–1 game against Singapore, the goalkeeper Fabien Barthez saw his wish of being allowed to play as a striker come true.

'Barthez was an especially good outfield player though he thought he was better than he was,' said his boss of the smoking Frenchman. Barthez wasn't one for convention.

'He turned up with his girlfriend, the supermodel Linda Evangelista,' recalled defender David May. 'Her eyes were electric blue and I thought, "What is she doing with that baldy?"

Fabien settled in easily. He was a top lad and was good to have around. He didn't want to train, though, and when he did, he didn't want to go in goal. He just wanted to play five-a-side as an outfield player.'

Verón, a record signing from Lazio, was a major star and shirts with the Argentine's name became immediate bestsellers in Old Trafford's Megastore, which had moved to a bigger, more prominent position by the main forecourt at the stadium. And not just because the Argentinian went in to buy so many.

'I bought many myself,' Verón told me. 'I went to the Megastore and bought them for everybody I knew in Argentina. It wasn't like today; you couldn't find the Manchester shirt in Argentina.' Verón also visited the club museum. 'I saw the Estudiantes crest with my dad's face as a cartoon,' he said. 'That was emotional. I felt like I was walking in the footsteps of my father.'

'Verón was a different level,' says O'Shea. 'And we were so good that he had to be good to improve us. We saw his technique in training as he scored goals with the outside of his foot, did rabonas, where the kicking leg is crossed behind the back of the standing leg, hit the ball into the top corner all the time. He's still the only fella to this day who everyone has stopped training for to clap one of his goals – a rabona from 25 yards into the top corner. It was pre-season at Niketown in Oregon.'

Expectations were somewhat lower for O'Shea.

'A test for a young player is how they do in first team training,' he says. 'I can remember training with them and the manager saying, "John, get closer" and I was thinking "Get closer? I'm giving everything I can and doing my best."

'"You can kick them!" Fergie would shout.

'"I'm trying!" I'd reply as I tried to get near lads like Cole and Yorke. The standard was in front of you every day. United thought I had potential and by 2001 Ferguson was saying, "We've seen you develop physically, you're ready to go now." I'd got a bit of recognition playing for Ireland under 21s and the full side, now it was time for United.'

Despite this, O'Shea's lift-off was not immediate, 13 appearances in 2001–02 with no first team action for months at a time but starting a league game for the first time, at home to West Ham on 8 December 2001. United lost it 1–0 as he played at left-back. He kept his place and played 90 minutes in the following game, a 5–0 win at home to Derby, playing as a central defender alongside Laurent Blanc.

United, the strong favourites to retain the league after signing Verón and van Nistelrooy, finished third behind Arsenal and Liverpool. Rio Ferdinand was signed in the summer of 2002 for a British record transfer fee rising to £33.3 million and world record fee for a defender. Did O'Shea see that as a threat?

'When you talk about Wes, for example, you'd say, "Proper solid, loves a tackle." Yet Rio would be as strong. He was a classy player who read the game well. He didn't wait and smash a player; he'd just get to the ball first by reading it well. A good operator who'd talk and organise. In later years, he'd end up complementing Vida so well.'

O'Shea played 52 times in 2002–03, including 16 Champions League games, the final two against Real Madrid, with the Spaniards eliminating United despite losing 4–3 at Old Trafford in the second leg after a 3–1 win in Madrid.

During the second leg, O'Shea nutmegged Luís Figo. Read that sentence again and enjoy it.

'I played 802 games all in – but people talk to me about that more than anything else,' he laughs. 'It pops up on socials on the anniversary every year. What happened was that Butty switched it to me, I was left-back. And Figo, not a bad player, in fact one of the best in the world, tried to shut me down. I just knocked it through his legs, kept hold of the ball and played it through to Giggsy. I was just quietly buzzing to myself that it came off. I've never spoken to him about it, though I've seen him a little bit at UEFA events. I don't think he's too worried about being nutmegged by me.' An advert in 2023 showed the event in cinematic style.

'Myself, Mikaël [Silvestre], Rio and Wes Brown started at the back in that game. Madrid were at another level in terms of technical play, speed, movement and strength. The manager said to us after we'd been knocked out, "That's the standard you need to reach if you want to be getting to European finals."

'But we knew we were at a top level. When everyone was fit and we played 11 v 11 in training, the standard was electric. The manager had to cut them short because we'd be kicking off with each other, it was that competitive. With me, I wouldn't have let anyone take the piss. If there was a strong tackle that I felt had been a bit naughty, I would have been putting it in the mental notebook to get them back – though maybe not instantly. I was a bit more calculated than that.'

Life was going well for O'Shea. He laughs as he says: 'Yvonne [his long-term partner] joked that she was waiting to see if I was any good before moving to Manchester from Ireland. I persevered to get her to move to Manchester and things worked out. We've got a brilliant relationship – she's been a diamond for me as I've moved clubs and houses.

'And then every so often there would be a new three- or four-year deal for me, which I was happy to sign. I was not going to say no and I was sensible with what I did with my money, being balanced on where I put it. I've made some good – and a couple of bad – investments over the years.'

Season 2002–03 was also the first time O'Shea was a title winner.

'We were written off so many times during the season, but the run we went on towards the end was incredible. We had the best parties when we found out we'd won the league. Leeds beat Arsenal at Highbury through [Mark] Viduka and an Ian Harte free-kick. We were the champions. Our phones started going and we headed into Deansgate and a bar called The Living Room, which was a place to be. It was incredible. All the lads singing. Gary Neville's dad, Neville Neville, singing United songs – all of them including "You've got Curly Watts as a celebrity fan because City are a massive club".'

That song was popularised by United's fanzines *Red Issue*, *United We Stand* and *Red News*. Other lyrics included: 'You've got the tallest floodlights in the league because City are a massive club' and 'You've got undersoil heating on Economy 7 …' or 'You've got the widest pitch in the league'. United fans hammered City fans in song. The words in The Inspiral Carpets' 'This is How it Feels' were changed from 'So this is how it feels to be lonely. This is how it feels to be small. This is how it feels when your word means nothing at all' to 'So this is how it feels to be City …'

A few months later, United stopped off on the way back from a US pre-season tour to open Sporting's new stadium in Lisbon, built in time for Euro 2004.

'I was slightly jet-lagged,' adds O'Shea, 'and not many of the boys were interested in playing the game after flying back from a tour in America late in the night.'

O'Shea had to mark an 18-year-old called Cristiano Ronaldo.

'Plenty of artistic licence has been used about what happened,' he says. 'Rio Ferdinand joked that I needed oxygen at half-time, but it was like any other half-time.'

Ferguson joked O'Shea had been given a migraine and that he kept shouting 'Get Close to him, Sheasy!' to which O'Shea replied: 'I can't!'

'I took it as a compliment that the manager was prepared to rate a player by how well he did against me. It was clear though how comfortable he was to go with either his left or right foot. He was strong in the air even at that age, and he had the confidence to try the same trick again. I was delighted when he signed for us and he became a brilliant, dedicated teammate who developed quickly.'

O'Shea's own cult status was already assured.

'When Johnny goes marching down the wing, O'Shea, O'Shea,' they sang. '... When Johnny goes marching down the wing, the Stretford End, they fucking sing, we all know that Johnny's gonna score.'

'It just gave me extra motivation,' he says. 'You think that the fans are thinking "This kid is doing alright." I think it was Pete Boyle who thought it up.'

Boyle, who often wrote and starts terrace songs, did.

'I was working as a DJ in Manchester and getting sent songs,' he explains. 'I made a 90-minute cassette of classic cover versions to listen to in the car. The Clash did a song based on the American Civil War song "When Johnny Comes Marching Home", the Levellers did a version too. I was driving to work when it came on and I started singing along and changing the words to "When Johnny goes marching down the wing, O'Shea". I went into the Bishop Blaize pub and started singing it at the next game. People laughed, they weren't sure. But by the end of the season when we beat Charlton to win the league [2002–03], the whole of Old Trafford was singing it. It had taken off at Real Madrid away, but it really took off against Charlton. I went out that night and you could hear people singing it all around town on a big night where we'd all but won the league.'

'It was such a weird feeling when thousands of people were singing it,' says O'Shea. 'United are huge, but within that you have a core fanbase that travels home and away around the world.'

Financially, O'Shea was fine for the first time.

'The manager always said that we'd be rewarded according to how we did in training and games. He rewarded us for being fit, healthy and a committed team player. Roy Keane helped us out initially, going to see the manager on our behalf to get us more money. Aside from that just having Roy in the team was a huge deal. And Denis Irwin, two Cork men. They would wind me up about being from Waterford – in a good way. It was brilliant for them to be supporting me, but they also needed to know that I was up for it and good enough for them to push me. Roy was different to Denis in character, but he wanted nothing but the best for you. He bollocked me loads of times – the only times you knew you'd let him down was when he stopped bollocking you because you'd given up. He wanted you to keep standards up and I saw him do that close at hand for the Irish team. He'd had that incident in Saipan [sent home after a row with manager Mick McCarthy], he had a break and then he came back in. I roomed with Roy for a little bit too. I made him plenty of cups of tea. I was a bit of a night owl and wouldn't go to bed as early as Roy. I'd tiptoe back into the room softly so that I didn't wake him up.

'Roy Keane set the highest standards. He was so good, even the way he hit the ball – hard and accurate, soft and accurate. The pass was always at the right angle for the player to receive it. He read the game so well too. He found space because he knew where the ball was going to go and where he needed to go. You know you're becoming a better player when you get time on the ball yourself, you create the time being in the right position by having the right touch. I saw him at his peak when I came into the team. He'd anticipate to break up attacks, with speed. Some player.'

O'Shea's close friends were the lads in a similar age group: Darren Fletcher, Wayne Rooney, Wes Brown, Rio Ferdinand and later, Michael Carrick and Nemanja Vidić.

'Our wives got on well too, the spirit was good. Then Patrice, Ji and Carlos Tevez had their own little three amigos group.'

O'Shea felt established.

'My relationship with the manager was him saying, "You'll play enough big games", and that was always the case. The key to me was seeing how hard I'd had to work to get in the squad – and that I'd need to stay at that high level to do that. You couldn't take the piss going out too much, given the quality you were up against. If friends came over then we'd go out occasionally and give it a right go if the time was right to do so, then it would be back to work and full focus.'

In 2004–05, O'Shea was linked with Newcastle and Liverpool.

'Nobody said anything to me and I don't know if the clubs spoke. The only time I knew of another interest was when Robbie Keane asked if I'd go to Tottenham, but that was 2007. And Kevin Moran was my agent, trusted right from those very early conversations with my father when I was 15.'

One of O'Shea's highlights of the 2004–05 season was a goal at Highbury.

'The manager told me, as I came on, to sit in front of the back four, don't move. Sit in there. Keep it simple.

'"No problem, gaffer." But we broke forward. Gabby Heinze skipped away from a tackle and played it inside to Scholesy. There weren't many of the other lads who were able to see a pass, so I thought I'd take a chance. Scholesy flicked the ball around the corner and found me. That's what's he did. Then I chipped it. People couldn't believe it but I'd done a few in training when we were doing extras. And most of the players were doing extra in training, usually finishing drills, shooting from different angles, from the left and right, low and high. I saw [Manuel] Almunia and thought, "He's going to come out here." I managed to clip it nicely and did the business.

'That's the game where Roy and Vieira came head-to-head in the tunnel before the game. Gaz Nev played a classic move. He was cornered in the tunnel by the Arsenal players who said: "We're gonna get you for what you did at the game against Antonio Reyes." They felt he'd nailed him a few too many times.

'We came in after the warm-up and Gaz said: "Fucking hell! I've just been pinned up in the tunnel." Roy said nothing to anyone. His mind was calculating what to say or do. Then he went down the steps. He waited until he got next to Vieira. His timing was perfect. I couldn't see it, but I could hear it as he had a go at him. We were all like "Here we go, that's our captain". There was always an edge between us and Arsenal.'

In 2004, I interviewed Roy Keane in a Philadelphia hotel where United were staying for the pre-season. It was supposed to last for 30 minutes maximum, but whenever United's media officer Diana Law, daughter of Denis, came over to call time, Roy politely waved her away. It's probably the most engrossing interview *United We Stand* has ever got and Roy knew exactly who he was talking to – match-going fans.

'People mention Chelseas, Liverpools and Newcastles pre-season but we have to be realistic,' said Keane. 'For me Arsenal are our biggest rivals. They have been our biggest challengers in the last 11 or 12 years. I know games against Liverpool, City and Leeds mean a lot to the fans and I can understand that but Arsenal are our biggest challengers.

'The rivalry is based on respect. And I think it goes both ways. There have been one or two incidents over the years but things like that happen. I'm sure they have a respect for us too.'

'Do the players leave what happened on the pitch?' I asked Keane.

'A lot of people were disappointed with what happened at Old Trafford last season [in the so-called Battle of Old Trafford in September 2003] but Arsenal got their punishment and they deserved it,' replied Keane. 'You must move on in football. Sometimes the media don't always want to move on and the coverage of events like last season can be intense. We must accept that.'

Keane also had a better grasp of fan culture than most players. When I asked him why players give it the 'I've supported United all my life' story before they sign, he replied: 'Well, I didn't. I was a Tottenham fan because I wanted to be different. And because of Glenn Hoddle. But all my family were United fans! It's all a game.

Players may think that if they have a bad game then the fans will leave off them if they think they're a big United fan.

'I speak with fans all the time. I was in a bar the other night [in the US], the one night we've been out on this trip so don't think we've been out on the piss. Some people really annoy you but there were a couple of lads with Manchester accents. Lads who weren't about to start tugging at my collar. I knew they were United fans and I said, "Alright, lads." They knew the score. They just wanted to leave us in peace. I've got time for people like that.

'I've had people who I admire but I give them a bit of peace. Years ago United were named team of the year and Muhammad Ali was there at the presentation. And I thought: "What wouldn't I do to get a snap with him?" But then I thought, give the bloke a break. I can understand the kids, they aren't a problem ...'

Keane could also speak his mind with his own players. O'Shea was one of them reportedly criticised in a still-to-be broadcast MUTV interview in October 2005.

Says O'Shea: 'David Gill and the manager spoke and agreed that the video shouldn't go out, but because of that the story has become bigger than it should. You hear players mentioned that Roy didn't even talk about. I wouldn't have had a problem if the video was shown. It was harsh, but it was right – we'd lost 4–1 at Middlesbrough and he felt, as he had at other stages, that the team needed to pull their finger out, work harder, train harder. So we had a meeting. It's nuts.

'Roy got everyone in the dressing room and said: "This video has been pulled but I have no problem saying it to any of your faces. I was speaking about the game and felt I needed to say a few things." Then we started talking about training and what we could do differently. Roy said to John Campbell, the kit man at the training ground, a little Scottish legend he was: "John, go and get the manager because we're talking about training different things." The manager came down with steam coming out of his ears. Roy explained that he'd spoken to the lads and told them what he'd said. The manager asked where the apology was. Roy asked what he had to apologise for. That's when it all kicked off. So, we all wanted to watch the video and started going upstairs to see it.

'We watched the video together, but if you saw that Middlesbrough v United game and asked someone to critique it, what they'd do is exactly what Roy did. Harsh, but fair.

'The manager came in the next day and said: "We have to move on. I've probably lost my best ever player" and I was thinking, "Jesus Christ!" It was crazy.' Keane moved to Celtic.

O'Shea was now 24.

'A little older, racking up the appearances, still involved but also knowing that there will be competition arriving every year because the manager wanted to be winning the league again.'

United finished third in 2004–05, only the third time they had finished outside the top two since 1991. The team reached the 2005 FA Cup final, played well and lost to Arsenal. A few days before, the Glazer family took control of Manchester United amid sustained fan protests.

'We were distanced from it,' explains O'Shea. 'But among the players there was a feeling of "new owners, new investment" and that the manager would get support. We weren't told that the ownership could be tricky, that there were debts that would need paying or financing.'

But there was a brighter outlook on the playing side as Cristiano Ronaldo and Wayne Rooney were on their way to becoming among the best players in the world.

'They were incredible. United would get the best players around from different clubs. And because they were so good they tended to settle straight away. Wayne had a relaxed nature. He was a fighter, but even at 18 he'd say to the manager: "Where am I play-ing this weekend?" I'd laugh, there's not a chance I would have said that at 25, let alone 18. Wayne wasn't being arrogant; it was self-confidence because he knew how good he was. The manager would generally wind him up and say: "You'll be having a rest this weekend, son." That kept Wayne going, but the manager knew what he'd get at the weekend.'

Rooney and O'Shea remain close friends. Rooney was a prankster, Catalan defender Gerard Piqué too.

'Wazza could prank himself, he'd break his mobile every two weeks at one point. Get angry and smash his phone. And he did tricks. Shoelaces would get cut; any bad outfits would get hung up outside the dressing room. Once or twice my outfits were singled out. One was a leather jacket where I thought, "You know what, I'll pull this off." I wore it once and it was like "Woah!" I barely wore it again.

'I was usually safe but when big Edwin came along the lads were all over him. He'd wear these big boots and jackets. He didn't care. He was too clever and knew that they were like children who'd get bored after a few weeks, which they did. The lads knew they were getting nothing out of Edwin, gave up and moved onto someone else.'

Long were the odds on O'Shea ever replacing van der Sar in a game, but he did against Spurs away in 2007 after the Dutchman went off with a broken nose. All the substitutes had been used; the travelling fans were singing 'Ireland's number one.'

'We were leading comfortably and one of us had to replace Edwin. Rio wanted to but I explained that I'd played Gaelic football until I was 16 or 17. If it was catching, punching or kicking it, I was going to be alright. At least that's what I said. Then I was in net, getting a load of abuse when I took a goal kick. I started to panic, but I shouldn't have. I'd taken goal kicks all my life. But I did alright. There was a little one v one with Robbie Keane and I took the ball off him. I knew we'd both be going on international duty together after that one and that Robbie liked a goal, so he wasn't too happy. I gave the shirt – Edwin's shirt – to charity back home, the Irish Lifeguard and Rescue in Waterford, so some good came from it.

'Gerard Piqué was going to be a top player, but I would have always said that he wasn't going to be as good in the Premier League as in La Liga because of the more physical nature of the Premier League. Barcelona was tailor-made for him. He'd be playing for the club he supported alongside the more experienced [Carles] Puyol. Gerard would have still done well had he stayed, but Barcelona was perfect, especially because Rio and Nemanja's partnership was so hard to break. Plus, the manager had Jonny Evans so he was thinking, "These are good kids", but Gerard had a good time at United. He settled in well, he'd come around to our house to play poker, he was a great lad who was fun on a team night out.

'Nemanja and Patrice arrived at the same time. When Nemanja joined, I asked Bojan Djordjic about Nemanja and he told me that he'd won the double at Red Star and was a top player, yet when he came in he struggled – as did Patrice. I was thinking, "These boys are struggling a bit" but winning the League Cup in 2006 really helped them lift their confidence, plus they learned English.'

Some players got their English better than others.

'Anderson came back one pre-season and he'd had a good summer. We were all having our body fat taken and the manager just happened to be passing as Anderson was putting a t-shirt back on. The manager shouted "Anderson!" Quick as you like, Anderson replied: "Ah, boss, Mama's potatoes." The manager burst out laughing and to be fair to Anderson, he would put a graft in pre-season. He was a top player, unlucky with injuries, but what a player. He'd boss Stevie G and [Cesc] Fàbregas in some of those games. The manager was proud at how multi-national his team had become and some of his best team talks were about the diversity in the dressing room, including at Moscow.'

United changed tactically, especially in Europe.

'The manager learned from his experiences and Carlos Queiroz made a difference. We'd be going into games thinking "We're going to win 1–0 away here" and we did, even in difficult places like Lyon. We knew we had power and speed to counter-attack, so we'd be tight and compact until we got a chance. And we'd get a chance.

'Carlos Tevez was one of the worst trainers ever. He'd love his nights out too – he'd go mad for a couple of hours and then bang, he'd go home. You couldn't fault him in games. He did so much for the team and he was a great kid. I would speak to him in slow English.'

O'Shea was a major player for United. He played 54 times in 2008–09. From emergency goalkeeper to emergency striker, it helped that he was so versatile – Ferguson reckoned he could play 'four or five positions with distinction'. Presumably centre-forward wasn't one of them.

'I played up front against Reading and should have scored. The keeper, Marcus Hahnemann, might say it was a great save, but I should have hit it better. Reading, under Steve Coppell, had been promoted and were a fit team full of enthusiasm. We did everything but score. The manager trusted me to understand different positions.'

Ferguson also trusted his judgement in other areas.

'I liked the horses, Scholesy did too and the manager. We were on one pre-season in Tokyo when the Galway races were on. I had a horse with a trainer called Eoin Griffin from just outside Waterford. Not my horse, but I told the manager and Scholesy about my horse, which was 16/1. We were on the way to training on a bus in the morning. Unlike now, you couldn't watch it back then, only listen.

'I was in the middle of the bus; the manager was at the front and Scholesy at the back. The rest of the bus was half asleep with jet lag. The horse was in with a chance! I could see Fergie at the front and Scholesy at the back, listening and bobbing up and down like they were riding the horse. Then I got the cheer and the thumbs up from both. When I found out what some people in football bet on horses, I wasn't giving them too many tips.'

O'Shea played in huge games, scoring the only goal in the 2008–09 Champions League semi-final first leg at home to Arsenal. He started in the final against Barcelona too – unlike in the previous season in Moscow.

'You're always pissed off not to start, but I felt that the manager was fair to me,' he says. 'The lads who'd done the business during the season and been consistent with it started. Wes was right-back that year, whereas I played right-back in 2008–09 and started in Rome. We missed Darren Fletcher for that final. He brought intensity, especially in Europe. You see it with the Italian teams and the players they have in midfield now. Energetic, they close you down and press. Given so many managers want to play out of a press, Fletch would get in any team. He linked, he passed forward with intelligence, he was brilliant and we missed him against Barcelona.

'The manager always said that he went into finals wanting to win them, that he didn't want to sit back. But, in hindsight, with the two Barcelona finals [2009 and 2011], I wonder if we could have done things differently – like we did when we played them in the 2008 Champions League semi-finals over two legs.

'We started well in Rome. Well, for ten minutes. That Barcelona team were so good. Obviously the individual brilliance of Messi means nobody knows what he's going to do. There's one move where he drops the shoulder and goes the opposite way to where you think. There's Xavi and Iniesta too. I had to face him in the Euros. He constantly manipulated the ball, always looked for angles. Barcelona was also physically strong; they could mix it and that's what the best teams can do – play and mix it.'

O'Shea didn't make the squad the next time United met the Catalans in a final.

'Probably my lowest point as a United player,' he concludes. 'I'd been injured and out for about three months. A dead leg that had gone wrong after I was injured in the Ireland v France World Cup play-off. It had gone into the front of my quad muscle and caused calcification. There was a bone growing in the middle of my quad that shouldn't have been growing. I was otherwise fine with injuries, but I was struggling to walk. I had to leave my left leg to waste so there was no muscle and the calcification could be dissolved and the muscle would build back up, but then I was out of sight and out of mind, with other players coming up. I worked my balls off to be able to be ready to play in the 2011 final but didn't make the matchday squad. The manager told me in my room at the Landmark Hotel, where we often stayed, the day before the game.'

It wasn't only about the game.

'When he was telling me, I knew there was a bit more to it because he also said: "and then we'll have a look for next season." And I was like "Hang on a minute, we were talking about the European Cup final and now you're talking about next season." He didn't go into detail but I wondered why he'd added that on.'

Dimitar Berbatov didn't make that squad either.

'He was angry,' recalls O'Shea. 'He was going to leave. We had to calm him down, tell him that everyone wanted to play and to look at the bigger picture, but he took it bad.'

O'Shea's time at Old Trafford came to an end in 2011.

'I was away with Ireland and the manager called me. He said he wasn't sure he could give me the amount of games that I'd be happy with. I had a year left on that contract, but I went into pre-season anyway, where I was called to see the manager on the first day of pre-season. He told me that Sunderland were going to make me an offer. I weighed things up. Sunderland had just finished tenth and I had just turned 30. There was a four-year deal on the table for me. I decided to leave.'

Of O'Shea leaving, Sir Alex Ferguson said: 'The horrible part of management is telling players who have given their all for you that there is no longer a place for them in your plans.'

'I went into the manager's office and we had a chat for half an hour about my time at the club. He'd say: "You played in some big games." It was surreal because I knew I was going, but I felt appreciated, which was important. And, deep down, you always knew that it was going to happen one day because I'd seen it happen to really good players and people.

'Was it worth waiting a year and seeing what came up in a year? Then, I thought no. Now, I think yes, because I would have backed myself to get enough games and helped the team win the league. That didn't happen because I left, but I felt if Wes and I would have stayed that season [Brown also left for Sunderland], we would have had enough experience to help us get over the line.

'You're always fighting to stay at Manchester United and I fought successfully for 13 years, nine with the first team. I'm incredibly proud of what I did, that I could compete at that level and reach Champions League finals, win five Premier Leagues in nine years. Incredibly proud.'

8

IS A RED

Gary Neville

Most of Manchester United's players saw the new Millennium in at a party in Ampersand behind Manchester's Deansgate.

'It was one of the best parties we ever had, one of the best nights of my life,' explains Gary Neville. 'Most of the lads were there. We were top of the league; treble winners and we'd just become world champions in Tokyo. We'd come through our first Champions League group and were about to go to Brazil. Me, Giggsy and Ron Wood [a local businessman and United fan] organised it. The day before, my brother Phil got married to Julie and all the players were there. We drank together and partied together. Then we had another party on New Year's Eve. We had 210 tickets to distribute – 70 each. Football was stopped so we had no game on New Year's Day. That meant we could relax, which wasn't normal around Christmas. We were surrounded by friends, family, teammates. It felt like one big family. I know it's a cliché, but we were a family on the pitch, a family in the club and a family off it. Six or seven of us had come through the ranks; our families travelled to games together. Most of us were Mancunian and United fans. I saw no difference between us and non-Mancunian players like Roy Keane and Ole Gunnar. We weren't just players; we were fans who genuinely loved the club.'

Neville was euphoric.

'The mood was unbelievable post-treble. We were unbreakable for the first four or five months of the '99–00 season. I felt like I was at a peak of my life, that nothing could go wrong, that my confidence was high, that we had won the treble and could do it again. We had the strongest bond that you could have in a football team, it felt impenetrable. We were so tight that if you criticised one of us then you were fucked.'

I did criticise one. Not badly, but it wasn't praise. As a guest on Sky Sports' *Soccer AM* programme in September 1998, I was asked if United fans were satisfied with the form of striker Teddy Sheringham, with the questioner suggesting that he'd hardly replaced Eric Cantona. I gave a balanced answer which reflected the mood at the match around fans – Sheringham still had to convince after a so-so first season following his 1997 move from Tottenham Hotspur. Watching was Gary Neville and he was not impressed, at all.

A few weeks later, United beat Liverpool at Old Trafford on a Thursday night. I went out with a mate, my sister and her friends the following evening. We went to Barça, a canal-side bar in Castlefield district that saw the first spurts of Manchester's three-decade building boom. Then it was flanked by car parks and post-industrial detritus; it's overlooked by skyscrapers now.

By chance, the entire Manchester United team were there. And I knew that almost immediately when what felt like the whole team were giving me daggers looking my way.

Very quickly, Peter Schmeichel came over. Gary followed. Rai van der Gouw. Ryan Giggs and Andy Cole too. All of them were on my case. My mate always stood his ground next to me, two against the world. It was full-on, with moments of hilarity.

'Your problem, Andy, is that you didn't make it as a footballer,' offered Schmeichel.

'Wait a minute,' interjected Chris, a friend of Giggs, 'I played against Andy, that was never happening!' Giggs agreed, correctly. At no point had I been marked as a football talent.

The upshot was that Gary Neville and I wouldn't speak for 16 years.

'That argument falls into the category of what I'm talking about,' explains Neville. 'In punditry terms, you went early on Teddy because later that season he ended up scoring in the FA Cup final and the equaliser in the European Cup final on the way to winning the treble. In '98 after he replaced Eric, he was deemed to be the reason why United were knocked off their perch in '98 as Arsenal won the double, with the reason being that Teddy had not stepped up to the plate. You contributed to that on *Soccer AM*. I remember watching it by chance one Saturday morning. You were very well respected; you had a column in the club magazine and you'd interviewed us. What offended me was that you'd done an interview with Phil and I at our home a year or so before. You had access to us and the dressing room. Then you went on Sky and criticised one of us. I felt very uncomfortable with that. I saw you out in Castlefield. You hadn't stuck a knife into Teddy, you didn't mock him, you said he'd not replaced Cantona. I felt that was an incorrect analysis of the situation. We'd lost Roy Keane to a cruciate injury, we'd lost Giggs, Schmeichel and Pallister to injury, it wasn't Teddy's fault; that was a shallow analysis of the situation.'

I'd only wanted a quiet pint, not a ten-men hairdryer.

'But it was the Ferguson mentality,' says Neville. 'When I look back now it was probably unreasonable, but we had a siege mentality. The clear principle was that if you were on our island, then if you let one of us down on the island then you'd get kicked off it quickly. It was us against the world. There was an unreasonableness to us, it came from the boss who talked about togetherness and unity, it came from the expectation that we had to win no matter what. Anyone who criticised us could fuck off. We had this constant messaging all the time. We were all for one and one for all and we were defensive of any teammates who were criticised. So, we didn't speak for 16 years but absence makes the heart grow fonder, Andy. You get older and as someone who now works in the media I understand how you would get drawn into a conversation on Sky where you could be critical. After I'd left the club I've criticised Manchester United heavily in the last ten years. I get it now, but as a 23-year-old you're not as mature. You're in the midst of this battle every day and we didn't care who we took on in our path.'

Teddy Sheringham was not involved in the argument, but, by chance, I got an invite to interview him two weeks later in London. He had an autobiography out. I lived in north London for a year during the treble season, but I was in Manchester and couldn't do it. We were a fanzine with no budget to send writers to London, but Steve Black, one of our long-time contributors, fancied his chances of jibbing the train and thus it would be at no cost to the fanzine. This, he did. At the interview, Teddy asked where I was. It looked like I'd bottled it, but I've never shirked an interview in my life. Teddy wrote a message for us at the start of our copy of the book: 'TAKE IT EASY ON ME … AND THE LADS, EH!!!'

Teddy, as it comes across throughout this book via numerous testimonies from his teammates, became not just a top United player but a top teammate. As Nev points out robustly.

'When you have Alan Shearer saying that Teddy was his best ever partner for England it shows how highly rated he was. He was a player's player; he knew where to be. He wasn't a Cantona or a Rooney. But he did an outstanding job for the team. He scored goals, he contributed to set pieces, both defensive and attacking. He made that third man in midfield when we were getting outnumbered. He was a very good player and I knew how good he was because I'd played with him for England. Teddy was a fierce competitor, tough on the pitch. People sometimes looked at him as a flash Cockney, but he was hard to play against.'

And Teddy was always fine with me, good-natured and honest. I did two trips to the Caribbean with him when he played in Legends matches and he gave me compelling interviews. In one, I asked him for three words which summed him up. He said: 'Competitive. Content. And I'm sure most Gooners [Arsenal fans] can think of another word beginning with "c" for me!'

But Gary and I didn't speak for the majority of his time at the club as he made 602 appearances (fifth on the all-time list and one ahead of Rooney) between 1992–2011. In 2022, he wrote in his book, *The People's Game*: 'I've known Andy since my early twenties, when he became familiar to United players on pre-season tours and from the interviews we would give to him, knowing we wouldn't be misquoted.'

That was nice of Gary to say, but that argument cost my good relationship with the Class of '92 lads for a decade or so. It was a shame: I'd known them since being young, I was a similar age and, as a journalist, I should have known them well during the greatest years of their lives. But I can remember asking to speak to one in the mixed zone in Philadelphia in 2004 and getting blanked. I was pissed off but I never told anyone and I never wrote negatives. It just meant that I'd have to work twice as hard to do my job properly. And life can be funny: on that same trip Roy Keane gave me one of the best one-on-one interviews I've ever had in my life.

Despite our differences, 90 per cent of the coverage Gary Neville received in *United We Stand* was positive, reflecting how he was an exceptional player for United, probably the club's greatest ever right-back. And one person who knew us both and who had witnessed the argument and knew almost all the players, long maintained that Neville was the most interesting United player, the best to deal with, the one who'd make it as a brilliant pundit.

'The problem with you two is that you share too many of the same personality traits,' he said. I once put this to Neville when we were speaking again. Of course he disagreed. But that was all 16 years after 1998.

So Gary Neville had started the Millennium on a high. It wouldn't last.

'Maybe for the only time in my career, my confidence and belief got so high that maybe I got a bit carried away and thought I was unbreakable, untouchable. I was established, I'd played in three tournaments with England and maybe I needed a clip around the ear that my dad would give me because a dip was always coming. Things were not going to continue going that well and I went downhill quite quickly and went through the toughest period in my career. I lost my confidence as a player.'

A game in Rio's Maracanã started it.

'The game against Vasco da Gama hit me. Me giving away the goals and us getting knocked out of the tournament. Scholes texting me "Fiasco da Gama" straight after, which I laughed at because I knew his humour. Then I came back to Manchester and played my worst football for the club, which continued right into Euro 2000, where I was awful for Kevin Keegan. I look back at that six-month period of my life. Take Real Madrid at home in 2000. I was going through a terrible period with confidence and felt like I didn't want the ball. I remember being on the pitch thinking, "This is a low moment for me." I was 25 and had never felt like that before.'

'I'd split with my girlfriend of seven years, Hannah, Ben Thornley's sister. I was suffering off the pitch and I struggled to separate the on-the-pitch stuff with off it. I felt that if I didn't change then I'd lose my place in the United team. The manager was loyal to me because I'd done well for him, building up credit for four or five years, but that wasn't going to last forever.'

For the first time in his life, Neville sought professional help.

'It was a scary time for me. It was the only time when I've been on the pitch thinking, "I don't want the ball". I was nervous, anxious, like I was going under. And, back then, there was nobody you could really go to. The only person I told was Doctor Stone at United. He was the only man at United who I was willing to go to with the truth. It wasn't for me to go to the manager, for example, and tell him about my breakup and how I was feeling. I'd never go to the manager or coaching staff with something personal. I had a rule: "Don't bring your personal shit in here". The 75,000 people who came every week weren't interested if I'd had a breakup, they wanted to watch Man United win and play well. I would never let personal circumstances come between me and playing for United and none of the other lads did either. It was an old school mentality, but that rule is wrong, I realise that now. You have to look after each other, particularly when one of you is struggling.

'I explained that I was struggling on and off the pitch and that I needed to sort myself out and asked how he could help me. The doctor told me to go and see a psychologist and to rest mentally and physically over the summer. I did. I had eight to ten sessions with the psychologist Bill Beswick and they gave me coping mechanisms that I use to this day, things which help me cope with the ups and downs of life. When something goes badly, we need to give ourselves messages. When something goes well, we need to give ourselves messages because doing well in life is as big a risk as doing badly. Doing well means you can get carried away, while doing badly means you can get more determined.

'What Sir Alex Ferguson wanted for us – and what I wanted for myself – was stability. I wanted the flatline, not to be up and down and full of shocks and surprises. I wanted to be consistent, as a footballer and as a person. My whole game was about reliability and consistency, week in, week out for my team getting the 6.5 or 7 out of 10, doing my job dependably, making sure that I defended the back post, close my winger down, be part of a good defensive unit, serving my forward players with good passes. That was my job. I wasn't a Cristiano or a Rooney, an explosive player that could live a life being up and down all the time. I needed stability.

'The first half of 2000 was an unnerving part of my life and I became a different player after that. I never took it for granted that my form would be good and that my place would be there in the United or England team. The break over the summer in 2000 helped get me right. I'd never worked as hard as I did in pre-season 2000–01 so that I could get back to where I was. I always worked hard, I was obsessed with the club and doing my best, but I'd been playing for four to five years from age 19 to 24 and got used to winning all those trophies. Maybe I needed to reset and I did.'

Neville was also unique in that his brother played for the same team.

'I had a great relationship with my brother – and my sister. We confided in one another, we trusted one another. But I also felt that I had six or seven brothers in that team.

'Phil was a fantastic footballer. He was better than me as a kid, then he got glandular fever and I maybe stole in front of him. But Phil was in front of me and played in the '96 cup final against Liverpool. We'd play so many times together. I remember one game which we both played in which I feel epitomises United more than any in the noughties, the game at Spurs in September 2001.'

Spurs 3 Manchester United 0. That was the half-time shock at White Hart Lane on 29 September 2001. It wasn't like it is now; Spurs had finished 12th months before; United were champions, 31 points ahead. United then signed Juan Sebastián Verón and Ruud van Nistelrooy and it was the former who changed the game.

'I've never been involved in anything like it,' Verón told me when I caught up with him years later in his native La Plata, Argentina. 'El Mister, Ferguson, was not happy at half-time. He said we had no respect for the people. We scored five in the second half.'

After a half-time tactical reorganisation and the hairdryer for the team, United were as emphatically excellent in the second half as they'd been bad in the first. Cole, Blanc, van Nistelrooy, Verón and then captain Beckham were the scorers. With nine shots on target to Spurs' three (all goals), United's dominance was clear.

'While it wasn't the most important game, that never say die spirit represented what we were,' says Neville. He certainly had his moments against north London sides.

Arsène Wenger accused Gary and Phil of 'deliberately kicking' José Reyes in the infamous 'Battle of the Buffet' match in October 2004. Did they set out to rattle Reyes?

'Arsène Wenger's deliberate kicking is our aggressive stance against an opponent. It's quite simple: Arsenal were a better team than us in playing football at the time and we knew full well that we had to find a way to win the match. We didn't need to over-step the mark because the officials were there to issue fouls, yellow and red cards. And even if we did kick Reyes, they had another ten players who could deal with it. I remember times when Martin Keown or Tony Adams or Steve Bould gave our forwards a whack. In an Arsenal against Manchester United game, you would expect defenders on both teams to be aggressive and from '96 to 2001 they were the best encounters because there were no holds barred, everyone was battling into each other and nobody was whinging. Then Arsenal changed. In 2003 they became a little more precious because they thought nobody could touch them. They didn't have players who could stand up for them as much and that's what we still see today. The fact that a manager thinks we kicked them out of the game is more a reflection on them than us.'

It all came back to United being united. If those kids were united, they could never be divided.

'Being part of the squad, with my brother and a group of other United fans who'd go and win everything, it's hard to put into words how good that was. This sounds depressing, but it can never be as good as '99. If you're a United fan who was there in '99, you were watching the most entertaining and exciting team, many of them local lads who'd die on the pitch for their team, who respected the badge and the club. Under a manager who dominated English football. It was a magical time and Manchester's music scene was alive in the 90s. Tony Blair had come in and that felt exciting and new. People remember us. If you were a Bayern Munich or Juventus fan then you knew about United. I'm getting goosebumps just thinking about it.'

Having said that about the 1999 line-up, Neville played in a later side which he thinks in some ways was even better.

'The team which won the league and Champions League in 2008, with Rooney, Ronaldo, Giggsy, Scholes and Tevez was probably the best I'd ever seen, but it was a different team with a different ethic. The '94 United team were groundbreaking and pioneering by winning United's first league title in 26 years and then the double, twice. The 2008 team were unbelievable but the '99 team had the homegrown heart, the best of British, the best of foreign and it achieved that magical season which I think reached the peak of Manchester United's history.'

There were many times when Neville used his organisational skills for the many parties needed to celebrate United's successes.

'The party for winning the league in '03 was an amazing one. That was the year fans started singing "We've got our trophy back". It was a new team, with Ruud and Verón. No player impressed me more when I first saw him train as Ruud. He scored a goal from 25 yards in his first training session and the way he kicked the ball left me thinking, "Wow, he's good!"

'We had the party in The Living Room on Deansgate. The one thing I miss most about Manchester United is the parties after we'd won the league. They only happened eight times for me.'

Only eight?

'Well, yeah. And eight times they were among the greatest nights of my life. I was with my mates playing for the club we loved. We'd have the fucking nights of our lives. We'd drink until we could not take another sip, we'd all be falling out of there. It felt like we'd run the marathon and there was no further to run. We could drink without recourse from the manager or anyone thinking that we'd been unprofessional. Yet it was still a safe environment for family too. My parents and sister came, Keaney's brothers, Butty's dad and brothers, Giggsy's mum, Becks' parents and all our partners. The coaches would come – not the manager – the kitmen. It was wonderful and I'll never experience them again.

'I remember The Living Room after we won the league one year. Cristiano, Anderson and Nani were there. The DJ, Keith Fane, started playing Latin songs, like "Bamboléo" by Gipsy Kings. We'd all been singing the songs in English, but when that came on all the other lads joined in. All the Spanish and Portuguese and Brazilians, the players, their friends and families were up on their feet singing along. The British and Irish lads went over. It was amazing, the warmth, trust, spirit. We trusted each other with our lives. When I was captain, I was always a believer that the music in the dressing room had to represent the regions of the world where our players came from.'

Trust. It's a thread of Neville's conversations. Did Neville trust the media?

'No. There were certain journalists that I trusted but we were inherently untrustworthy of the media because that came from the boss. He'd say, "Leave the media to me, they can't help you win football matches." He played on the mistrust of the media, on the negative headlines. He would lap it up in terms of creating a siege mentality of us against the world.'

No player attracted as much media attention as David Beckham. I remember interviewing Giggs in 1996 and him being relieved that Beckham was starting to get so much attention that it took it away from him. As a journalist who has divided my time between my home city of Manchester and Barcelona since 2001, I've never fielded as many phone calls as when Beckham was linked to the Catalans in 2003. Nobody messaged then.

Neville had also been David Beckham's best man and best friend, but he could see the tension between Beckham and Ferguson.

'David Beckham was an amazing footballer. The celebrity is always thrown at David, but he had so much quality. He was like De Bruyne in quality terms. City fans might ridicule that statement, but he had the quality, the energy. Maybe De Bruyne could dribble more, but Becks maybe had more stamina.

'Beckham had the precision of passing from wide areas that I've not seen any other player have other than De Bruyne in the Premier League years. I could see he was on his way out of Old Trafford because there was tension building and relations became fractious and that was sad for me. We were two opposites, yet the same in our support of United, in how our families were dedicated to us and supporting us every week. I became close with Becks when we were aged 17–18 and had gone full-time professionals. We played on the same side of the pitch and knew each other inside out. I felt like I knew everything that he was going to do next, on and off the pitch. I knew where his head was and what his mindset was. He knew where I was – there was a telepathy on and off the pitch. Beckham was a 50/50 partnership where I defended for him and attacked for him – and he defended for me and attacked for me.

'Later, Ronaldo was "I attack, you defend"! Even though I would go forward, I knew I had to be more responsible because I knew he wasn't going to defend. On the other hand, I didn't need to attack for him because he was that good. With Andrei Kanchelskis I had more a supporting role because he was a flying winger, with 25 per cent of me attacking and 75 per cent of me defending and vice versa. Then, with Antonio Valencia, my legs had gone. I needed him to defend and attack for me and I sat there hoping that he'd do that and cover me. He was 90 per cent and I was 10 per cent.'

Beckham and Neville have been close for decades.

'We knew when we needed each other, when we were struggling. We were so close and had a relationship that was different to the other lads. Phil could be a lot more humorous with Becks, whereas Becks and I wouldn't take the piss out of each other. We were mates and the relationship was built on trust, respect and care. All six of us were close, but within the six were individual dynamics. Phil and Scholesy were close. Giggsy and Butty would take the piss out of each other all the time and with Becks they'd talk about his accent or his clothes, but I never did that.

'Denis Irwin is the best full-back that I ever played with, an unsung hero, but Park Ji-sung is the most underrated player. Owen Hargreaves played a big part in that side which won in Moscow and Ji didn't even make the squad in Moscow, but he epitomised the collective of that United side. He did a job for the team, sacrificed himself for the team, covered for other players. He was like Darren Fletcher, unselfish and an important player who would sacrifice himself for the team so that other players could go and win the game.

'Patrice and Rooney would make me laugh a lot. They kept me young towards the end of my United career. I knew my career was coming to an end but along with Ronaldo and Rio, they were funny as fuck. They'd take the piss out of each other something rotten. Scholesy and I would sit in the corner chuckling, because Wazza can snap and so can Patrice. We'd become the less dominant in the dressing room; the days of the six of us bringing the energy to the dressing room were over because half of us had left, so we'd laugh at how the younger players were always poking and pushing each other. Funny.'

Neville was not one for doing pranks.

'Why would I want to hide car keys or take the laces out of someone's trainers? I was not Maysie or Butty. Giggsy and Scholesy would take my car keys three or four times per week. I was 35, captain and yet I hid my locker number from them. Scholesy was a sneaky fucker who'd watch me enter a new code in and then three hours later, I'd go and get my car keys and they'd be gone. I'd shout: "Scholesy, you are a little twat. Give me my keys now." I'd then be waiting for 15 minutes as I looked for them. As I did, they'd go "cold", "cold", "warmer", "warmer". It was a liberty, a liability, every single day. They were constant.'

Giggs says in this book that he was first in the dressing room each morning.

'That is a lie. I was in first. He might have been in first for the few years after I left, but when I was there, he was usually second.'

Neville built extensive connections with all kinds of players. Darren Fletcher mentions in this book about one with Darron Gibson.

'I did have a strong connection with Darron Gibson, but I also believe that in my own way I had a strong connection with a lot of players, especially when I was captain. With Darron, he'd walk in with those big dark eyes and I'd say, "Gibbo, stop looking at me like you want to kill me." He'd tell me to shut up. He was a young player and I felt I knew how far I could push him, but it was all done with humorous intent.

'Vidić was another. He'd walk in and I'd say, "Vida, you look like you are going to eat someone alive. You need to relax." And he would reply: "Gary, I do not need this now from you. Leave me alone." I'd pull back. I wasn't going to mess with Vida, but he was a brilliant lad, a great competitor. I loved all the different cultures in that dressing room and tried to find the sweet spot with each player. Berbatov used to walk in and I'd call him Danny Zuko. He'd have a black leather jacket, sometimes black leather pants. He looked like something out of *Grease*. He was cool as fuck.

'Coley, who I sat next door but one to in the dressing room, was immaculate. He smelled beautiful. I used to wonder: "How do I smell like Coley?" Before anyone had moisturising regimes, he'd smell so beautiful with this butter that he'd put on himself. He'd be perfectly dressed and everything would fit perfectly, everything would match, the watch would match the strap on the belt and the jacket. His hair was perfect. Then you have me and Scholesy in the corner from Oldham and Bury and looking like a dog's dinner.'

There were one or two players who thought Neville was doing a prank when he brought a priest to Carrington.

'I was captain and it was Christmas. I'm not religious, but I wanted the football team to sit together quietly for 15 minutes to reflect and think. That's not easy with them lot.' Patrice Evra, for one, was impressed.

There were landmarks throughout the noughties covered by this book. Another was the 50th anniversary of the Munich air disaster in February 2008. With Manchester City scheduled to be opponents at Old Trafford for a Premier League game a few days after, many feared the worst – that City fans might sing songs mocking the tragedy. United lowered the temperature by taking down a banner, which hung permanently from the old Stretford End with transferable numbers. It said '32 Years', the period since City had last won a trophy. It was soon back up and modified to '33' at the start of 2009.

In the event, after Ferguson and City's manager Sven-Göran Eriksson had laid wreaths either side of the centre circle, City fans behaved impeccably throughout the memorial silence. They also saw their side win 2–1, a rare Blue victory for the noughties.

Inside the ground, United and City supporters held up special commemorative scarves that had been handed out before the game. Banners around Old Trafford paid tribute to the 23 people. A lone piper led the United and City players out on to the pitch, where they were greeted by a guard of honour of United's youth and reserve players, and mascots wearing shirts bearing the names of the victims, which included former City keeper Frank Swift.

'The team wore 1958 old-fashioned shirts with no sponsors on and a black armband [City wore similar],' recalls Neville. 'I remember doing pictures with Scholesy and Giggsy before the game by the Munich clock. I didn't take many good pictures as a player, but that was one I was proud of. Munich is a thread through the spine of the Manchester United fan and player. We must never forget it. Munich shouldn't be something to be in awe of or to give us fear. It shouldn't be a burden, but when I put the blazer on to represent United, I knew what that blazer meant, what the badge with the old Manchester crest meant. It gave us responsibility.

'It's still the crest on the blazer today and that should never be taken off the blazer. There are certain things about the club: the values, the principles, bringing young players through, how we play, that are more important than winning. Manchester United have the best stadium, the best training ground, the best facilities, the biggest fanbase. And 6 February every single year and knowing what those lads went through, how the fans suffered. These things are more important than us winning. Those things are what we stand for and the more I played for United, the more I felt responsible for what we were.'

City had other successes against a dominant United. In 2002, for the last derby at their former Maine Road home, Neville was captain.

'At 1–1 a ball was played over my head. Ninety-nine times out of a hundred I'd have cleared it to safety, but I dawdled and then decided to lay it back to Barthez, knowing he was comfortable on the ball. Disaster. I scuffed the pass, and Shaun Goater pounced. As errors go, it was a bad one in any game; in a Manchester derby it was unforgiveable. So much for a captain's performance: the manager subbed me after an hour. We lost 3–1, and the boss was steaming as we came into the dressing room. You could see him looking around, ready to explode but not certain of his target. Then Ruud walked in with a City shirt over his shoulder. He'd been asked to swap on the way off and hadn't thought anything of it. But the manager had. He told him never to give those shirts away. That they were Manchester United shirts, not his. That they should be treasured and that if he saw anyone giving one away then they wouldn't play for him again.

'I also had a very funny spat with Robbie Fowler when he played for City. I was pointing towards the fact that I felt his waistline wasn't quite what it had been. He was pointing to the size of my nose and something else which I'm not going to go into. It was quite funny. I was marking him on corners. I would step across people and it would piss them off when they were trying to make a run for goal.'

Neville was seen as the embodiment of much of what United stands for when he was a player. United fans would sing 'Gary Neville is a Red, He hates Scousers.'

He got a lot of stick after kissing the United badge in front of Liverpool's fans at Old Trafford following a late Rio Ferdinand winner in January 2006. He later insisted it was 'absolutely' worth the £10,000 he was fined.

'I don't regret that celebration. I celebrated like a fan because I was one. Bryan Robson was my hero. He epitomised everything that I believed a Manchester United player should be in my childhood. He had thunder, guts, courage and obviously an ability to play. It felt like he had a never-ending willingness to want to win. He put his body on the line for the badge, the shirt. That guided me in my early days into thinking what I wanted to be as a football player. Norman Whiteside and Mark Hughes were also heroes, but Robson was the standout. In terms of others, you never see your parents and grandparents as heroes when you're younger, but as you get older, you reflect and in terms of the time and effort realise that they too are heroes.'

The fan who became a player.

'It was an absolute blessing that we were fans. The care and passion we had for the club meant we were sold into it straight away; we needed no convincing. Every time we lost it was a disaster, every time we won we celebrated like a fan. Even players who grew up not supporting United became supporters. Some grew up as City or Liverpool fans and changed. Manchester United grips you and you can't do anything about it. And I made my choice. Footballers don't make sacrifices. It's choices. You choose to be a football player so you must be professional. Any football player who says he has to make a sacrifice to play for United is talking through their arse. If you don't win on a Saturday, you don't go out. If you win, you can go out. If you are playing on a Saturday then you don't go out on a Wednesday, Thursday or Friday. That's your job.'

That job could be tough, especially at the start.

'In my first year I cleaned the apprentices' dressing room,' he says. 'That was the worst job because they were the last to finish and they didn't really care, they just threw everything on the floor. But because I was the foreman and the captain of the youth team, in the second year I had to clean the coaches' boots. Then I'd knock on Eric Harrison's door and find out what time we could leave. I never knew what was going to happen. Sometimes he'd keep us waiting an hour, others he'd let us go. It depended on what mood he was in.

'I wore my heart on my sleeve. It might be different now because of my role in the media, but when I played for the club I had an unbelievable relationship with United fans. That was special. I never once played a game where I didn't clap the fans at the end of the game. I told the other lads that they must do that too.

'Now, I can be critical of the club, which some United fans find difficult to come to terms with, but I desperately want the club to win and I want the club to get back to where it was. I'm not impatient about the winning, but I am inpatient about doing things the right way, having the right stadium and training ground.'

Neville talks about giving supporters greater influence and his ideas for the future of the game that played into football having an independent regulator, about learning lessons from abroad. What about Germany's Bundesliga? There, they have rules to ensure that the club's members retain overall control via owning at least 50 per cent + 1 of the club's shares

'I'm not a 50+1 man, though I know many are. English football has always had wealthy owners. Mr Davies, a hundred years ago, saved Manchester United. We're too far gone to get back to 51/49, but I think we could get to a point in the future where fans have a meaningful stake in a football club. That might be 25 per cent, 15 per cent or 10 per cent. Fans have a seat on the board and there are strict rules on the board from the regulator around what owners can and can't do. That might mean a club can't move out of a city. Or change the colours of the kit, which I did at Salford City. I look back now and think to myself, was that the right thing to do?

'We came into a Step 8 club but should I have been allowed to do that as an owner of a football club? The fans are passionate about issues like affordability, ticket allocations and prices. Fans are not going away; they're always going to be there as the most important component of the game. Fans can have great power if they come together collectively. Owners should serve the club and try and create a successful team, but also work closely with fans and get to a point where they almost become joint owners even though they're not.'

Post 2014, Gary and I buried our differences. He called me, we met up. We got on. We started to do stuff together and travel. I'd see his life, sometimes close at hand. Met his wife Emma and liked her sense of humour. He hosted a 25th birthday party for *United We Stand*. He asked for feedback about Hotel Football, a football-themed hotel overlooking Old Trafford part-owned by Gary and some of his fellow Class of '92 cohort. One of the suggestions I made was that every fan going in on a matchday should put £1 in a bucket, with every penny going to a local charity. This happened.

I found him more relaxed in real life. Generous too. When, in 2018, I decided to go to the World Cup in Russia at the last minute, I knew that I'd know half a dozen players who were working there for TV. And because I'd left it late, I had no accreditation. Neville was the only one who really tried to help me. First he came to meet me, then he rang around and got me a ticket for the World Cup semi-final between England and Croatia. It was in Moscow that he started to see Roy Keane more.

'My relationship had changed with Roy from the beginning. Despite playing together for so long, I started to feel like I got to know Roy towards the end of his time at the club. I was getting more mature and experienced; we were injured a couple of times together and when you are injured you train together and work each other hard. We both had a very strong work ethic.'

Neville became United captain when Keane left in 2005.

'I wish that would never have happened because I wanted Roy to stay. He was the most influential footballer – by a mile – that I have ever seen. He set the highest standards.

'We did separate for eight to ten years because that's what happens in life, but we met up again in 2018 as we were both covering the World Cup in Russia for ITV. Our relationship has grown again and become strong. I know Roy and I trust Roy and I think he trusts me. He's a great storyteller. He's definitely misunderstood at times, just as Sir Alex was with the hairdryer, where people think it was ferocity all the time, whereas most of the time it's storytelling with humour, defending your principles and values.'

In 2017, Gary had invited me on a trip to Asia with the Class of '92 lads. I turned up and was in economy. That was fine, I travel economy. But the Class of '92 lads were in business class and Gary insisted that I wasn't left alone. He paid for me to upgrade.

In 2015, he took the Valencia job. I started to see a lot more of him and knew a lot about what was going on there – but kept it private.

I went in the press lounge after his first game and sat near the front. This was going to be Gary's first post-match press conference and I raised my hand to ask the first question of his managerial career. He looked up, saw me and laughed. His answer was serious, but Di Law, daughter of Denis and United's press officer for much of the noughties who helped him in Valencia, told us both to grow up after. We kept our heads down as she said: 'What are you two like? Will you ever grow up? I saw you both smirking.'

I became invested in how he was doing and was proud that a Manchester lad was now in charge of Valencia, with Phil as an assistant. I could see how hard he was working, learning Spanish for two hours every day. He was offered a car and security after one game but I told him that we should walk to a bar and see the supporters. He was well up for this. He didn't want to be in an ivory tower and respected them.

I'm mild mannered but would have ridiculous arguments with Gary, like who was the most working class.

'You played cricket, Gary, it's for middle-class people.'

'My dad drove a lorry day and night to buy our cricket pads,' he'd reply, taking the bait. He's a better laugh and more relaxed than people watching him on screen would ever think.

In January 2016, Valencia came to play Barcelona in the semi-final of the Copa del Rey. Things hadn't been going well.

'Can you pick me up at the team hotel please?' Gary messaged. I could. Spain's fourth biggest club from the country's third biggest city existed in a perpetual state of crisis. In the previous months, Gary had told me enough to build up a picture. Such as when he walked the corridors at the Paterna training ground fellow members of staff would stop speaking as he came within earshot. And there were leaks all over, enough to stop a great club from a great city sailing as it should. That former players and officials, many of whom still lived in Valencia, were queuing up to have a pop through the media at the manager was nothing that hadn't happened before. But, new to the place and not knowing the language, Gary, relentlessly undermined, had little idea of the politics.

Valencia fans are hard to please but Neville did his best, giving up his busy, engaging life with four or five business projects and moving his family from a city they'd always lived in at short notice. He loved the city of Valencia and the people he met in the street. And he did no hiding.

I drove to get him along the busy Diagonal which cuts across the Catalan capital. A dozen Valencia fans hung around the lobby like they had business there. I messaged Gary and told him I was waiting. He came down and the Valencia fans spotted him and rushed towards him. Gary smiled, posed for a few pictures and a letter was thrust into my hand to pass onto him.

Handwritten in English, it read: 'Just want to take your attention for a minute, Mr Neville. I'm a Valencia fan and I'm proud of it, as my grandpa was. I just wanted you to know that all Valencia fans will be by your side always. Even if you lose we will be there because Valencia is not just our soccer team, it's part of us, our lifestyle. Most of us are sad when we look at the club situation. We have passed through many difficult times but we're still there and always will.'

And so on.

I started reading it to Gary. He'd heard it all before. Footballers or managers don't like any implication that they're not giving everything.

Gary cut to the chase: 'Is he after a ticket?'

Ah, the small print. 'I'm afraid I won't be supporting you at the stadium because I am a student with not so much money. I will leave you my number in any case …'

He got two tickets.

'Something to eat?' I asked as we drove away.

'Anything,' said Gary, who was clad in his Valencia tracksuit. That meant sitting outside a bar on pretty Enric Granados for two hours over coffee. Pedestrians occasionally did a double take. Was the manager of Valencia just outside a street café having a coffee before playing Barça?

'Can we walk to the ground? Get something to eat on the way?' asked Gary.

'Well, we can, but you're the manager of Valencia and the crowd will be building.'

'Andy, can we walk to the ground?' he asked bluntly.

'Fucking too right we can,' I replied. 'I just need to pick up my computer as I'm covering the game and tell my wife. You can tell her that I can't pick the eldest from school, then we can walk.'

So we walked up the stairs to our flat. My wife and her friend were there. They didn't expect to see Gary and were very polite. I believe we could even have got away with a three-week stag do in Vegas with him asking so nicely.

We set off on the four-kilometre walk towards Diagonal, past Lionel Messi's restaurant, and stopped at an Italian called No Solo Pizza. We were hungry and the owners, Inter Milan fans, were happy to have us in there. Gary marvelled at the wine selection and discussed it with the owner. They may well have been speaking in Basque for all I knew.

We carried on walking. Valencia fans did more double takes.

'Vamos, Valencia!' they'd shout from cars.

'AMUNT!' came the Valencian cry.

'Hello Mister!' said curious fans politely in English.

'Hola,' replied Gary. This was surreal and it's not every day that you get to walk to a game with one of the managers.

I liked it that a manager could be so close to the people who paid his wages. Most didn't see him; they weren't expecting their boss to walk past.

Gary's Spanish was basic at the start but he learned quickly and practised different verbs each time I saw him. And all the while he tried to help his family settle, to rehouse his daughters in their new school.

After one game, he suggested that I spent the following season in Valencia writing a book about the year in the life of the club. I loved that idea, in part because if the manager was on board then the access would be incredible. I started to envisage travelling to Galicia on the Valencia team plane or Malaga with their ultras on a bus. A literary agent was very keen. I looked at apartments in Valencia but two problems would arise: my wife didn't want to move to Valencia and Gary would soon be gone.

What happened in Barcelona had a bearing. Gary needed a black tie. It wasn't for a funeral, but to go with his match day suit. We stopped in the L'illa shopping centre close to Camp Nou and bought one Adolfo Dominguez for €40. The shop assistants recognised him and fussed around him, but I don't think he noticed. He had other things to think about like stopping the best team in the world at that moment.

Gary went into the hotel to meet up with the team, I made sure the letter writer got two comp tickets and walked to the stadium alone.

The last time Gary had visited Camp Nou as a player was to win the treble with Manchester United.

There was a healthy British interest in the press box because of Gary and it being a semi-final against Barça. On another occasion that he played at Europe's biggest football stadium, he was part of an epic match as United drew 3–3 with Barça. And on his first trip he came to Camp Nou to sit on the bench and, for the only time in his career, was glad he wasn't on the pitch as Stoichkov and Romario battered United 4–0 in 1994.

In 2016 it was even worse as the game quickly degenerated into a disaster for the visitors.

'When you give the ball away close to your own goal three times in the first 15 minutes, you get punished,' observed Gary afterwards. 'We were 4–0 down with ten men and I'd used all three substitutes. I thought: "We're in the coffin here and they are putting the lid on and slamming the nails in." Neymar was taking the piss; Barcelona were outstanding and in their best form of the season and I felt helpless that I couldn't do anything. I'd watched Messi, Neymar and Suárez closely working in the media, now they were doing to my team what Man United did to West Ham when we scored seven, to Bradford when we scored six or Forest when we got eight. I stood there thinking: "You're getting a bad taste of your own medicine here."' Barcelona scored three more goals. Neville had not been part of a team that conceded seven since he was nine. It was the worst Valencia defeat (7–0) for 23 years and not the kind of scoreline normally associated with semi-finals.

In the press box, I felt some of the British journalists were mocking Gary. I didn't like it and, for the first time as a journalist, felt conflicted and defensive over someone I wanted to succeed, but it was their right – and their job – to pass comment.

In the press room, the Valencian media contingent was waiting for him. The mood was not forgiving. The first question wasn't a question: 'You must resign, Mister.'

'Is that a question or an order?' Neville asked himself. 'I said I'd carry on working. The next two questions were the same. People think the British press are bad, but when the Spanish media go for you, it's unrelenting. That said, they ask superb tactical questions, the football ones you don't want, where they've spotted mistakes and want an explanation. They know how to push the button and I respected them for that, but I left that press conference in Camp Nou thinking, "I hope I never have to face one like that again."'

Gary remained positive in the press conference.

'Positivity has been immovable in my life,' he said in English, which was translated to Spanish. 'When I have moments like this I don't enjoy them at all. I stood out there both halves feeling helpless, trying to change it in some way, knowing the tide of the game was against us. We were playing against a fantastic team – keep that in perspective – but the scoreline is unacceptable. But they [Barça] don't lose games. The reality for me is that I last had doubts as a player 18 years ago and from that moment on I developed a mechanism to deal with situations like this.'

His team, exhausted and demoralised, arrived back at the training ground at 2 a.m. to a reception from 250 hostile fans, with an ashen-faced Gary at the front. 'World War Three was breaking out; they were shouting that we were all mercenaries,' was his take.

Then he lost his job. I did his first interview post Valencia for *The Sunday Times*.

'People may say, "Gary Neville's had a tough six months, he's finished, he's crap, what does he know about football?"' he said. 'But I don't see it like that. I suffer disappointment, I reflect, but I don't dwell. I can compartmentalise things quickly. I did that as a footballer and my character or personality hasn't changed because of what's gone on.'

He gets knocked down, he gets back up again. And again, like he did in 2000, to win yet more trophies than he could ever have imagined.

9

ONE LOOK AT CITY ...

Dimitar Berbatov

Summer 2008. Manchester United are champions of England, Europe and soon to be the world, yet Sir Alex Ferguson decides he needs to strengthen an attack comprised of Cristiano Ronaldo, Wayne Rooney and Carlos Tevez. True, the post-Moscow summer had been soured by Ronaldo's posturing towards Real Madrid and the prospect of United losing their first Ballon d'Or winner since the 1960s, but Ferguson persuades him to stay a little longer. However, another striker, Louis Saha, is on the way to Everton.

That summer's transfer story became whether Dimitar Berbatov would join United. Spurs didn't want to sell and demanded a record £30 million-plus fee. Manchester City, suddenly flush with cash after a takeover, also showed interest.

It was against that backdrop that I set off on the pre-season tour of South Africa. Despite leaving 42 hours before the first match in Cape Town, I nearly didn't make the game.

'I'm sorry, Sir, you'll not be boarding the aircraft to Johannesburg.'

'But ...'

'I'm sorry.'

This was the culmination of a conversation at midnight on Thursday, shortly after I'd tried to board the Air France 777 to South Africa at Paris Charles de Gaulle.

As I handed in my final boarding card, an airline employee flicked through my passport. He paid particular attention to each visa stamp. Was it because I'd been to Cuba, Israel or Saudi Arabia? No, it was because there wasn't a free page for my South African visa. There were half pages – and a previous South Africa visa took only half a page, but the official maintained I wasn't allowed to fly with my passport. As my head started to spin, I heard: 'You'll have to try and get a new passport and we'll put you on tomorrow night's flight.'

'But I'm in Paris. How can I get a new passport in a day?'

'We're sorry.'

I was escorted out of departures to an Air France desk, where a lad who lived in Manchester overheard my conversation. He'd missed his connection to Rio de Janeiro and Air France were putting him up for the night in an airport hotel. He was a United fan. With no space in the airport hotels, he said that I could crash in his room. I appreciated this gesture by Alex Clarke immensely.

First thing in the morning, I rang the British Consulate in the French capital.

'We can't promise anything, but come down,' offered a soothing voice. I took a train into Paris, thinking about lost flights and interviews. The staff in the Consulate were highly efficient and promised me a brand new 48-page jumbo passport within four hours for €194. I called my mum and praised the Consulate.

'They knock the British for many things,' she said, 'but we're good at things like that.'

I walked the trendy arrondissements around the Consulate, the Champs-Élysées and Saint-Germain in the same clothes I'd been wearing a day earlier as my luggage was held in the airport.

The Brits were true to their word and at 5 p.m., Friday I headed back to the airport, hoping to finalise my flight connection to

Cape Town, the destination of United's first pre-season friendly at 3.30 p.m. on Saturday.

The first Air France official told me it would cost €3,064 as my ticket needed to be upgraded to Business Class. I laughed. The second took an hour, but did it for free. My new flight meant I would arrive just an hour and ten minutes before kick-off. I boarded the plane, with officials barely glancing at my new passport and not checking any pages. I rarely sleep on flights but managed eight hours as we flew south before switching for a connection to Cape Town, where a hire car was still waiting for a drive across the Cape Flats townships and arrived minutes before kick-off.

United will never play in a setting more magnificent than the Newlands rugby stadium in the shadow of Table Mountain. A brilliant light bathed the pitch and many of the 50,000 supporters in the sell-out crowd for the friendly against the Kaizer Chiefs, before the sun slipped behind the mountain and into the ocean beyond Robben Island, where Nelson Mandela was incarcerated for much of his 27 years in prison. Mandela was busy hosting his 90th birthday party.

Around the pitch, local photographers tried to engineer staged photos of middle-class United supporters surrounded by the hardcore fans of the Chiefs. Flamboyant and exotic to European eyes, they sported masks and miners' helmets, some brandishing dead animals while blowing vuvuzela horns and whistles to create a uniquely African atmosphere. Standing behind a red, white and black tricolour with 'Beswick' written on it are some of the 40 travelling United fans.

The post-match press conference wasn't about the game, but United's pursuit of Berbatov. Ferguson was cagey, he knew there was an almighty tussle going on to try and get the player out of Spurs.

The following day, I fly to Durban. Mike Dobbin is at the airport looking rough – despite not being out drinking with the other fans.

The 61-year-old did not miss a single United game for decades and while he would have hated to be referred to as such, he was likely United's most loyal supporter. Dobbin watched more than 1,000 consecutive matches in all competitions including friendlies. In total, he watched United in 45 countries from Bermuda to Nigeria, Brazil to England. He saw United at more than 250 different grounds and the last European away game he missed was Milan in 1969.

The annoyance of a delayed flight to Durban was compensated by three hours chatting to him about his life as a Red, including being the travel secretary of the United London Fan Club, a group he joined months after its inauguration when he moved from Manchester to London in 1965. Quietly spoken, he liked classical music, opera, his collection of football memorabilia included most United league programmes going back to 1947.

Dobbin told me of his plans for the next few days. It pained him that it was impossible to see the final game of the tour in Pretoria and travel to Nigeria for a friendly a day later – the team would fly direct. Dobbin described it as 'unfortunate', so here's what he did: he flew back to London, went straight to Oxford to watch a United XI before driving back to Heathrow and flying to Nigeria.

Unbeknown to Mike Dobbin, he had pancreatic cancer. He died in January 2009 – a month after seeing United crowned world champions in Yokohama. He was in Japan to see it, too.

Driving away from the airport in Durban, I received a phone call, a representative from Nike.

'We need a Spanish speaker now to interview Carlos Tevez,' he said.

'Can you do it?'

I could and drove to the heavily guarded United players' hotel to be ushered to a room, where various stylists, photographers, assistants, advisers and advisers' assistants were fussing around the diminutive Argentinian. He couldn't communicate with any of them.

'Can you tell him that the glycerine we are spraying on his face will not do him any damage?' asked a stylist as soon as I'd arrived. 'But that he must close his eyes.'

'Er, hello Carlos. Nice to meet you. This stuff they are spraying on your face will not harm you.'

I'd never spoken to Tevez before and didn't know him. There was a flicker of interest that I could communicate in his language, then genuine engagement when talking about fan culture in Argentina. He relaxed.

'What have you heard about here?' he asked, referring to players.

'Everyone is saying Berbatov,' I said.

Tevez nodded and said nothing.

Afterwards, I had a drink in the hotel where Ferguson had spent much of the day sunbathing. The United staff were having a quiz on the club's history and arguing about who United's manager was before Sir Matt Busby. It was wonderful to see.

The 'will he, won't he come' Berbatov saga continued for another six weeks. It would be unbearable in the social media era, with demands for incremental updates even if there were none. As the man at the centre of it all says: 'When you follow your own path, you must make decisions like this. I wanted to win trophies and play for the biggest club and the biggest club in England is Manchester United. United had been interested before and I thought: "If they come again, I'm not going to miss that chance." My agent called and said that United were interested again. I didn't believe him at first, but I trusted my agent and he said: "You can stay here [at Spurs] in your comfort zone or make the next step in your career." It was not a difficult decision. Manchester United were the English and European champions. They had the best players; they had Sir Alex Ferguson and Old Trafford. How could I not be seduced?

'When I signed for United, I felt like it was a reward for everything that I'd been through in my life. Like Nemanja Vidić, I came from a small town in a small country in Eastern Europe, but we had reached the top.'

Berbatov had absolutely no doubts.

'When United wanted me I was like a horse with blinkers on. I was not interested in anyone else. City [managed by United legend Mark Hughes] offered more money, but the numbers went in one ear and out the other. Their team was weaker and their history couldn't compete with United's. I didn't understand all the drama, the secrecy that summer.'

The saga ran and ran until transfer deadline day, 1 September 2008.

'Daniel Levy nailed us to the flagpole when he took us all the way to the last day of the transfer window before agreeing terms for Dimitar Berbatov,' said Ferguson. 'When we got wind of the fact that Levy was trying to sell Berbatov to Manchester City, we stuck in our oar, chartered a plane and flew the player to Manchester, agreeing on terms with the player and, as I thought, a transfer fee with the club. Then Levy came back to us and said he needed Fraizer Campbell, one of our young strikers, as part of the deal. David Gill demurred, so Levy then upped Berbatov's transfer fee a little. Finally, in order to get the deal over the line, and add insult to injury, we sent Campbell on loan to White Hart Lane and paid the increased fee. We were up until midnight signing and faxing papers to make sure all the paperwork went through before the deadline expired. The whole experience was more painful than my hip replacement.'

Ferguson likened dealing with Levy to being on a Big Dipper, having experienced it signing Michael Carrick.

'You come off dizzy. You can't discuss both sides of the issue with Daniel. It's about him, and Tottenham, nothing more, which is not a bad thing from his club's perspective.'

Berbatov will never forget that day either.

'My agent Emo was like a professional phone dispatcher. Manchester City, Manchester United, Daniel Levy. I kept saying to him: "There is only one goal for me – United." The club sent a plane for us. During the flight to Manchester I barely said a word. I was picturing myself on the Old Trafford pitch raising my new jersey. But I was also extremely nervous as I was going to meet the greatest football manager face to face.' The signing was greeted with optimism, yet caution, from fans. 'Interesting ...' said the front cover caption of *United We Stand* fanzine.

'We all thought that Berba was a quality signing,' explains Wes Brown. 'I'd played against him and always tried to be physical – and he didn't like that. But he had class, flair and a lovely touch. He was the closest to Verón with his touch and style, using the outside of his foot. He looked smooth and he played in his own rhythm, which I thought was special. I know we already had world-class strikers but he gave us another dimension because he was one of a kind. He's into complete football and liked people to have good touches. He was good on the ball with flair. If I did a little dribble going forward then he'd say: "Wes, leave this for us players and get back there." He said it in a funny way, like an actor.'

'We welcomed his signing,' says John O'Shea. 'I knew about his character from Robbie Keane at Spurs – and that he had different characteristics from the other strikers that we had. Play was going to go through him a bit more, like it had with Mark Hughes and Eric Cantona. Berba was one of the best players in the league and United wanted the best players in the league as was the case when Michael Carrick was signed. Berba was a cool, strange kid, in a good way.'

Brown got on with him. 'He's more chilled than me, which is saying something. He would have been a movie star if he wasn't a footballer with that Andy Garcia look. He had the face for *The Godfather* or *Goodfellas*. He could be so quiet that people wouldn't know if they could go up to him.

'He'd always ask me to do things for him, which was fine until I twigged that I was older than him and it should be him doing the jobs for me. I told him this and he laughed. He's an intelligent man and I'd see that in later years when we played together in India.'

What Berbatov considers his greatest moment in a United shirt came quickly.

'My first training session,' he says. 'I was going to the training ground thinking "How the fuck am I here?". I was about to meet Sir Alex and all the players. They were the best team in the world and I was thinking that I was at my personal peak to reach that level. From an early age I wanted to play for the biggest team in the world. That team is Man United and I was so happy to join them. I would watch the way Giggs carried himself around the training ground and played at such a high level even though he was coming close to 40. I could go to players like that and ask for advice and I was soon doing yoga.'

And then he was playing for real.

'When I stood in the tunnel as a Manchester United player, I saw Ronaldo, Rooney, Giggs, Scholes, Neville, Vidić, Rio, Evra, Edwin van der Sar. I said to myself: "Berba, you need to cherish this moment forever, my friend." And then I looked at the opponents. They were already beaten.'

His debut was at Liverpool, his first goals at Aalborg, Denmark, in the Champions League on 30 September when fans in the small stadium sang 'Dim-i-tar, Berb-a-tov. One look at City, And he said fuck off.'

'I don't like songs,' he says. 'I don't think they are necessary. But I remember that game. I missed a sitter and I was thinking, "Berbs, what the fuck? This is not going to be your day." Then I scored two goals and I felt like "I am here".'

He made a positive first impression.

'Seeing Berba on the pitch was like watching a beautiful woman,' said Patrice Evra. 'He was a pretty footballer, elegant with the best first touch. Dimi is shy and quiet, but I really warmed to him. I set myself a challenge to make him laugh, to make him my brother. It worked. He still calls me his brother from another mother and we became great friends. He wanted to be an actor and asked me to get him tickets for the Cannes Film Festival. He's an artist, too. He is a very private person, but also very funny and intelligent.'

Exalted expectations at Old Trafford meant the jury was still out for Berbatov after a year. A satisfactory first season saw the five times Bulgarian footballer of the year make more assists than any United player and net 14 goals in 43 appearances. A start on the bench, in both Champions League semi-final games and the Rome final, illustrated how the £30 million signing from Tottenham failed to establish himself in Ferguson's first XI for the biggest matches.

Berbatov's arrival also relegated Tevez.

'I signed Dimitar and the emphasis was on him and Rooney as the forward partnership,' said Ferguson. 'Watching Dimitar at Tottenham, I felt he would make a difference because he had a certain composure and awareness that we lacked among our group of strikers. He displayed the ability of Cantona or Teddy Sheringham: not lightning quick, but he could lift his head and make a creative pass. I thought he could bring us up to a level and extend our range of talents. He had talent in abundance: good balance, composure on the ball and a fine scoring record. He was a good age, tall, athletic. I felt we needed a bit more composure in the last third of the field, the attacking third. So Berbatov's arrival relegated Tevez to more of a backup role.'

Tevez wasn't happy, he wanted to play more. He needed to play more since he got his fitness in games. Ferguson was faced with the conundrum of accommodating both and admitted: 'It was a mistake on my part, in the sense that Berbatov was a player I fancied strongly and wanted to see him succeed.'

United won the Premier League and reached the Champions League final again in 2009.

'Personally, my first season at the club was OK,' is Berba's take on all of this. 'When you have the players that I had around me, I needed to save that moment in my head. I watched them play around me and felt that I was at the theatre. Sometimes you need the roar of the fans, but you don't need to scream to appreciate what is happening on the pitch.

'I had cost a lot of money and I felt the pressure sometimes, even though I didn't want to admit it. Sometimes you put pressure on yourself, we're all human. You need to be mentally strong, but sometimes you doubt yourself, you over-think.

'I would see people who understand football speaking about me and think: "You are speaking shit!". A player would take notice of someone who had played at a high level over someone who has never kicked a ball in his life. But I was a striker and people expect strikers to score goals. But I didn't see myself as a striker. I liked to play with the ball and have the freedom to move around. If every player is on the left and I am on the right, you need to trust me that I have seen something the other players have not seen. I like it when the coach knows this and allows me to express myself. I felt that Ferguson trusted me.'

His new manager immediately made an impression on him.

'When he walked into the room, people would stop talking. He commanded so much respect and attention because of all the success he'd had. He was good with words, probably from all the books he read. I'd go to his office and he'd have Napoleon's biography on the table. In general, he'd speak with me one way, maybe different to how he spoke to others. He was OK. I learned a bit of how to be a manager if I am to be a manager one day. Maybe I would learn some of the things and techniques that he put on us.'

There was a lighter side to their relationship.

'He'd tell me what a good striker he used to be,' he smiles. 'He'd say: "Berba, I was so good, I scored so many goals!" We laughed.

He knew how to speak to people in their language, even if he was telling them that they were not going to play. He'd say it in a way that you didn't feel it was a personal criticism. He'd say: "You're not playing today but you're playing next week." And you'd think "Maybe he's right." You need to have this psychology in football because there will always be someone saying: "What the fuck? I deserve to play!"

'Sport is healthy but it can be the opposite of that at the top level. You have so many injuries, you put your body through so much. You wake up at two in the morning and you cannot move. Top-level football gives you fame and money, but it takes away a lot, too.'

At United, everything is magnified, the praise and the criticism. Everyone has answers.

'I tried to explain this to my mother who works in the medical profession. Imagine being the best doctor, hugely respected in your field, and performing a successful operation. Only for someone with no medical experience to come and start telling you how to do your job. How the fuck is that possible?'

But there were plusses.

'You know Maradona once came to training at United. We were kicking the ball around when one of the players said: "Fuck me, is that Maradona with the boss?" Training stopped. We all looked at him. He slowly walked to us. We gathered around him and said hello. His English was not good but he had huge presence. Players loved him. Maybe he had something which makes the players love him and want to die for him. And that's not bad if you're a manager either. He's like [Hristo] Stoichkov. He's like a rebel who says what he wants but if you respect them then they will treat you with the same respect. But you go there and try to be too familiar with these guys, then they'll kick you in the arse.'

He is reflective about what being a world-famous footballer brought to him.

'Fame is good if you know how to use it and know how to behave. Most people don't know how to behave and handle money and fame, especially money. Fame and money can destroy you. Fame comes normally after you have put a lot of hard work in, when you didn't try and become famous, but to do something like be a top footballer. Then, one day, you walk down the street and the guy walks past and says: "Great game today, Berba." Or you're sitting there and you can hear people talking about you, even though they think you can't. And they're saying: "There's Berba, great goal today." It makes you feel positive because you've done something to make people feel happy.

'I don't like persons from *Big Brother* who are famous for no reason. How did this make their country or their family proud? This is easy fame, but it's not. I came from a background where we didn't have bread. I know what it's like to live with money and no money. Fame and money step by step is better.'

His was no overnight success story. As a child, once he'd queued to buy bread at 6 a.m. in communist-era Bulgaria, he could focus on the day ahead. Football mattered. He talked with his father, a footballer, about Bulgaria's finest. 'Stoichkov, [Georgi] Asparuhov, [Lyuboslav] Penev,' he recalled. 'Asparuhov died young in an accident with his best friend, Kotkov, another excellent footballer. Both wanted to play outside Bulgaria, to improve their game and their life, but they were not allowed to.'

A very young Berbatov was building a reputation of his own in Blagoevgrad, a town of 70,000. He was quiet, self-contained.

'My friends would play teams from the other tower blocks,' he explains. 'They would say: "Berba is coming with his team, we need to prepare." I was ten. We played six-a-side, which I still play. I started to pick up a reputation on the street. I had street cred. Like drug dealers, my reputation grew on the street and into other towns. I walked to school with my chest out. I was a hustler, I hustled for football. There were others. Some of them had scars.

You could see how hard-working they were. You could guess their occupation. I played with guys like this. They don't spare you; they kick the shit out of you. You get a good life lesson from this. There were better players than me but I was lucky, I made the right choices in life.'

Berbatov trained with older boys, played in the junior teams of local team Pirin, then for CSKA Sofia under legendary boss Dimitar Penev. He didn't want to leave. CSKA's lack of money meant he did, for Bayer Leverkusen.

'I was lonely, but that would help me. You need to count on yourself because maybe nobody else can help you. Then you become stronger and maybe you can help others.

'I was alone and didn't speak German. I was 19. You know how difficult the German language is? Some words are like sentences. I went to training and then home. Every day. I went a long time without speaking to people.

'I am quiet, but if want to say something I'll say it. I played in the second team at Leverkusen and started to learn German. Berti Vogts was the coach and he paid more attention to the senior players so I thought: "I'll show him." I was the young boy who thought he knew everything. I would speak to myself at home and say: "Why the fuck are you not playing?" I had conversations with myself. I still have them. They help me put ambition in myself, but going home when there was no internet access and with nothing to do in Leverkusen apart from watching movies, I'd listen to music and it meant I talked to myself a lot.

'Klaus Toppmöller became coach and told me that I was going to feature more and he backed up his words as he started to integrate me in the team slowly. I calmed down a little bit.'

When he had free time, Berbatov returned home to Bulgaria, where his grandad insisted on walking him around the local market, 'proud and walking slowly, like he was a general.

'Then I'd go back to Germany. In hindsight, Germany is a great place for a young player to go and develop. German teams give youth a chance. And young managers.'

Slowly, and eschewing any distractions to concentrate on football, he established himself in the Bundesliga, helping to knock out Liverpool and Manchester United on the way to a final with Real Madrid.

'I scored against Liverpool, a great 4–3 game. We had a good team. The luck was with us in most of the games in the run to the final, but not in the final itself against Real Madrid at Hampden Park, but I was playing in the Champions League final aged 21,' he smiles. 'The manager told me that I was going on with 30 minutes to play. I was too young to appreciate that I was playing in the Champions League final. I almost scored too and we almost beat Real Madrid if it wasn't for that fabulous Zidane goal. I was in the centre of the pitch and saw the ball draw down. That left foot of his. Bang!

'They had Ronaldo, Figo, Raúl. I was afraid to touch them. I was in awe of them. I let Figo go past me because I didn't want to touch him, but it happens in football. Years later at Manchester United, I saw teams lose the game at Old Trafford in the tunnel before kick-off. They were almost asking for autographs.'

It took a while before he became a first choice United striker.

'We lost the title to Chelsea in my second season but won it again in my third. That was one of my best seasons in football, 2010–11. I kept scoring hat-tricks. I have those balls at my home, all signed by the United players. I treasure them.

'One hat-trick was extra special because it was against Liverpool. The second goal was special. Nani crossed the ball and I saw Wazza in front of me. I saw by his body movement that he was going to try and go for the ball. I said: "Wazza, leave it. Wazza! Wazza! It's me." He left it and afterwards he was very proud as he said: "I left you the ball." I controlled the ball with my thigh. I would be lying if I said I did this intentionally. The ball was falling and my thought was that was the best option. The decisions were made in nanoseconds. It was automatic, I didn't think about it. And the way it went in off the post and down made it cooler. By the roar of the crowd I knew it was in.'

Wes Brown remembers it too. 'His hat-trick against Liverpool was exceptional. He could finish with flair, he had the complete package. People think that Berba was slow but he wasn't, it was just the way he moved around the pitch reading the game.'

Berba was settled at Old Trafford.

'I was friends with everybody. I didn't go to dinners with them and everyone has their private life, but at training I was ready for the challenge. And at the heart of United, this huge club known around the world, it feels like a family. Lots of the staff have been there for decades and they cared so much about the club. The chef's ringtone was "Glory, Glory Man United". They cared about the team and doing their job, so that made us care about the team and do our role.'

I previously met Berbatov in Marbella in 2015 when he was doing pre-season training with Indian club Kerala Blasters. His WhatsApp icon was him with the Premier League trophy at United.

'I'm proud of those trophies. I was the first Bulgarian to win it. I was so happy that I went home and made love to my girl!' he said, never short of a killer quote for a journalist.

He agreed to meet, but asked a favour. A signed shirt from Lionel Messi, explaining: 'Because he's the fucking greatest. Ronaldo is brilliant, Messi more my kind of player. He sees the game so clearly. He can score, create, he's the complete player, the best probably. If you ask someone older than me they will say Pelé, Maradona or Puskás or Di Stéfano. But for my generation it's Messi or Ronaldo. They're pretty much even, but something with Messi makes me shout "Messi! Messi!" when I watch Barcelona on television. I've played against him up close and personal. That was enough. He also has great players around him, Xavi, Iniesta, Busquets. I like Busquets the best after Messi. He's tall like me, yet he's so smart on the pitch, always one or two steps ahead of the other players. I didn't start in Rome [in 2009] against them. The first ten minutes, it was all United. We had chances. Barcelona were better after that. Carlos and I were left on the bench and we wanted to play. It was the second final that I'd lost too, so it was more painful. I got on the pitch in the second half, but by then it was too late. Barça were passing the ball around us.'

Almost all the players mentioned came to Berbatov's charity game in Sofia in that summer. Gary Neville and Vidić hadn't played any football before that. They got especially fit for it. They could have fobbed him off with an excuse.

We met again in Manchester, then again in Singapore in 2019 at his hotel. He was engaging and looked better than ever, like a James Dean in a simple white t-shirt.

Part of the conversation in Singapore went like this.

'What was your worst moment at United?'

'I bet you are expecting what I am going to say. Or not.'

'I was most pissed off with you when you missed a sitter against City in the FA Cup semi-final of 2011,' I said. 'That allowed City to move towards a first trophy in 35 years.'

'But if you were in my shoes could you have taken that chance? I'll tell you to save you thinking about it. Probably not. If you cannot do something better than me, why are you pissed? Why are you judging me?'

'I'm not judging you; I was annoyed. And I'd be annoyed at any other player. It wasn't personal against you.'

'That's stupid.'

'But when has football been rational?'

'People need to think first. I would love to put all the people who were pissed off with me and asked them to take the same chance. I would have laughed harder than I laughed in all my life.

But, at the same time I try to understand that fans get annoyed. Anyway, it was not that day.

'And there was worse,' he continued. 'That City game was a shit game, but it was not as shit as losing the title to Man City in the last minute [in 2012]. I couldn't believe it was happening. We were celebrating winning the league and then suddenly "What?!" As a team, that was my low point at Old Trafford. Personally, when I miss a chance or don't play well, you always feel bad. But when Agüero scored that goal, that was terrible for all of us. We were in the dressing room and someone had said that they had finished and we celebrated. And then someone said: "No, they have scored." The journey back to Manchester was terrible. Normally, when you lose, you try to joke because there will be another game. But this one was in the last minute of the last game of the season. Shit happens.

'No, the worst was when I didn't play the Champions League final [in 2011]. I was told in the dressing room before the match.'

'I felt sorry for you that night,' I said.

'I don't want people to feel sorry, but I was upset because I was the top goalscorer for the team that season. I felt confident. I thought I could score goals from the halfway line. But every time I didn't play well, I disappointed myself, those people close to me and the fans. That is such an awful feeling and every player has it.'

Ferguson has given his side of the story of leaving Berbatov out of the squad. 'He obviously took it badly and I felt rotten. Wembley has a coach's room, nice and private, where I explained the reasons for my decision. Dimitar had gone off the boil a bit and wasn't always the ideal substitute. I told him: "If we're going for goal in the last minute, in the penalty box, Michael Owen has been very fresh." It probably wasn't fair but I had to make those decisions and back myself to be right.'

Ferguson agreed to write the foreword to Berba's life story, *My Way*. Berba wrote it all himself. Footballers don't write their own books. Berbatov wrote 443 pages and published it himself. His way, indeed.

'I loved writing,' he says. 'A lot of things popped into my mind when I wrote. Sometimes I sat there from 2 p.m. until 5 a.m. It's my story, I need to be in control of it. The book is how I speak. I hope people understand my sarcasm and the irony. I hope it is not lost in translation from Bulgarian because I am an artist. On the pitch and outside the pitch.'

'His goal record at United stands testimony to his goalscoring ability,' writes Ferguson effusively. 'He started 108 games and scored 56 goals. He was a good professional and never gave me a second of bother … it was a pleasure to have him for four years. His goalscoring achievements are highlighted in his five goals v Blackburn Rovers and his hat-trick v our great rivals Liverpool, the second an overhead kick which sent Old Trafford into a frenzy. I don't think I will forget his mastery of skill when he managed to waltz along the byline, leaving his opponents in their wake to set up Cristiano Ronaldo for a simple tap in.'

Ferguson's more detailed explanation of why he left Berbatov out of the 2011 Champions League final prefigured some of the reasons for the Bulgarian's departure the following year.

'As the shape of the team changed and we had more options up front as goalscorers, Dimitar's appearances became fewer and this was a constant problem for me as he was still a top player and this problem wrestled with my conscience.

'The moment arrived which still lives with me today and gives me terrible memories – sometimes when making decisions as a manager you can make mistakes and that was the case when we played Barcelona at Wembley. The structure and tactics of our opponents meant we adjusted our tactics to play a single striker on the bench. I still see the disappointment on Dimitar's face. It's something I'll always regret; he deserved his place in the team. However, he never held a grudge, which marks him out as a special human being.'

Berba left in 2012.

'We could see it coming,' recalls Brown. 'In his last couple of seasons he'd sit at the back in training and play as a defender. He was very good at the back, but it was also probably his way of showing his frustration. He wasn't the type to snap or lose his head, it was a tough time for him as it is for any player who is out of favour. We've all been there.'

'Nobody wants to leave United,' Berbatov agrees. 'But footballers want to play and I was not getting enough chances to play anymore. I told Sir Alex and he said that he could not guarantee me this as they had bought Robin van Persie. Competition is good, but my ambition to play more meant I left. I don't want to sit down and do nothing, even though I could have won another champions medal. I had an offer from Fiorentina and Juventus, but after so many years in England I wanted to stay in England and not learn a new language, new training methods and style of football. I'd already learned English from movies and talking to myself and I wanted to use that.

'I scored 56 goals and cherish them all, like every striker. I don't remember them all, but occasionally I'll see my goals and think, "Oh my god, how good was that?" It's a nice feeling.'

He joined Fulham and he knew their manager Martin Jol from Spurs.

'"Berba!" he shouted like a big bear when he called me. "I want you in my team." I could not say no to him. London, England, Premier League, Martin Jol. Lovely.'

Ferguson later wrote about the move: 'Berbatov's stylish but languid approach did not work out at United, even though he scored 21 goals in 2010–11 and was joint top scorer in the league. In 2012 we sold him to Fulham for £3 million.'

* * *

Another United signing along with Berbatov from that summer of 2008 was Rafael da Silva, who'd arrived with his twin brother Fabio from Brazil.

I went to see Rafael and sat, for 90 minutes, talking over food in Lyon's beautiful old Gare des Brotteaux; Rafael was open and enthusiastic about his life as a footballer. The Brazilian worked hard, he got his rewards and he recalled making his United debut in a 2008 friendly at Peterborough: 'It didn't matter that it was a friendly, I knew then that I could play for the first team.' The son of a maintenance man, Rafael grew up in Petropolis, a city of 300,000 in the mountains near Rio de Janeiro.

'My father was like an Englishman, very strict, punctual and hard-working,' he explains of his childhood. 'He didn't go to school and couldn't read – he only learned after we'd become footballers – but my parents worked every day for us, seven days a week, both of them.

'They didn't earn much money and we lived in a small house in the grounds of a rich family home. The family would come at the weekend, to swim and relax. Dad was the maintenance man. I could see the huge inequality of Brazilian life every week between the family who owned the house and our family. I never ever thought that I would be in a position to buy a house, let alone a big one like they had. The greatest achievement in my life was to buy a house.

'I was good at school, but Fabio was better,' he says. 'I would sometimes copy his answers in tests, though he'd think that I was just looking over his shoulder to see how he was doing. We played football a lot, using flip-flops to mark the goals. Sometimes we didn't even have a correct ball. Now, we make sure the boys in Petropolis have proper footballs. When they see us, they also see that they can make it as a footballer in Europe. We've shown them that it can be done.'

The twins' older brother was also a footballer.

'Luis Enrique – he went from Botafogo to Italy and was at Brescia for six months, then he stopped. He missed home; he got messed around by agents, given promises, and my family put their trust in the wrong people. His misfortune helped us, made us use lawyers and do things properly when we had offers.'

The twins didn't start out as defenders.

'Fabio was a striker, I was a midfielder. When I was 12, our coach at Fluminense (a great old Rio club) put me at right-back and my brother at left-back. It was a hot day and I wasn't used to it because Petropolis was cooler. The grass was long at right-back and harder to run in. He said it would be for ten minutes. Fifteen years later, I'm still there.'

There was no shortage of Brazilian full-backs to idolise.

'Roberto Carlos, Cafu and Belletti,' smiles Rafael. 'Brazil has a history of great attacking full-backs. Dani Alves, Maicon, Alex Sandro, Marcelo. We could speak for ten minutes only about Brazilian full-backs. They're suited to modern top-level football because they can attack as well as defend.'

Rafael supported Botafogo, another legendary Rio side, as a boy.

'I still support them. When I was younger I went to the games with my friends. Sometimes we'd take the bus and get into the stadium early.

'I didn't like to watch them against Flamengo because the supporters were crazy in those games. My father, who also supported Botafogo, never went to the stadium. He loved to watch football, but he thought the stadium was dangerous. And it was. Now, it's even worse, the area around it is dangerous.

'I'd go with my friends. We'd sing the songs. I'd cry when Botafogo lost. I still sing their songs [he started singing about wanting to see them win a trophy again]. I want to play there one day and the club know that.'

United spotted the twins playing for Fluminense in a youth tournament in Hong Kong.

'I couldn't believe it,' he says of United's interest. 'I was 15 and we played in the Nike Cup. A guy came up to me and asked if I'd like to go and visit Old Trafford. I thought it was a joke. There was nothing formal, but I went to Manchester with John Calvert, who worked for United, and it was all amazing. I trained with the first team. Fluminense had good facilities but in Manchester everything was perfect.

'When I went back to Brazil, they started to talk to me about signing for United. After that trip to Manchester I was sure that I wanted to play in the first team of United.'

Fluminense weren't so keen and stopped the twins playing.

'It was a long, bad story.' He shakes his head. 'They stopped us because we'd agreed to come to United. Fluminense said that we should stay with them and spend six months or one year in their first team. United accepted that, then Fluminense changed their minds, but we still ended up coming to Manchester. When we did, we hadn't played football and were out of shape. I don't think we impressed so much at the start.

'Fluminense? We were there for seven years; we still have good friends there. And we were happy that they received money for me and my brother.'

There were other Portuguese speakers when the twins arrived at Old Trafford.

'Ronaldo called us and asked us to join United. He knew that Arsenal wanted us too, but we had given our word to United and my parents said that was important. Nani was also there and the Brazilian Anderson, of course. Those three helped me, my brother and another Brazilian, Rodrigo Possebon, a lot because we couldn't speak any English.'

Nor could Anderson. 'That didn't stop him offering to be my English teacher!' laughs Rafael. 'I'm serious. He would listen to someone then translate what he thought they had said. It was hilarious. He would get angry in games and try to speak, but he couldn't speak English, he'd get so frustrated.

'Anderson was living with Ronaldo. Great players. I arrived in January and the team won the Champions League in May. I was training with them all. I was sure that I was playing for the best team in the world. I could see that they were going to win the Champions League. They were all so angry that they'd been beaten by Milan [in the semi-finals] the previous season. They were so focused on winning.'

Rafael's debut came later than summer.

'At Peterborough in a friendly with my brother,' he recalls. 'Fergie said a lot of good things about me. I'll never forget that day. I felt that I could play for Man United after that game. Darren Fletcher came up to me – I love Fletcher, he was so helpful to me – and he said: "Not bad for a first game, eh?" He always tried to help me. For example, I was still learning English and in one game I didn't play well. Fergie was telling me off and I was replying to him smiling with my thumbs up, because Brazilians do that. I thought I was showing respect. Fletcher said to me: "You don't do that."'

Rafael won the league in his first season, 2008–09, and was shortlisted for the PFA Young Player of the Year, won by Ashley Young.

'I was patient – you must be when you are young – because you're not going to play every week. You have to work to play, that's it. And I had Gary Neville in my position. When I arrived he joked: "You want to retire me, eh?" I could push Gary and Fergie knew that. I was aggressive, fast and wanted to win. I felt like a Man United player but I needed chances. I did get chances because Gary had injuries and at one point so did Wes Brown and John O'Shea, who could also play right-back. Whereas my brother had fewer chances because Patrice hardly ever got injured.

'When I got my chance I took it. I'd get the ball and look to play it quickly to Cristiano, or Scholes or Giggs. So many players you can give the ball to. Fergie always wanted me to get forward. He never said: "Today we're going to focus on defending". Never. When we played City away, he came to me in training the day before and said: "You're going to play tomorrow. You'll be against Robinho. You know what you must do." I knew I had to attack him as much as he attacked me.

'I played very well and we won. City and Liverpool, they were the two games I most wanted to win. I felt that people wanted to win against Liverpool more than any other game.'

Ferguson was the major influence on Rafael's career.

'He did everything he could to help me, even when things didn't go well. In 2010–11 I made some mistakes and got injured a lot, but he never gave up on me. He renewed my contract when I wasn't playing well. He saw how hard I was working and I would like to think I repaid him. At the start of 2012, he came to me and said: "You cannot be making mistakes any more. You are mature now." I'd made too many mistakes before that.'

Some of those were more memorable than others.

'Being sent off against Bayern Munich [in April 2010] was the worst,' he says. 'I fouled van Bommel and then I did a stupid challenge when I didn't need to because we were attacking. Then I grabbed Ribéry.

'I went back to the dressing room and cried. Fergie was angry but I don't think he said everything that he wanted to say to me that day, he took it easy on me. I was so disappointed in myself that night and he saw that. He said that I had dominated Ribéry – and that made me even sadder because I played very well that night. But I made two mistakes.'

There was another sending off against Spurs in 2010–11, when Rafael was a league winner again. That season, he also got concussed at Blackpool.

'My mum and my wife were watching on television and they were worried,' he remembers. 'They tried to call me and couldn't get through. They became desperate as my phone was in the dressing room and I was in hospital. I was unconscious on the pitch for two minutes and the game was held up for ten minutes, but I was OK. I was concussed a few times at United. I went into one challenge against Giroud at Arsenal and can't remember anything about what happened next. I came round towards the end of the game and thought we were winning. We weren't.'

The twins also played left and right wing against Arsenal in an FA Cup win that season.

'We loved it and we won! Fabio scored, too. Who needs Cristiano and Giggsy when you have us two?'

By the time Ronaldo left the club in 2009, Manchester City were beginning to rise. Rafael didn't see their success as inevitable.

'They started slowly and there's always a chance that it is not going to work out. Other clubs have had money thrown at them and not worked. But you have to say today that they are a very, very good team ... but they buy everyone!'

And United?

'Of course United buy players, but they also promoted lots of players from the youth system. City don't do this. It's bad; you have to give opportunities to young players from your city, from your house. Imagine if you have children and you don't make them go to college. You must trust your children, to give them a chance, but City obviously think differently.'

While Rafael won three Premier League titles at United, he didn't play in the two Champions League finals during that time.

'I was on the bench in Rome [in 2009],' he remembers. 'Maybe people were thinking "Barça are brilliant", but I was not. I wanted to win the Champions League in my first season. I'd won the league; I'd played in the game where United became world champions – which is very important when you are South American.

'We became world champions, had hardly any celebration and went straight back from Japan to play against Stoke, but I knew I wouldn't play against Stoke because of Tony Pulis's style of football.

I'm not very big. Fergie would always say to me before Stoke: "You are not going to play today. You know why?" I knew why. I'm not two metres tall.

'For the second final at Wembley, I did not expect to play because I had been coming back from injury. But my brother started and I was so nervous for him. I was always like this with him then. He didn't sleep the night before and it was not a good night for the club.'

Fabio starting the Champions League final and Berbatov not even making the squad. That's not something anyone could have foreseen in 2008.

10

HE COMES FROM SERBIA!

Nemanja Vidić

Nemanja Vidić has the distinction of having the highest win percentage of any established Manchester United player in history. Of his 300 games for the club, the Reds won 204 of them – 68 per cent. The most important of those arguably was in Moscow on 21 May 2008, the Champions League final against Chelsea.

The Serb knows the Russian capital well. He'd once called the city home. In the early hours of 22 May, he joined some old friends and family back at the team hotel. United were champions of Europe for the third time and their captain was considered the greatest central defender in football.

As the players celebrated, Vidić's father decided to do things slightly differently.

'My father was mesmerised not by the players who'd just become European champions, but Bobby Charlton. At the party, he followed Bobby around; he'd watched him on television in 1966 when United played Partisan Belgrade in the European Cup semi-final. That's how good the football teams were in Yugoslavia back then. Red Star won the European Cup as recently as 1991.

'Mum didn't really care about football, but Dad knew about Charlton from the Munich air crash. Everyone in Serbia knows about the plane crash because United had played Red Star and the plane took off from Belgrade before stopping in Munich. And here was my dad standing staring at Bobby Charlton, with me having to come and translate as he told him how great he thought he was!

'Everything was like a dream in Moscow. I didn't sleep that night. It was a long party, which started late. I was drinking fast. I can handle my drink. Maybe that's why I forgot that Didier Drogba wanted to punch me during the game.

'Russia had been good to me. When I moved there as a player, it was the first time I'd left Serbia and Moscow was hard at first. I didn't know the language or have friends. Over time, I learned about Russia and enjoyed it. I was happy to come back with Man United to a stadium I played in many times before, especially for the Champions League final.'

Vidić didn't take a penalty.

'Giggsy was ahead of me in the list. I think he was seventh. I said that he had more experience and should shoot. Giggsy scored his and I was next, but I wasn't needed. Giggsy was still sharp when he was 40, he could still change direction quickly. We only knew the first five takers; it was less organised after that. Players were putting their hands up to offer to take a penalty. Maybe mine didn't go up as quickly as the others because I would have been nervous taking a penalty. All players have some nerves taking penalties. Thankfully, I wasn't needed. I think you can practice penalties many times, but they don't replicate the pressure of what it's like to take them for real. There was a lot of stress for the team and for me before the game so we were very relieved to win. In the weeks before the final, I had problems with my back. I was advised to rest completely from playing football but knowing that I'd face Drogba, Sir Alex Ferguson would not accept that. We got through it.'

Vidić was United captain, but no social convenor.

'I had a family and they didn't see enough of me because I was spending more time with my teammates than my wife and kids. We were playing two or three games a week and then I was playing for the national team. It was very intense for years. I saw enough of my teammates; I respected them and understood them but I didn't need to see them even more.

'I was also proud – and I know Ferguson was – that we had 12 nationalities in the dressing room. Of course, the French go well with the French, the Spanish with the Spanish speakers, the Portuguese with their speakers, the English with their humour.

'My family were made to feel welcome in this environment. At Carrington they asked if I wanted Serbian food. They were really advanced like that. I was OK with the food in England, it was good at the training ground and I had a wife at home who knew how to cook, especially Serbian dishes. She makes an excellent Punjene Paprike – peppers stuffed with meat, onion and spices.

'On matchdays, my family came to watch me play. My wife recently said to me that she missed going to games. She would bring my sons to Old Trafford, there would be excitement and tension. If we won a game, then it was a happy time not just for the team but for the family too. She missed it. What could I say? I miss it too. We have happy memories of United and Manchester, our kids were all born there in Wythenshawe hospital, all of them United and Serbia fans. And I learned some English ways. I didn't even know what darts was. In Serbia, my friends do not even consider it a sport. When I started watching in England, I loved it because of the atmosphere and especially when they got 180. People sing and jump. I started to play at home with my brother when I visited. I had a pool table and darts board. I respected the culture in England and darts is part of that.'

And Vidić did socialise with teammates. A bit.

'Rio. Edwin. Robin. Michael,' he says when pushed. 'I went out with them a couple of times. Dinners. I came to United as a mature person. I'd done my discos in Serbia and Moscow. At the biggest club in the world it was important not to spend time on the stupid things. I wanted to show the whole world how good I was in the most important years in my career and I was lucky to play eight years for Man United.

'My point is that we all had the same target then. We were there to play for the biggest club in the world, we knew what the aim was – to win the biggest trophies. We had to play well, week in week out, but there were always setbacks. I had many times where I played when I didn't feel well or sharp, but my teammates would see that and help me. We had an incredible team spirit and that helped us win trophies – and trophies are the only way to get recognition for Man United.

'At smaller clubs you don't have the same aims but you still have aims and expectations, but at Man United, where every team plays 100 per cent against you, you should always play like it's your last year: 90 per cent is not enough and the current players should play like that. You should be scared that you're not going to be there next season and you have to fight to stop yourself going because it's only when you leave Man United that you realise how big Man United is.'

I didn't know Nemanja Vidić when he played for Manchester United. Not really. A few chats in mixed zones, the odd question in a press conference as in Kiev in 2007, impressive as he conversed in three languages. It felt a lot safer there than it did outside the stadium as a 500-strong group of self-styled Dynamo ultras appeared, all chants, flags and salutes. They'd marched through Kiev's grandest shopping avenues, dodging the rash of flash cars and enjoying the attention bestowed on them by statuesque female shoppers. I stood back and watched them pass from the safety of a doorway.

Then a cry went up by the main entrance to the stadium, close to where booths were selling match tickets for the equivalent of £4.

'United! United!' There was an urgency about the police because the cry was so unexpected. As far as they knew, the 1,200 travelling United fans – an impressive figure given the distance and cost – had been safely led into the other side of the vast stadium. I went towards the group of Reds, hoping to clock a familiar face. They chanted for Nemanja Vidić and Wayne Rooney, but I didn't recognise anyone. 'Where you from?' I asked one. 'We are the Polish Reds,' he replied proudly in perfect English, 'and we hate City and all Scouse bastards!' Before they knew it, a Ukrainian police unit were escorting them to their own section.

Vidić, signed a year earlier from Spartak Moscow for £7.2 million, became one of United's most important players and, to this day, the only defender to be twice-named Premier League player of the season. We all admired from afar but his job was to play football and win, not to cultivate any journalists.

I did, however, know Gerard Piqué when he was at United and he'd tell me about Vidić.

'I learn from him and Rio every time I watch them play,' he said. 'Just as I do every day in training. It's the nuances, the little details which help improve my game. They share many similar qualities: both are tall, quick, hard players who read the game well and anticipate attacks, yet there are differences and they complement each other.

'Rio is technically better on the ball, a leader in the team who always talks. He is deceivingly strong – I see that in the gym at Carrington, but on the pitch he'll get closer to strikers to stop them turning, whereas Vida is more aggressive. He sees every game as a battle in which he must win. Vida is solid. You would fancy him to win any 50/50 ball. You would still fancy him if two opposing players went for the same ball as him. They are two of the best centre-backs in the world and probably the best central defensive partnership in the world, certainly a reason United don't concede many goals.

'Off the field their personalities differ. They get on, which is important, but Rio is a joker in the dressing room. He likes to speak to everyone and make sure everyone is OK. He loves playing cards and everyone knows what kind of music Rio is into. Rio dresses in a street style, very hip hop, or whatever you call it in England.

'Vida is more serious. He's more into films than music and his English is still improving, partly because he watches a lot of films in English. He dresses in a more conservative English way, but he has a strong presence inside the dressing room because he is really respected as a player. I find him interesting and intelligent. He tells me about growing up in Serbia, about the wars, the NATO bombs in Belgrade, the recent split with Montenegro and the mood in his country.'

And other United defenders past and present talked to me about him, too.

'Jaap Stam came in and did very well, but he was never really replaced until Nemanja arrived in a move that turned out to be great value for money,' said Paul Parker. 'Vidić is very consistent and rarely makes mistakes, but if he does, then his recovery rate is very high. One advantage Vida has over Steve Bruce, who he reminds me of, is his pace. Another is his experience of playing international football and club football in several countries. You need that now at a club like United.'

Then, in 2014, the former Ipswich Town striker James Scowcroft bumped into Vidić, who he didn't know, in Palma de Mallorca. Scowcroft, a United fan, introduced himself and they had a chat. Vidić had just left United and Scowcroft said he should do an interview for the fans – via *United We Stand*. Vidić wasn't on social media and he was initially reluctant. I'd later find out that can be his nature. But he agreed and we had a chat on the phone. It went well. Fans liked what they read, including him making clear that, in reference to his song 'Nemanja, woaah, Nemanja, woaah, he comes from Serbia, he'll fucking murder yer' that while he liked the fans singing it, he'd never actually murdered anyone.

A year later I went to Milan to interview Vidić, where he was living after playing with Inter. He came to my hotel to collect me but didn't recognise me. Some interviews last 30 minutes and it didn't get off to the best start when he said: 'I don't want to do this interview. I don't like talking about the past. I'd rather talk about the future … when I have something to talk about.' Then he took me out into Milan and we spent hours talking in his favourite Japanese restaurant in Milan's fashionable bar-lined Via Carlo Ravizza. I'd just been at the Belgrade derby and he was keen to hear my thoughts. Which were that the atmosphere was among the best in the world but it was crazy since I'd witnessed sustained violence for 45 minutes.

'It's loudest in Belgrade,' he said proudly. 'I stood with the hard-core fans of Red Star when I was a young player at the club. I moved to Belgrade at 15 to play for the youth team. I sang with them and I loved being with the Delije because I was a fan of the club since being very young. It was crazy on the terraces and you jump around and sing the whole game. And I remember Celtic Park and Anfield, the fans are close, it's like they are breathing on the players. But there's something I like about English stadiums that not many people say: the moments of silence in a game when the crowd fall flat. That's the moment when the players have to earn the roar of a crowd by doing something which excites them, a tackle or a pass. They love a great tackle in England and so do I. And when you've earned it, it feels better than non-stop noise regardless of how you are playing.'

I found him fascinating. He spoke football as expected, about Serbia, Kosovo, where his wife Ana came from. I told him I'd taken a bus to Kosovo, one with live chickens onboard being carried by a passenger.

I went back to Milan a year later and we spoke for even longer. His theories on football, life. He was fiercely protective over his family. Private too. He spoke to no journalists. I was reading a book about World War I and how Serbians resisted the attacks of the Austro-Hungarian empire armies at the Drina River at the start. We spoke about this. He was proud of his country, his people.

'Was it true that Sir Alex Ferguson had to talk you down from going back to Serbia to enlist in the army?'

'Good question. Fergie said this in his book. The story is that Sir Alex and I walked onto the training pitch and he asked me what was happening in Serbia. He could see that I was angry and sad. It's our land, it had been our land for centuries and we had to leave that land. Fergie could see that I was passionate and angry and that's how he interpreted it. But the truth is I never spoke about going back to serve in the army.'

I told him that with his football career over, he should travel to see the world. He told me that I sounded like his wife and asked why I couldn't just relax and stay at home. He can also take a joke.

'Nemanja, what do you think first attracted your wife to the captain of Red Star Belgrade?'

'What are you saying? That I'm not good-looking?' Pause. Smile. 'She was attracted to my intelligence and my dancing.'

We continued to keep in touch. Fast forward to late 2018. My dad died on 6 November. I'd said my goodbyes but I found out as I landed in Milan ahead of a game in Turin between Juventus and United.

'Come to mine,' said Vidić. 'I'll take you to Turin.' How I needed that. I went back to Milan in 2019 for another interview, then, when he moved back to Serbia, to Belgrade. And with each visit, another layer. Always fascinating. Always hours. Never rushed. Never an agent or an advisor interrupting. Just an adult thinking for himself.

He showed me around Belgrade. Serbians are not unattractive people.

'I should go back to my hotel now,' I'd say.

'I thought you British people knew how to have a good night.'

'I'm up early.'

'Where do you go next?'

'I'm flying to Rome. To interview a player near Naples and see Monte Cassino, one of the great World War II battle sites on the way. Do you want to come?'

He shook his head like I was a madman.

I asked him if he fancied climbing Mount Kilimanjaro for charity. He gave a two-word answer, which I expected. I told him I'd tell his wife and she'd agree with me that it was a good idea.

'I've climbed the highest mountains on earth with Man United,' he said. 'I can't climb any higher than that.'

Serbian journalists asked why he spoke to none of them but spoke to me. Promoters asked if we wanted to do an appearance show together.

'I'm not a performing monkey.'

But then he had said in that first meeting: 'I'm not really a fan of commercial activities, but professionally you have to do it – it's part of your job. Football is a business. The media and the clubs and the players get so much money. I had Puma as a sponsor and nothing else. I didn't want the distraction of more sponsors. Some players wanted more sponsors and enjoyed doing that type of work. I didn't really enjoy it, no matter how much money was involved.'

In 2022, we were going to meet in Belgrade. He suggested Montenegro and that I should bring my family. He brought people along to meet me. He couldn't do enough for my family either.

And we spoke a lot. Little stories from his life, so different from most professional footballers. About how he'd seen missiles coming over his town in '99 and how he and his friends had all run in different directions – one towards the missile – before they later met up at the bus station. His town was bombed.

'When they started bombing, I went back to my hometown. We didn't know how bad it was going to get. When the bombing was about to start, we heard sirens and went to the bomb shelter to hide. When the sirens were off, we tried to live a normal life. It wasn't easy, but we tried. And humans are animals. We adapt to anything.

'One day, I was in the playground near my home playing football. The sirens went off and I ran away to safety, but we couldn't have official matches while we were being bombed. We still had informal games.

'I didn't feel like I was living in a war zone, but my town was bombed five times. They took out the strategic targets, but they were in the centre – the telecommunications centre, which was 200 metres from my home. I heard the big crash in the day. Nobody died, thankfully.

'We don't like speaking much about it. I'm not politically orientated anyway, but bombs are sad to see, not just in Serbia, but anywhere in the world.'

By the Adriatic, he introduced me to his friend Budimir Vujačić, a former Yugoslavia international who'd played for Partisan but also for Sporting in Lisbon under Carlos Queiroz. And that's where I started to piece together the story of how Nemanja Vidić had come to play for United. The pair had kept in touch and Queiroz, who was now at United as an assistant to Sir Alex Ferguson, respected Vujačić's opinion on players. He told him that they were looking for a central defender. Vujačić, who was based in Milan, watched Vidić on television marking Oliver Bierhoff and decided to take a night train to Naples in October 2002 to see Serbia play Italy in a European Championship qualifying game.

'Budimir is the opposite of me and likes the adventure of travel, a bit like my wife,' smiled Nemanja.

Down in Naples, Vidić was boarding the team coach. He remembers the journey very well indeed.

'"Don't sit there, it's not your place," said a voice from behind a seat. It was another player. I couldn't see who it was and didn't really care. I said nothing and found another seat. I was an outsider, the new boy. I'd just climbed onto the coach before my international debut. I was 20.'

The bus was escorted along a motorway by the blue flashing lights of the carabinieri from the hotel on the slopes of Mount Vesuvius and then through the back streets of Naples towards the Stadio San Paolo, where Maradona was king.

'As we approached the stadium, Italy fans showed us what they thought of us, lighting flares and singing. Naples had a reputation for being a hot atmosphere, but inside the bus was quiet, me especially so. But my life was changing quickly and now I was surrounded by huge names of Serbian football as the bus journey ended on a slope down a ramp into the vast, scruffy, stadium. It was old and rundown. I was disappointed by it, the Marakana in Belgrade was better.

'In the dressing room, I looked around at my new teammates. Siniša Mihajlović, the free-kick king and a big star for a Lazio team which had spent more money on players than any club in world football when he was part of it around the turn of the century. He had one of the best left-foot free-kicks, maybe in the world.

'Mihajlović had been man of the match for Red Star when they beat Bayern Munich in the semi-final of the 1991 European Cup, scoring the two goals, the winner in the final minute, which put Red Star into the final. I didn't tell him that I watched the game so many times on a VHS that my dad complained that I kept breaking the video machine.

'And then Mihajlović scored in the final against Marseille to make Red Star champions of Europe in Italy. A hero. The Champions League started a year later and no team from Eastern Europe has come close to being European champions since.

'Our captain Predrag Mijatović had been at Real Madrid, where he came third in the Ballon d'Or behind Ronaldo and Zinedine Zidane. The best first touch I've seen. Zoran Mirković had played for Juventus alongside Zidane. Darko Kovačević, the big striker, had been with that Juventus team too.

'They were experienced, hard and wise professionals and now I was expected to play with them. It was all happening so fast.

'A few days before, my Red Star coach Zoran Filipović called me over after training and told me that I been called up for the national team. I was delighted and asked him if he was sure.

'"Yes and I told them that you are ready to play," he replied. I was still surprised and expected to be on the bench.

'Our coach was Dejan Savićević, a legend of a player. A genius – they called him that in Italy. Some older Man United players and fans told me he was the best player they'd ever seen at Old Trafford when he turned out for Red Star against United in the 1991 European Super Cup final. Years later, he'd ask me to get a CD of that game from Old Trafford and I called in a few favours.

'Most of the other Serbia players were ten or 12 years older than me and I knew them by their huge reputations, not personally. As they talked among each other, I kept my head down as the fans outside put theirs up. I was happy with my life, for which I had no future plans. Red Star Belgrade was my life and I hadn't even thought about playing for my country since I was so happy playing for my club. Playing for your country, I thought, was something older players did – like the ones around me in their tracksuits.

'In the dressing room, Savićević was not big on detail for individual players, it was all about the group. There was no individual advice for me, beyond the supportive words of "Do well."

'It was 12 October 2002 and the season was young but my name was being talked about in Serbia. I'd played two games for Red Star against Italian side Chievo in the UEFA Cup and for the first time in my life, I came up against a player where I thought: "Now this is difficult."

'Our biggest opponents in Serbia were Partisan and while there were a lot of talented players and the rivalry was intense, they were in the Serbian league and not the top, top level. If you wanted to be recognised as a top player then you had to play against the top players from the top leagues in Europe and before long I would be put against one.

'Oliver Bierhoff was a big German striker playing for Chievo of Verona, a big player, a top scorer in Serie A, the man who'd scored the first golden goal in football in the final of Euro 96. My job was to stop him scoring and I did well, I felt tested and yet comfortable against him. We drew 0–0 at home and won 2–0 away in the UEFA Cup first round, a huge result.

'It sounds impressive but the reality was that I was young and inexperienced; Bierhoff was at the height of his powers, really good in the air, and I had to show how good I was. He was tough, a grown man, I was a boy. My muscles were not fully formed, he was physical. I was energetic and strong in the air; he was intelligent and knew where and how to move. That's the most important thing for a forward. All Chievo's balls were played to him, so I was busy. But they didn't score in 180 minutes.

'People recognised what I'd done and if I could do well against Bierhoff, then the logic in the media was that I could do well against Italy away. Inside the team, our logic was that when you play a game against Italy away then you know you are going to be dominated because Italy had very good players – Francesco Totti, Alessandro Del Piero, [Alessandro] Nesta.

'The coach read the team out in the dressing room and I was genuinely surprised to be named in the starting line-up. I said nothing, but walked out to do the warm-ups, where the noise was building. Naples had a reputation for being loud and intimidating, but when you have played at Red Star you don't really get intimidated. Outside of Serbia, in my career maybe I was only ever intimidated at Celtic Park with United for the first ten minutes of a game when the fans breathe fire towards the players. I loved playing at Celtic and felt it was like the mentality that I had grown up with.

'In Naples, I was playing for Serbia and Montenegro. The national anthem was the old one from Yugoslavia. I didn't sing it. I didn't connect with it, it didn't give me a boost, because it was the anthem we'd had before the break-up of Yugoslavia. Before long, we would sing a national anthem for Serbia, but I knew in Naples who I was playing for: my people, my family, the Serbian people.

'I admit I was a little star-struck doing warm-ups and thinking "Wow!" as I looked at the guys around me. My teammates were not rude, but they didn't really speak to me. Only one, Zoran Mirković – or "Bata" to us – took me to the side to explain how [Filippo] Inzaghi, who I'd be marking, played. He told me I'd be fine playing on my debut against one of the finest strikers in the world. He could hardly say I wouldn't be, but I trusted him, even though Bata played for Partisan, our deadly rivals, not Red Star.

'"Every ball which comes towards his feet, which he likes, I will be there to help you," said Bata of Inzaghi. And I knew that he would. Bata was brave on the pitch; he'd put his head where it hurt. Honest, tough. He supported justice. A man of principle, he would die to defend justice. Maybe he saw something in me, but I listened, I felt supported and I appreciated it, this unusual Partisan and Red Star alliance, enemies for our clubs, allies for our country.

'The referee blew his whistle and everything in the stands became background noise. I saw and heard nothing of what happened off the pitch after that.

'I started the game well, though, with my first tackle. Inzaghi. I went in strong and won the ball. It was a difficult tackle, the type where you risk to commit. Same for my second tackle. My confidence soared. I could do this. "You can fucking do this, Nemanja!" I thought of the people watching me back home. I wanted to make them proud, to punch the air as they watched the game on television at home or in the bars of Užice or Belgrade. And I did this by following some advice I'd been told as a boy at Red Star by a coach, Zoran Antonijević – the assistant in '91 when Red Star were champions. He'd told me: "The first touch in the game is the most important. Control the ball, pass the ball, grow into the game. First touch, pass, jump, tackle. They all must be good." I followed that throughout my career.

'Then there was a problem. Bata was hurt. He looked at me and shook his head. He went off injured. Only nine minutes had passed and I was without my guide and all alone, with Del Piero and Inzaghi, then [Andrea] Pirlo behind them. Shit!

'Inzaghi wasn't a great player on the ball, the type of player to dribble past you or create, but in the box he was the most difficult player to keep an eye on. He had perfect movement; he was always in the right place. It's hard to stop a player like that, you must have a feeling for the space. In the box it's not about the physical stuff, it's about your positioning. I think my greatest strength was my positioning and timing. There were players who were faster than me or jumped higher than me, but I had good timing. But so did Inzaghi. He was like a snake who could sit under a rock and not move for 89 minutes and then "bang!" he'd score. I had to be careful with him.'

He was. Italy would win every home game in the group, they beat Wales 4–0 with an 11-minute Inzaghi hat-trick. Every game, except one. Against Vidić.

'I received a lot of praise for my debut that night. My teammates finally spoke to me. They said: "Great game, kid" as we left the field. I later found out that they'd been worried about me because I was not experienced, I could have made mistakes which cost them. They thought that because they didn't know me, they didn't watch the Serbian league closely. Now they could relax. While still on the pitch, a few of the Italian players said positive things too, which meant a lot to me.

'I switched on my phone on the bus away from the stadium and didn't realise how many people I knew. The phone buzzed with text messages. Everybody was saying: "You're the man". It felt good.

People in Užice were happy, they felt part of my success and I felt so much positive energy. I called my mum.

'"You played a great match!" she said. I was laughing and replied: "How do you know, Mum, you know nothing about football!"

'"I watched! I watched! I saw how you played! Everyone in Užice says you played a great match."

'"For you, Mother, I always play well." If we had lost 5–0 she would have said that I was the best player on the pitch and just a little unlucky but this time she was right and there was a sense in the Serbian media of "Wow, this is a player who can play for a top team in Europe!" My life was about to change even more and there was a big increase in demands for interviews and people wanted to know more about me. I did some, but I was never open to the media – not throughout my whole career. I'm private. I refuse offers all the time to go on television.'

That game in Naples was an important landmark, but what Vidić didn't know at the time was that someone was watching very closely in the stands: Budimir Vujačić.

After the game, Budimir took another night train to Bari to get the boat back across the Adriatic to his home in Montenegro.

'He told me later that it was on that train that he woke up from his sleep and thought: "Nemanja Vidić would be perfect to play alongside Rio Ferdinand for Manchester United." I knew none of this, but he called Queiroz from Bari and said: "You have to look at this player."

'"Are there any big games coming up?" Queiroz asked him.

'"Red Star v Partisan at the weekend," replied Budimir.

'"We'll send Manchester United's chief scout Mick Brown to Belgrade to watch. I will put you in contact with him."'

Vidić returned to the training ground at Red Star, where his coach smiled and said: 'I told you that you were ready.'

'I started to get a lot of interest from clubs who wanted to sign me. Parma, in Serie A, were the first club to come to me with a definite offer and I signed a pre-contract with them. Serie A was shown on Serbian television and I'd watched some of Parma's great teams with players including Thuram, Cannavaro, Buffon, Asprilla, Crespo and Verón. I knew a lot about them and that they had a history of developing the careers of young players and helping them reach the highest level. I was happy to go there, but there were other eyes – not that I knew.'

United watched Vidić in the derby.

'We drew 2–2 and I did OK.

'Mick Brown told Budimir: "I like the way he plays" and he advised Sir Alex Ferguson to watch me. Ferguson booked a trip to Paris to see me play against France a month after my Serbia debut with a view to signing me.'

Word was spreading, but in Paris Vidić played in a three- rather than a four-man defence and Ferguson decided against pushing to sign him because he felt he'd not seen him properly and he was in a team playing defensively, rather than how United would play.

'The timing wasn't good either – United's defence had improved and was looking very good and he would use the money for another part of the team. I was ready to go to Parma, who were owned by Parmalat. Silvano Martina, who would become my agent, said he'd watched me play a few games and said he'd like to represent me in Italian football. A former goalkeeper from Yugoslavia who'd played in Serie A and represented Gianluigi Buffon, Martina knew Italy. Buffon had been at Parma too and he knew them. Buffon was more than three years older than me and I admire the fact he was still playing when I retired in 2014. But I also regret that I didn't play longer because of mistakes I made as a young player.

'Martina was the first person to bring me a concrete offer outside of Serbia, where everyone wanted to be my agent.'

This was not always a positive thing.

'An offer came but that didn't go to plan as I got the news that Parma were about to go into administration because of a huge fraud involving their owners Parmalat and the deal was over. I was 20, I didn't care. I was playing every week for Red Star, winning almost every game and going out after every win.

'My teammate Nenad Lalatović was a defender four years older than me and was the main guy I knocked around with. He liked me for several reasons: I was a talented young player but also because I was a defender who'd come through the youth system like him. Lalatović was a good player and a big help to me early in my career. He was Belgrade-born and captain of Red Star Belgrade.'

And still the clubs came.

'Internazionale tried to negotiate for me, but didn't offer the same money as Red Star wanted. Marseille tried to buy me but Red Star refused at the last minute because of the fans who felt that I was too young to leave their club.'

By 2004 more offers came in. Carlos Queiroz was now manager of Real Madrid and he asked about Vidić, but he would only stay in that job one year and his relationship with Madrid's president was not perfect.

'Shakhtar Donetsk made an offer and Lalatović flew with me from Belgrade to Donetsk, my first ever time on a private jet. Never again. It was so small and I was sweating as the plane moved around. The sporting director didn't say a word to me, didn't ask me anything, didn't show any interest in me. I wasn't going to join them after that, no matter what they offered. And they kept offering more, despite me failing an initial medical.

'At Belgrade, there was an offer from Spartak Moscow. I was interested. Russian football was growing a lot, their offer was the same as the original Shakhtar one (and 50 per cent of what I'd finally been offered in Ukraine) but I made sure the clause was in there though, that I could leave for $10 million.'

After playing two seasons in Moscow, Vidić eventually arrived in Manchester.

'The first one and a half years were hard. We found it hard because we came from a different culture. I'd lived in Belgrade and Moscow. The change wasn't big. Then I came to England, where everything was different. I found it hard. I started to enjoy Manchester, especially when my three kids arrived. All our three boys were born in Manchester. We lived in Wilmslow, which was great for families. I didn't go to Manchester city centre much. I had peace in Cheshire and really enjoyed it. I wouldn't have stayed for nine years if I didn't, although the weather could be hard. I made some good friends and found the people to be friendly.'

Vidić built a solid partnership with Rio Ferdinand.

'Good on and off the pitch. We didn't socialise together much but we had an understanding and liked to talk about football. It's important that two players who play alongside each other get on well. I'd say the same of central defenders and forwards, you need to get on. Ninety per cent of the conversations I had in my life with Rio were about football. Rio was keen and driven, he wanted to talk. He'd not won any trophies for a couple of years at United before I arrived and he was desperate for a partner.'

Vidić respected Ferguson immensely.

'He was inspirational for the players. He knew how to get the best out of players. He could find inspiration in anything – including the chair I'm sat on. He'd tell you how much the chair cost to build, how many hours it took to make, where it was made. That would make you think, "Hmm, someone has worked hard to make this chair. I have to work hard if I'm going to have any success." His philosophy was to work hard, give your all and have no regrets when you're finished.

'His reputation as a hardman was right and I saw the hairdryer, but it was rare. If you strum the strings on a guitar too hard all the time then they'll break. But sometimes to get the best you need to play them hard. Even when he was angry, it was usually because he felt that you could do better. He was usually right. At other times, he could put his arm around you. Some players needed that, others don't. Ferguson knew how to read players. He understands people and knows who needs what.

'He had good coaches around him too – Carlos, Mick Phelan. I once scored a goal for Mick. Fans still tell me about the celebration. I didn't score many goals. I'm not a forward so I have no need to plan my celebrations and any celebration came from pure emotion. It was the last minute against Sunderland. Mick told me to go up front. I was jogging forward and the ball came to me and I scored. I ran to Phelan to say, "That's your goal." René Meulensteen became first-team coach in 2007. He liked to do a lot of technical and skill work. He helped develop young players. He was good at his job, but the combination of them working together and with Sir Alex was what made it so successful. I think the manager tried to vary the characters he worked with to bring variety. You need a mix of personalities and we had that, on and off the pitch. First of all, the atmosphere was really good. Of course, we had good players and we had good characters. Then we had good players who were also characters. We didn't think, "we're going to win the league and the Champions League" – we just took everything game by game and we got better and better.

'I think we played our best football in 2006, 2007 and 2008. We still had success later and reached two more Champions League finals, but that team was so quick around the time we won in Moscow, the football was attractive to watch.'

Vidić – and Patrice Evra who also came in January 2006 – signed at the right time, though he nearly went to Liverpool.

'Liverpool manager Rafa Benítez called me and I nearly went there. I was interested to go, but my English was not good and I was struggling to communicate. Then Man United came. Fergie called me in my apartment and said: "I want you here. I watched you for Serbia against France." United were decisive. Everything was done very quickly, two days.'

Weren't your first few weeks awful?

'It was more than weeks; it was four or five months. I was struggling to stay on my feet in training, training with great players. They were fast, strong and quick. Ronaldo, van Nistelrooy or Rooney would run at me in training, Saha too. They were too much.

'I arrived in Manchester unfit because I came in January, the break in the Russian season. I did a two-week fast fitness course and they wanted me to play. I wasn't ready. I wasn't as good as I wanted to be, nor the club wanted. But I worked hard, was a team player and slowly rose to become captain of Manchester United. Even with my ability you can become captain of United; you have to work hard enough.'

Another new arrival, Evra, who was to play on his left, also shared Vidić's initial nightmare.

'Patrice and I both had a tough beginning in Manchester. Neither of us was ready to play for United, both physically and in terms of experience in England.

'Sir Alex sent us to play for the reserves and we played at Blackburn. We played 45 minutes when René Meulensteen, the manager, took us off, saying, "Enough." Patrice and I showered and said: "What have we done coming here?"

'People were saying: "Who are these two guys? If they can't play for the reserves, how can they play for the first team?" It was a difficult time, but we both worked hard, improved and established ourselves. It was a good lesson for us, that start.

'Then I played against Peter Crouch. Even in Serbia, which has many tall people, I'd never seen a two-metre-tall player before. He played for Liverpool and we played them in a cup game at Anfield. I was thinking, "Wow, what can I do today with this guy?" Then I saw Bellamy next to him, not a great player on the ball but very, very fast. He would run into space, Crouch would jump into the air. I'd never seen football played like this. I'd never had a number nine and a sharp, fast, player next to him. I knew how to deal with them individually but not both of them at the same time. I played alongside Wes Brown, it was a tough game, a long game. We lost 1–0. You have to work hard in life. That's what I want young people to know who read this: work hard.

'But Patrice and I built a trust. I'd tell Patrice to go forward – and that meant I could cover him behind. If Patrice went forward then he was free to go. The space he left was then my responsibility and he would be right to blame me if there was a problem. It took time to get like this but the trust did build.

'I never had a problem if a player lost the ball. The problem was how we reacted after the player lost the ball to make sure we won it back. And then, when we got it back, what options were we giving to the players to pass to. Modern football is all about movement off the ball. It doesn't matter how good a passer a player is if he doesn't have a player in space to pass to. If a team is concentrating on movement and the timing of when to move, that's where a team can get an advantage.'

After a year, Ferguson said of his Serbian signing: 'We've done well there. He has that mentality of the proper, really authentic defender. Watch Vidić in training, and he'll batter Louis Saha and then pick him up, as if to say, "This is my job, this is what I do." I'll be yelling from the touchline, "Watch the tackling, watch the tackling," and Vidić will shout, "Sorry, boss, sorry, boss." But he's not sorry at all, he just loves defending.'

One of his best challenges was against a young Kyle Walker at White Hart Lane, when the Spurs player went six feet high in the air.

'I remember that one. Kyle went honestly for the ball and so did I. It's why I liked that challenge, it doesn't matter who won, what mattered is that we both went for the ball. I love that about English football and hope it never changes.'

The jigsaw that would make United English, European and world champions was coming together, with Cristiano Ronaldo United's first Ballon d'Or winner since the 60s.

'Ronaldo was the best player I played with. He was professional too. He worked hard to get to where he did. Maybe he came across like someone who didn't work hard, but he did. When training was finished, he'd push the ball and do stepovers across three pitches. He didn't do it at full pace, but to get the movement of the skills smooth and exactly right. He practised his free-kicks with both feet; he worked all the time on his body to get the physique that he has now. Of course he has talent, but he worked hard to make himself so much better. I respect him a lot for that.'

And Vidić was respected himself.

'Vida was brilliant,' says Darren Fletcher. 'If he was playing against a strong player, he'd do weights all week. If he was playing against a fast player, he'd do fast feet work. That was his way of preparing. He was intense and Vida and Rio were so important to the way we played, always vocal, telling us to move left, right, up or back towards them. They were loud, aggressive and always organising the whole team from behind. If they did that well then it meant they didn't have to defend as much but even if they did, Vida was the best defender in the Premier League at defending the penalty box; there was nobody better at intercepting, heading and set pieces. He also had a ridiculous knack of not only clearing the ball, but finding a United player when he did – his stats for this were unbelievable.'

Vidić proved his worth against some of the toughest opponents in world football.

'Didier Drogba was physically the hardest, Suárez and Agüero were the best,' he says. 'Drogba would be even better if he didn't get so many injuries. They were the top three that I played against.

'Fernando Torres always created a chance to score, but Drogba was on you for the full game. He was a very clever player who would get into the brain of the defenders. He was strong, but he was always thinking ahead. He would think "if the defender pushes me now, I will go down" or "next time I will go strong". He used his strength well; he was really good in the box at Stamford Bridge, a close, tight stadium. Drogba was on you for the full game. He was always around the box and very difficult to stop from scoring. People say: "You had a difficult game against Torres", but it was just the one game and the story has grown. I went to head the ball but changed my mind and tried to pass to Edwin. I misjudged the distance. Torres was in a better position and scored. He scored a few against us.'

Vidić tasted the highs but he inevitably remembers the lows at United with bitter regret.

'Losing the Champions League finals in 2009 and 2011,' he says. 'Even though we had won the Premier League, we went on holiday thinking like losers. And the FA Cup final, 2007. We played Chelsea and lost to that Drogba goal in extra-time. I was very disappointed and the FA Cup is the only trophy we did not win.

'Maybe losing to City in April 2012 because that contributed to losing the league. I don't like to lose. There's a lot of stress in football. Pressure to win, pressure with social media, especially at the big clubs. Players have to learn to deal with this. Some have ability but they don't have the mentality to cope with the pressure and succeed. I learned early on how to deal with pressure when I played for Red Star, a team who are always expected to win.'

Vidić is happy being at home in Belgrade, happy too when he thinks of United.

'I was very proud to play for those fans and would like to thank them for the support they gave me over the years. I always did my best. I had the best time of my career there and we still have a house there. The only thing I had a problem with was the weather, nothing else. I really enjoyed Manchester, the social life, the people, the organisation. For the football player and if you are a family man, Manchester is perfect. And my time at United was perfect.'

11

GIGGS WILL TEAR YOU APART (AGAIN)

Ryan Giggs

Ryan Giggs (né Wilson) was the best player in our junior football league at my age group. Well, him, Simon Davies and Adie Mike. All made it as professionals. Adie played 19 times for Manchester City. Simon played 20 times for United then had a long career before he ended up at City as a coach. I was the worst player in a good team. Our goalkeeper, Richard Bibby, also became a professional at City – and his parents became host families for a lot of young City players. Richard and his former teammates still have a WhatsApp group called 'The Real Class of '92'.

No matter good you are, it's hard to become a professional footballer at a big club. I played as a right-back and once tried to mark the man who'd go on to play 963 times for Manchester United. Tried. I never got past half-time. I couldn't get near him and could see my father, a footballer from a family of footballers, wincing. At 15, I decided it might be better to write about football than play it.

Giggs was storming through the youth teams and it was a buzz to watch him go on to play all those times (with friendlies it's well over 1,000 matches) for United. Sir Bobby Charlton's 758-games appearance record for Manchester United was long considered insurmountable. Giggs passed that mark in Moscow in 2008 when he won his second European Cup.

How does he feel now it's long over and he's got time to reflect?

'I always looked forward when I played, now I feel like I can enjoy looking back on my career. I might see a clip on the TV and think "I remember that". It's a nice experience when you do retire and see the response that you get in the streets. When you're playing, it's all about how you're doing and the mood at the time around the team. It can change week to week. Comments go from: "You're not in great form" and "You didn't play well at the weekend" to "What a goal!" It's a rollercoaster. Now I get good comments in the street – and not just from United fans but opposition fans saying "I remember when you did this". It's a much more enjoyable experience. I've just been to Turkey and waiters would come up to me and say: "I fell in love with football when you were playing" or "You're one of the reasons I started watching the Champions League." People are usually polite and don't want to stop you, but now I have two-way conversations. When I was playing it was just a "Thanks". You get more comfortable where you are in life.'

At the end of November 1999 Ryan Giggs had just been crowned man of the match in Tokyo as United beat Brazilian side Palmeiras in the Toyota Intercontinental Cup, where the Champions League winners took on the victors in the Copa Libertadores. His prize was a car – a Celica coupe, and he was presented with a giant gold car key.

'It was too big to bring home so it stayed in the hotel room,' he laughs. 'Then we went to Brazil [for the inaugural Club World Championship in January 2000] – and there was a lot of hype around the trip. The players were devastated that we didn't enter the FA Cup. We were saying: "Just play the reserves and we'll back for the second round."'

The *Daily Mirror*, edited by Piers Morgan, ran a 'Save the FA Cup campaign'. They even dedicated one front-page headline, asking, 'Is there anyone left in Britain who does not think Man Utd should be in the FA Cup?' The headline was surrounded by opinions from the great and good of British society: such as a lottery winner, an IT girl, various C-list celebs and supermodel Caprice, who opined: 'They should think about the fans.'

'While we wanted to play in the FA Cup, playing in Brazil seemed like a great adventure,' Giggs continues. 'I'd never been there and I was excited to be part of this new tournament … until we landed and we saw how hot and humid it was. The trip ended up being a holiday. The football was hard work, the training was really hard, even though we trained early. The temperature would be shown on the lamp posts – it would be 33 before training and 39 after. Ridiculous. We'd try and find some shade – and fail. We came off the training pitch and demolished these huge watermelons that had been left for us. They were no conditions to play football in so the football was a disaster. We ended up hanging around the pool, going on the beach, having a night out. And by the time we got back, we were in a better position than when we left because other teams had dropped points. We went back having had a holiday, ready to win the Premier League again, which we did.'

There was perhaps a bigger priority: retaining the Champions League.

'After '99 and given our team and our ages, we felt we could go on and dominate for a few years. It had been a struggle in the mid to late 90s in Europe, just as it had to win the Premier League before '93. We felt that just as we'd won a lot of Premier Leagues, we could do the same in Europe.

'In 2000, Real Madrid beat us. In 2001, Bayern Munich, when the prankster Karl Power jumped in on the photo. That was a mad one. I watched him walk over to join our team picture and thought: "This must have been agreed, it must be allowed, it must be for charity or something." There were better teams around then than now. The biggest teams were around, but you also had Valencia and Deportivo, who were really good. It felt more difficult than it looks now. It was really difficult to win the Champions League back then and because we weren't winning it, the manager made huge changes to the team, which he was never afraid of doing, and to our style of play, bringing in lads like Seba Verón – the type of player we'd not seen at the club before and who I wondered where he would play. He let Becks go, [Jaap] Stam too. Then, with Ronaldo and Rooney, I think he had his eye on building a team to win the Champions League again – more of a 4-3-3 than a 4-4-2 – and I'd never really played a 4-3-3 before and I struggled in it because there was no obvious player to hit or a runner. The manager said that Eric, Teddy or Yorkie used to drop in so it was more like a 4-3-3, but they were all forwards really. Seba Verón wasn't a runner and it didn't really work with him playing as a "10", a position that had become the norm with Salah or Eden Hazard or Foden there.'

Giggs tried to help. Just as he'd taken new signings Eric Cantona out or Andy Cole to Liverpool's Cream club in the 1990s, so he took Verón out around Manchester.

'I felt that I was a local lad and I wanted to immerse them in Manchester's culture or out with my mates. Seba liked a drink and a night out, but I couldn't speak Spanish and he couldn't speak English, so it was hardly riveting conversation. We'd nod and smile and I'd say things like "River Plate" or "Boca Juniors" and he'd nod. Or "Passarella" or "Kempes". Another nod. I ended up speaking more to the translator.

'Like the other South American lads, they'd have a crazy streak. They don't drink like us, so they'd order a straight whisky or something. They don't take their time over six or seven beers. So all of a sudden the whisky would hit them and they'd be jumping on chairs. Even the sensible lads.'

Verón's best game was at Spurs away in 2001, when the team came from 3–0 down at half-time to win 5–3.

'I didn't play in that and stayed at home. I was following the score from home – teletext, online updates as the game wasn't on telly – and at half-time was telling my mates how much the team was missing me and that this is what happens when I'm not in the team,' laughs Giggs. 'At full-time I was worried that I wouldn't be in the team the following week. The amount of forward players on the pitch was staggering: Seba, Becks, Coley, Ole, Scholesy and Ruud. Ridiculous.'

Teddy Sheringham, another forward, had left United in 2001.

'There's a few players in your career who you have a special connection with and I had a connection with Teddy, I really liked to play with him. He was just a solid player: tough. He could turn a bad ball into a good ball, which is probably why I liked him. When I played on the left, if I wasn't taking someone on, then I could play a pass into the number 10's possession knowing it would stick. Even though Teddy had limitations pace wise, he was such a good player to play with.'

Ruud van Nistelrooy's arrival changed the dynamic for Giggs again.

'He was the best finisher. Coley, Sparky [Mark Hughes], Eric – even Cristiano. All good finishers. Ruud would do exactly in training what he'd do in a game. He wouldn't pass to you if the shot was on. And if the shot was on then he'd score. He had every finish in the bag: side foot, pings, dinks. He'd do it every day in training.'

Another player who rated himself as a finisher was goalkeeper Fabien Barthez. In one pre-season friendly in Singapore in 2001, Ferguson relented and let his French World Cup winning goalkeeper play outfield.

'We won the league in the first season with him and his stock was high. His kicking was unbelievable, accurate and far. With Pete [Schmeichel], he'd catch the ball and throw it to you. With Fabien, he'd have the capabilities to find you with his feet to launch a counter-attack. The cracks started to come after an amazing first season and he didn't end up being an amazing keeper for United in terms of how he's now regarded. I liked Fabien as a person. He was different. Quiet, not offensive, not a bad teammate. Didn't speak great English but I liked him. He was a good character and when Laurent Blanc came, Fabien had a mate who was very similar. They already knew each other from France, they'd have a fag in the toilets at games.'

A fag in the dressing room toilets before games …

'Some people said they had one at half-time. I never saw that, but I did see them smoke before a game. They had the cheek to call us for eating baked beans and Laurent would go mad if one of the players had beans on toast before standing next to Laurent and farting. He'd go off his head, yet they were having a fag. It was just their way.'

Giggs learned from Blanc.

'He had a big effect on me. It was round about the time that my hamstrings were starting to get on top of me and impact on me. I saw the way Laurent looked after himself in training. It was all about quality rather than quantity. His diet was spot on. He also went to a detox clinic in the Italian Alps that I attended for three or four summers because of him. Zinedine Zidane went there and it helped him with his knees early on in his career. I'd go for five days before pre-season. You wouldn't eat a lot, you had massages and blood tests, supplements. You'd come out feeling amazing and I felt it helped me. Roy Keane came with me one year.'

The summer of 2001 saw coach Steve McClaren depart as Ferguson's assistant to be his own man at Middlesbrough.

'Steve had fresh ideas and different views when he arrived to replace Kiddo [in February 1999]. He brought in a psychologist, Bill Beswick. I never used him myself and I'm not sure the manager was having him, but I quite enjoyed his talks to the team. As a footballer you train every day and everyone says it's the best job in the world, which it is, but you still need to stimulate players who've won things and who are still hungry and want to improve. That's not easy, but Steve did that. He continued to make training as competitive as possible, he added variety. If he did try and change things that the players weren't having – and footballers can be entitled and say "Well, we don't normally do this" – then he'd usually recognise that and change. He wouldn't be stubborn enough to persist and that's a good skill to have. I thought Steve was a brilliant coach who took a lot of pressure off the manager because he more or less managed the week. He also had a hard act to follow in Kiddo, someone the local players looked up to because we'd come up with him and felt that he looked after us.'

Despite signing Verón and van Nistelrooy on top of having won the three previous league titles, United finished third in the league in 2001–02. It was also the season which fans expected to be Sir Alex Ferguson's final one.

'Arsenal were very good,' explains Giggs. 'They bought Pires, Henry and it was tough for us to keep the motivation to make it four on the trot. Everything has to go for you. I wouldn't say the manager was getting tired, but I think he was desperate to win more Champions Leagues. That was his thing.

'When the manager said he was going to go, I had no reason to believe otherwise. We all thought he'd leave, but I don't think it hit home that he was actually going because it was always something months ahead – it never got to the stage where we turned up for pre-season and it was someone else. I just respected his decision and got on with my job.'

In February 2002, Ferguson changed his mind. How did the players feel?

'Gutted!' jokes Giggs. 'The prospect of more hairdryers. But by that time my relationship was changing with the manager. In the first ten years it was very much player/manager – and sometimes we'd get into heated arguments. Certain players would get it from the manager more than others, including me. Becks too. I got changed next to Becks in the dressing room. The manager would be having a go at Becks and I would be nudging him, whispering, "Don't respond, don't say anything." Becks would ignore me and have a go back. The following week, the manager would be having a go at me and Becks would be muttering, "Don't say anything." But I would. Another argument. That was our relationship for the first ten years. It changed when I became a more experienced player. He leaned on me a lot more when it came to decisions and putting his thoughts to me. He valued my opinion and my relationship was so much better from that point onwards.'

But it wasn't always smooth, for either him or Beckham.

'Becks left in 2003 and I honestly thought it was him or me who went. It was a bit of a shock when he went, even though you could see that the relationship between him and the manager had been strained for two years. The manager wasn't going to change, Becks is strong-minded and he wasn't changing his lifestyle. He was always a good professional, I never sat by his side with my watch, but he had a lifestyle that maybe the manager didn't always agree with. I was sad to see him go because he was a quality player, but I also thought, "Good luck to him." And because he left, I got to take some free-kicks for the first time in years.

'If he'd stayed then maybe I'd have been pushed out. There was talk that Inter Milan wanted me but nobody said anything to me. And I ended up having a good season.'

Giggs knew he had his manager's ear by then.

'If something was logistically wrong, I'd tell him. It might not be his fault, but I'd say that something shouldn't be happening. It might relate to travel or commercial demands. If I felt it was impacting on results then I'd go to him. He could still tell me off, though he wasn't always right. In 2011, he went mad at me after I'd had a night out in New York on the pre-season tour. Vida [Nemanja Vidić] and Berba [Dimitar Berbatov] had gone out to a restaurant called Lavo and a few of us joined them. At 11 p.m., a DJ came on and it turned into the club. People started dancing on chairs and I was pictured on the front page of a paper dancing on chairs. Just me, not the rest of my teammates. The manager battered me in front of all the players at the New York Giants training ground and said: "And you, I expect better." He threatened to fine me. And I had a pop back and said: "It wasn't like that."

'Later, I said that I didn't mind him having a go if he was valid, but this wasn't. I said that I'd never fought a fine, but that I'd fight this one. And he backed down and said: "Right, you're not getting fined. I've just got to let the young lads know that if I'm willing to have a go at you, then nobody is safe. Don't worry about it, I used you as a bit of a scapegoat and I apologise if I went over the top."'

Giggs as a long-serving player was due a ten-year testimonial in 2001.

'We played Celtic. Brilliant occasion, as I thought it would be, having been involved in those of Brian McClair and Bryan Robson. I remember my testimonial committee saying: "We've just sold 15,000 tickets to Celtic and they said if you can get us 20,000 more then we'll sell them." That was a wow moment, but also one of relief. You do worry whether anyone is going to buy tickets for your testimonial and there was a bit of controversy about whether I should have been having one at all. It ended up being a feisty game because Ruud, Scholesy and Neil Lennon kicked off a bit. I just stayed out of that one.'

Season 2002–03 was a difficult one for Giggs. He started to get stick from fans. Did that make him consider leaving the club?

'No. It's part of being a footballer. It was a bad time, though. I missed an open goal against Arsenal, I wasn't playing well. There were reasons for that and one of the reasons was simply that I just wasn't playing well. It happens. Another was that I was no longer that flying winger and I was trying to find a game where I could still be effective and relevant while still staying in the team. It's like a golfer trying to change his swing while still going out to play golf and hit the good shots. I had to take the hurt while I went from being a flying winger to being a left midfield player who played more in pockets of space. I was still quick and could still be effective. I could still run in behind defenders, just not like I could in the 90s. At 18 and 19 I felt I could beat anyone. Anyone. That changed.

'Overall, my relationship with fans was positive. You'd get stick if you were losing, but we didn't lose a lot. Fans were supportive when I was a young lad who came into the team and did well, even though my performances were up and down. Then I set a high standard. But I also put myself in a position where I met fans away from football and interacted. I'd go to the local pub, clubbing in the Hacienda or the Boardwalk and fans would speak to me. That wouldn't be the case now for a footballer.

'Yet I still maintain that it was one of my favourite seasons. We ended up winning the league and had a night out celebrating. I'd invited some of my mates, Nicky [Butt] would too. Friends who knew all the terrace songs.

'I scored 15 or 16 goals, my daughter was born, I scored against Newcastle in the week she was born. We actually moved into central Manchester on Deansgate. Nev lived in the same apartment block and we shared the driving. The city was changing quickly and still is, it's a better place than it was with better shops. It was a great season. It was never a big deal to get stick. If you're not playing well, you should get stick.'

Giggs' status as a local boy and one of the team's top players made him one of the main men in the dressing room, someone with the social skills and playing skills to influence and uphold what Manchester United was – and to keep humour prevalent.

'I'd sit opposite the door at Carrington,' he explains. 'Nobody was getting past me, I'd see everybody getting it, there was no blind spot. I was first to arrive because I'd drop my daughter at nursery and then go training to doing my re-hab with my hamstrings. I'd wear clothes which, at times, could get a bit of stick. So I'd be in there first and get the stick in first on everyone. Bad trainers or shoes? They'd be hung up in the middle. What motivated me was that so many of the lads who have left home were thinking: "You know what, I look good today, I'm safe." But they were never safe. No designer label was safe. Nicky and I were the main instigators: he was a top character. As were Cristiano and Patrice [Evra]. Cristiano could do really good impressions of people – he'd do Phil Neville's walk and walk behind him. Patrice barely spoke for six months, then he came out of his shell. These lads had a knack of seeing something in someone and then just taking them off.'

Giggs, his fashion ideas formed in Salford and the clubs of Manchester, the clothes worn by his mates, set the tone.

'You simply couldn't come in that dressing room wearing a leather jacket because one of two things would happen. One, the rest of the lads would start humming the theme tune to *Happy Days* because you were trying to look like The Fonz. Or two, motorbike sounds. I've been there when a player has walked in wearing leather and 20 adults have been making motorbike revving noises.

'If you wore something remotely different that, say, made you look like you were from the country, like cowboy boots, people would be asking you where your horse was.'

What on earth must these players new to the dressing room have been thinking?

'Ole Gunnar came with a new Christmas jumper on, which he'd bought from a local shop in Bergen or somewhere. He looked about 12. We didn't let it go, so much that if anyone came in with a lively jumper 15 years later, someone would announce: "Fucking hell, Ole's back." You'd have sensible people like Edwin van der Sar trying to rise above it all, but he'd still get stick and, because the Dutch have a bit of a different sense of humour, he'd laugh. There were so many smiles in that dressing room. There weren't many bad eggs and if they were, it would soon get knocked out of them. Teddy turned up in his Ferrari and got stick for being a flash Cockney, but he ended up delivering on the pitch. Rio came in and got hammered for the first few months for his clothes and flash cars. Every time someone beat him or he made a mistake, someone would shout: "How much did you cost?" He wasn't great in training but then after a month he was the best in training. If you deliver on the pitch then you soon earn respect and the stick goes away.'

There was a serious side to the unserious side.

'If someone turned up late, I'd go and sit next to them and – saying nothing – look at my watch. They were less likely to be late again. Scholesy would chop players down like a tree if they were taking too many touches in training. Young lads did – Paul Pogba did. Bang, he'd be down. He'd look at Scholesy, who'd say: "If you pass the ball quicker and move it quicker then I can't kick you to get the ball." It was a lesson to the player – you have to be good at timekeeping. You had to be organised and pay attention. If you turned up at a train station wearing a suit when everyone else was in a tracksuit then it'd be a disaster for you. Everyone would cheer and the first thing the player would do would be to change into a tracksuit in the train toilets. Nev had high standards and other players would see that. Those standards helped us be the best team in England and, at times, Europe and the world. Standards.'

Even Ferguson acknowledged Giggs' humour.

'Ryan Giggs was the most skilful in his mockery,' he said, having told the team he was staying on as manager in early 2002. 'Oh, no, I can't believe this,' said Giggs. 'I've just signed a new contract.'

Who made Giggs laugh?

'Keaney. Butty. Patrice. Rio. Brucey in the early days. Keaney could be cutting and has a dry sense of humour, but he got a bit of stick, especially when he first arrived. He'd come in with loads of balls and shirts to sign for back home. He soon learned but he could take it too. You could tell if Roy had secretly bought some new clothes and was giving it a good go, he knew that he'd get stick because it was a change from him wearing Hi-Tech trainers and tracksuits every day – his sponsor. New jeans, new brogues, the type him and his mates wore back home … he'd get stick.'

This was all taking place at Carrington, United's training ground since January 2000.

'The Cliff was an amazing place for team spirit, but you can be over-emotional about it. Footballers want the best facilities, pitches and training rooms. There were more players and the dressing room at Carrington is twice the size of that at The Cliff. I was so excited to move to Carrington because of all that – and it had a pool.'

Wayne Rooney first played at Old Trafford in October 2002. Giggs' impressions of the teenage prodigy were deceptive.

'I'd heard about him but I was looking at him thinking, "He's a bit stocky." That was until I went to close him down and he went past me like I didn't exist. I thought "Wow!" I wasn't expecting it. The England lads would tell me that Wayne was tough, old school, top level. Then he joined us. He was 18 but he wasn't shy, he'd happily sit in the middle of all the experienced players. He didn't give a fuck about anything or anyone – in a good way – and I'd never seen that before. He was so confident at a young age.

'Ronaldo was another world-class player. When he first joined it was skill without substance, but he quickly became a man and learned. He went through a stage where he was diving and that was knocked out of him by us more than anyone else. We'd say: "You can't do that because they will start to target you." The manager, meanwhile, spoke publicly about him needing protection. We know how skilful he was, that he scored with his right foot, left foot, headers, but he was so tough. Everyone was trying to kick the shit out of him and he didn't blink. But his skill was a level above everyone.'

In 2005, the Glazers' controversial and highly leveraged takeover of United went through. Giggs, like most of the United players, kept his head down.

'As a player, you're selfish and worry about how it will affect you. Would we be buying more players, would there be more money? I felt that I had to concentrate on playing well and staying in the team, no matter what else was going on. They were tough times because Mourinho had come in at Chelsea and took them to a different level. We'd been knocked out of Europe by Mourinho's Porto team in 2004. Benni McCarthy scored two headers. I couldn't help but think that Rio, who was banned for missing a drugs test, would probably have prevented both of them.'

Ferguson was angry, but even he described McCarthy's headers as 'out of this world'.

McCarthy was ironically a lifelong United fan and Giggs admirer who'd grown up in the vast Cape Flats township in Cape Town, where he played in leagues run by gangsters.

'I scored two against United and was heartbroken,' McCarthy told me. 'I support Man United and always wanted to play for them. I loved players like Mark Hughes, Andy Cole and Ryan Giggs. My dream was to score once at Old Trafford, not to knock United out of the competition and Mr Mourinho wasn't happy with my reaction and told me to cheer up. He told me that if I didn't then I'd never play in his team again.'

Porto came to Old Trafford with a 2–1 lead.

'At half-time, Mourinho told us to keep shape, keep it tight and prevent them from scoring because if they score we're screwed,' adds McCarthy. 'But if they manage to break us down and score, that's when we attack and play against them like we played in Porto. But if they don't score, a 0–0 draw suits us fine.

'United scored and we crapped ourselves, but before they could attack us again we went full steam ahead. I don't think they'd been bullied like that. Ricardo Carvalho was exceptional. Our defence was magnificent. Nuno Valente kept Ronaldo at bay.

'When Louis Saha, a dangerous player, was taken off, the game was over. We'd done our job and United were out. A great night for Porto, but a mixed one for me.'

Porto won the competition and Mourinho joined Chelsea.

'It didn't even register with us when Roman Abramovic bought Chelsea in 2003,' says Giggs. 'I was more bothered that Patrick Vieira agreed a new contract at Arsenal and hoped he'd go to Madrid like Becks.

'But Chelsea spent money like water. Nobody could live with them financially as they signed Mutu, Crespo, Makélélé. They took Seba Verón too, which I wasn't surprised about because I knew he wasn't happy.

'Chelsea became a really tough team to play against and it seemed like they didn't have any weaknesses. They were robust, physically strong, a winning machine. We had players leaving, but two very talented young players coming through in Wayne and Cristiano. It's fine now saying that everything was going to be alright, but it didn't feel like that at the time.

'Chelsea were different to us. Our rivalry with Arsenal was about two quite similar teams. Mourinho's Chelsea were strength and power. They'd bully teams. They did have skilful players like Duff and Robben, but it was more about Drogba, Terry, Cech, Lampard and Makélélé. Big, efficient characters. In the 90s, we'd go to Stamford Bridge and win, in the noughties we didn't look like winning when they became good. There was no space on the pitch so we had no choice but to try and raise our game.'

Chelsea would become the main rivals for the players, just as Arsenal had been, but for the fans it was more Liverpool, City (when they were up) and Leeds until they went down.

'The games against City were open. It didn't matter where the two teams were at, anyone could win it. But even when City started getting good towards the end of the decade, we still felt that we were so much better than them.'

Carlos Tevez, signed from West Ham in 2007, would become a key player for United.

'As a person he wasn't someone I got close to,' says Giggs. 'He'd grunt. I reckon that even if I spoke Spanish there wouldn't have been much interaction. He kept himself to himself, but he loved playing football. He was a bit like Wayne: hard, relentless. I'd played with a lot of pairings up front, but when I was on the left and looked up to see Rooney and Tevez hunting defenders down, I'd never seen that before. They were ferocious, they'd look after themselves and then, when they got the ball, they'd hurt teams. They were a massive handful for opponents.'

Tevez made his own mates.

'There was a weird three ball with Carlos, Ji [Park Ji-sung] and Patrice, who brought them together. They'd sit together, they'd do keepy-ups at the end of training.'

Another Carlos, Queiroz, had an impact of a different sort.

'Overall, he had a positive impact,' says Giggs. 'He wasn't a coach at home on the grass, more an assistant manager. He wasn't like Kiddo, René [Meulensteen] or Steve, all coaches comfortable on the grass. He was more strategic but at the start, the players weren't having him. I wasn't. We were in Amsterdam pre-season in 2002 and played Ajax. We stayed at the Hilton and I was trying, and failing, to make an ice bath in my hotel room. I'd gone to the physio's room and got some ice. There were two games in two days and I was asked to play in both, so I thought, "I'd better try one of these ice baths." I was just about to get in the bath – reluctantly – and there was a knock at the door. I thought "I'm saved here" and went to look through the keyhole and it was Carlos. Keep in mind that he had been at the club then for only a week, ten days. I opened the door and said, "Hello, Carlos." He said: "Can I come in, please?"

'He came in the room and sat down. I'll never forget this and he had some front on him, to be fair. And he said: "Where is the world star, Ryan Giggs?"

'"What do you mean?"

'"Where is the Ryan Giggs that I loved watching because I'm not seeing him?"

'I went on the back foot and said, "What are you talking about, Carlos? We're early in pre-season."

'"Yes, but last year you were not good," he said. "I want to know how to get the best out of you."'

Giggs wasn't happy with this.

'Thinking back, it was probably Ferguson who sent him in to talk to me, but right from the start it wasn't good for me and Carlos. I'd been in the team over a decade and this character had come and I hardly know him and he's telling me that I should be upping my game. I wondered who he thought he was. But, gradually, he started earning the respect of the players. He knew his football, he knew how to win games. It was a rocky road for Carlos. We did boxes training and if you get a ball in the nose, everyone laughs at you. It's horrible. Your nose is sore, your eyes are stinging and everyone is laughing at you. I got a ball in the nose and Carlos came over and called me "Giggs". I had to pull him and say: "Carlos, I didn't go to school with you, it's either Ryan or Giggsy." To be fair, it was just a foreign way and when I go away now I get called "Giggs", "captain" and "coach".

'But in the end I quite liked him. From his perspective, he couldn't believe that we didn't have sports scientists. He would take the warm-ups himself until he brought Valter Di Salvo in, who was very good at his job. Carlos needs to take credit for improvements in these areas because ultimately, he was good – really good, especially tactically.

'The training session Carlos gave before the Barcelona semi-final in Camp Nou in 2008 was one of the best training sessions that

I've ever seen. He put PE mats out on the pitch and told every player exactly where he wanted us. He told us where the Barcelona players would be, where they'd hurt us. I'd never seen that before. And he was right.'

Giggs never did get in that ice bath, but because of Queiroz's tactical nous, United got a 0–0 draw in Catalonia. That set up a home semi-final against Frank Rijkaard's side.

'That was the best atmosphere I experienced at Old Trafford – at least the last 20 minutes were and I came on the pitch for them. I stood waiting to come on, thinking how loud it was. The crowd saw us over the line, it was sustained. I saw Old Trafford erupt like that a few times – Steve Bruce's winner against Sheffield Wednesday in '93, Michael Owen's winner against City in 2009.'

Owen was another surprise recruit.

'When he was younger he was quick and would skip over tackles, he could finish too. He joined us when older and I could relate to his situation a little bit because he'd lost that blistering pace. What surprised me when he came to us was how intelligent and how good a footballer he was. The ball could stick with him – better if it was played on the floor – like it did with Teddy Sheringham. He was safe on the ball, he knew what he was good at and knew his limitations. He would get the ball, control it, pass it or try to score a goal. Simple, yet intelligent.'

Giggs also has praise for another Michael, Carrick, who came to United from Tottenham in 2006.

'The most underrated player I've been on a football pitch with,' says Giggs. 'A brilliant footballer. I loved playing in midfield with him and on the left with him. He always looked to pass forward with both feet. He was so calm, a top character. Perhaps he didn't and still doesn't get the recognition he deserves because he took Keaney's number or because he was a different player to Scholesy. When he didn't play well or if results weren't going well, he didn't go around kicking people or score a goal to get you out of the shit.

That wasn't him. But as a midfielder who'd take the ball from Rio or Vida and play it around the corner, do a short pass, long pass with either foot, be good at set-pieces because of his height. A brilliant person, too.

'Vida liked a moan. Hard work. I fell out with him once in training. I was old, maybe 36, and I went through three players and went to get past him and he took me out around my waist. I got up and squared up to him and said: "What the fuck are you doing, we're training?" He told me where to go. I told him that I'd smash him the next time the ball came our way. He'd scrape into a game with a niggling injury, but then when the game started he'd be brilliant. Since I stopped playing I've met him a few times and played golf with him. He was so relaxed and calm. The edge had gone which he had as a player, like he was always ready to kick off. I always liked his sense of humour though.'

By Moscow in 2008, Giggs was 34. At the start of the 2008–09 season, Ferguson said of him: '[Giggs] is a very valuable player, he will be 35 this November but at 35, he can be United's key player. At 25, Ryan would shatter defenders with his run down the flank, but at 35, he will play deeper.'

He was still starting most league games, though he'd only come on for the last 22 minutes in the final game of the season.

'I scored one of my favourite goals at Wigan, all my mates were in the United end, I matched Sir Bobby's appearance record and we secured the lead. Our coach went past my mates after and they had their heads out of their sunroof, singing away.'

Giggs has never lost touch with the lads he grew up with, which has helped him considerably, unlike other footballers who very often do not know who their genuine friends are.

He played less so in Europe in the biggest Champions League games, though he was captain in the 1–0 home win against Roma, just as he'd been captain that season against Sporting, Dynamo Kiev and Olympique Lyonnais.

'I didn't expect to start that game in Moscow and had no complaints that I didn't. Where would I have played on the left? The way the manager wanted to play, which was the right way, was to try and stop Ashley Cole on the left. That's why Owen [Hargreaves] played. Cristiano was on the left, Tevez and Rooney up front, with both of them on fire.'

The Welshman entered the pitch after 87 minutes, replacing Paul Scholes.

'I was always a decent sub because I could read the game and was always ready to come on, ready to take a chance or make a chance. I had a chance which John Terry cleared off the line. I should have scored really.'

With penalties approaching, Ferguson had to think ahead.

'The manager was about to put John O'Shea on, so I went over to him and said, "Sheasy won't take a pen. You need to put Anderson on" because Ando didn't miss penalties. He didn't score goals, he scored penalties and he had a mentality that nothing would faze him. His mentality would have been the same whether he was playing with his mates on a beach in southern Brazil or playing in the Champions League final. He wouldn't think of any consequences, just that it's a football. John Terry missed his spot kick then Ando stood up. He put his penalty down the middle, our sixth one, ran to the fans and got it going a bit.'

I've kept in touch with Anderson since he left United. He's from Porto Alegre, the same city as my wife. He's quite the character and in 2018 I stayed at his house and had a night out. We spoke about the penalty.

'I came on the pitch and didn't touch the ball before the game ended,' Anderson explained. 'It was straight to penalties and I was the sixth one. Ronaldo missed. The best guy missed. We all thought "Shit!" Tevez, Carrick, Hargreaves – great player – Nani. All scored.

'John Terry missed. If he'd scored, Chelsea would have won. I was not thinking about him. It was me next. It was the longest walk towards that ball. I started to think about my life. I had been born very poor. My life had been so hard. As I walked up, I thanked God for giving me everything. God told me that this penalty was like a sweet, a cake. It was my moment to be enjoyed. When God said this my nerves went away. I had pictures of my life in my mind. Very poor. No money. Fights with my mum. Sometimes nothing to eat. My father dying. Leaving home when I was 12. Gremio. Porto. I walked to the ball and crashed it. Cech is a big man with big hands. He touched the ball, but it went in.'

Giggs was next. What was going through his head stepping up to take a penalty to potentially win the European Cup?

'My preparation was spot on. I took 15 penalties in the week leading up to the game and scored 14. Always in the same spot. The one that I missed hit the post. So I was as confident as you can get taking a penalty in a Champions League final. The only thing going on in my mind was "Get your head over the ball". I hate penalties that are a yard off the ground because they're so easy for the keeper. As long as the ball is on the floor then you have a chance, even if it's not in the corner. I scored my penalty. Edwin saved Anelka's. We won and it was extra special for me because I broke Sir Bobby Charlton's appearance record and was presented with a watch by the manager, David Gill and all the players. That meant a lot to me. I've still got it.'

One last word from Anderson. 'When Anelka missed, I thought we had one more penalty. Then everyone started to run – we'd won – so I followed them. I have the picture. I jumped. Vidić jumped at the same time. His teeth went in my head by accident. Aaah, that hurt! But the celebration was amazing. The fans behind the goal. Crazy. And then the music from a Brazilian in the stadium. Gal Costa. I danced. Such a famous song in Brazil. I saw Manuela, who worked for my agent and was like my mother, and my girl-friend. They were crying. I drank until seven in the morning, celebrating. I drank on the plane to Manchester and then went straight to Brazil. When I arrived I joked that I wanted to go straight to hospital and to take blood because I'd drunk so much. My Champions League medal is safe. And my four Premier League medals. And I have 400 shirts that I swapped: Henry, Iniesta, Ronaldinho, Rivaldo, Cristiano Ronaldo. Many more.'

The game finished after midnight local time. Giggs, famously once never one to leave a night out early, took it easy.

'I'd done the wild celebration in Barcelona where I'd had half an hour's sleep and was in no mood for doing the same again. It was too late and I was getting on. We got back to the hotel in Moscow really late, about 2 a.m. I had a few drinks and was one of the fresher ones on the coach in the morning. I got a couple of hours' sleep. Others didn't, the lads who'd won it for the first time like Rio and Wayne.'

Giggs would start against Barcelona in Rome a year later, as Manchester United captain. His assessment is surprising.

'I don't think I should have started,' he says. 'Or if I was to start, it should have been on the left and not as a number 10. The gaffer promised Ji that he was going to start him after he'd not the year before. Fair enough, but I thought Cristiano should have played on the right against Sylvinho and maybe play Wayne up front with Ji behind him and me on the left.'

Famously, United got off to a positive start.

'We decided to press them and had a little success. We had a free-kick on the edge of the box and they couldn't get out, but that first goal killed us. Game over. Well, not quite. Not like it was at Wembley in 2011. That was about the only time where we went behind and I thought: "We can't win" but that was Wembley. In Rome, I felt we could get something, but Barcelona were so good. They had a lot of players at their peak. Yaya Touré, Piqué, Valdes, Henry, Messi, Iniesta, Xavi. It's the worst I've felt after a game. I nearly retired after that game. On the coach after I was thinking "That's me done" because I was so disappointed. I didn't want to feel like that again. Nobody had won two Champions Leagues on the trot and I felt we would with the team we had. And while Barcelona were great, they weren't quite as great as they were at Wembley two years later. Then you sleep and calm down a bit.'

Giggs was voted the BBC Sports Personality of the Year later in 2009, ending a successful decade for him.

'I said to my agent Harry that I wasn't going to go, but I think he wanted a night out because the awards were in Sheffield and he lived near Leeds. I told him that I had no chance of winning it and he said: "You never know." Harry wasn't really interested in football, more doing commercial deals. He only ever represented three players: me, Kevin Keegan and Bryan Robson. He looked after us all, he was like an adopted granddad and we became really close.

'Harry was enjoying it in Sheffield, but it was a weird feeling because Jenson Button was nailed on favourite to win. Anyway, I went over to Sheffield with Di Law, United's press officer, and we met Harry. There were whispers going around that it was going to be close and then as soon as Jensen came second I was thinking, "Jeeez!"

'I rang my mates as I wanted to go out celebrating. But it was a Sunday night. They said they had work in the morning and none of them wanted to come out apart from Gary Lloyd, a friend from childhood who has since passed away and who I used to go and watch United with. So me, Di and Gaz went in The Lowry hotel for a few drinks. It wasn't a bad way to end the decade.'

ACKNOWLEDGEMENTS

Huge thanks to all the players, club officials and staff I have spoken to over the years, and specifically those who gave their time for this book. Your stories are what make it.

To Jon at HarperNorth, Joyce Woolridge, Jim White, Joe Ganley, and Paul M.

And thanks, as ever, to Mum and Les.

Harper North

BOOK CREDITS

HarperNorth would like to thank the following staff
and contributors for their involvement in making
this book a reality:

Fionnuala Barrett
Peter Borcsok
Lauren Braggs
Ciara Briggs
Katie Buckley
Sarah Burke
Fiona Cooper
Alan Cracknell
Jonathan de Peyer
Tom Dunstan
Kate Elton
Sarah Emsley
Simon Gerratt
Lydia Grainge
Monica Green
Natassa Hadjinicolaou

Emma Hatlen
Grace Howarth
Megan Jones
Jean-Marie Kelly
Taslima Khatun
Petra Moll
Alice Murphy-Pyle
Adam Murray
Genevieve Pegg
Amanda Percival
Natasha Photiou
Florence Shepherd
Eleanor Slater
Chris Stone
Emma Sullivan
Katrina Troy

For more unmissable reads,
sign up to the HarperNorth newsletter at
www.harpernorth.co.uk

or find us on Twitter at
@HarperNorthUK

Harper
North